Second Edition

WORKING

WITH

CHILDREN

OF

ALCOHOLICS

Second Edition

WORKING

WITH

CHILDREN

OF

ALCOHOLICS

The Practitioner's Handbook

Bryan E. Robinson
J. Lyn Rhoden

SAGE Publications
International Educational and Professional Publisher
Thousand Oaks London New Delhi

For information:

 SAGE Publications, Inc.
2455 Teller Road
Thousand Oaks, California 91320
E-mail: order@sagepub.com

SAGE Publications Ltd.
6 Bonhill Street
London EC2A 4PU
United Kingdom

SAGE Publications India Pvt. Ltd.
M-32 Market
Greater Kailash I
New Delhi 110 048 India

Printed in the United States of America

Library of Congress Cataloging-in-Publication Data

Robinson, Bryan E.
    Working with children of alcoholics: The practitioner's handbook /
by Bryan E. Robinson and J. Lyn Rhoden. — 2nd ed.
        p. cm.
    Includes bibliographical references and index.
    ISBN 0-7619-0756-4 (cloth: alk. paper). — ISBN 0-7619-0757-2
(pbk.: alk. paper)
        1. Children of alcoholics—Counseling of—United States.
    2. Social work with children—United States. I. Rhoden, J. Lyn.
    II. Title.
    HV5132.R63   1998
    362.292'3'0973—dc21   97-33805

98 99 00 01 02 03 04 05 10 9 8 7 6 5 4 3 2 1

Acquiring Editor: Margaret Zusky
Editorial Assistant: Corinne Pierce
Production Assistant: Lynn Miyata
Typesetter/Designer: Janelle LeMaster
Indexer: Trish Wittenstein
Cover Designer: Candice Harman

CONTENTS ⚏

ACKNOWLEDGMENTS

We extend our thanks and appreciation to our graduate assistant Karen Flynn for her important contribution to this book—her insightful and perceptive assistance and input enhanced both the process and the product.

A SYSTEMS PERSPECTIVE OF THE FAMILY **1** ▪▪

The application of the family systems viewpoint is relevant to our understanding of the complexity of alcoholic families and our efforts to help children who face the fear and problems caused by parents who drink too much. Alcoholism is an integral, inseparable part of the entire family and that family's social network. Alcoholism may even be regarded as a discrete "member of the family," as it generates family dynamics and influences family functioning through its interaction with and impact on each family member.

Because the entire family revolves around the alcoholic's behaviors, the children are often second best, and the children's problems are often invisible. A comprehensive approach to helping children of alcoholic families must focus not only on the child, but on the child's natural environment or context, his or her family system, and the context of the family, the socio-economic-cultural suprasystem (Anderson & Sabatelli, 1993). It is within the complexity of these systems that the caring professional can identify resources and strategies for making children's special problems and needs visible and reducing their pain and suffering so that they can receive the help they deserve to lead happier, more productive lives.

CASE 1.1

Jack and Dorothy Smith, both in their mid-40s, have been married for 20 years. Although the Smith family does not often openly express affection, both spouses and their three children, Rick, Tracy, and Eva, know that family members love and care for each other. Now that their children are young adults, both Jack and Dorothy had anticipated sharing activities and simply enjoying each other's company.

Jack's work has been a constant source of conflict between him and Dorothy and between Jack and his now-grown children. Dorothy often felt like a single mother rearing the children. Although the three children are successful adults, they acknowledged to Dorothy that they never believed they could do anything well enough to please their father, and they even felt anger toward him because he wouldn't let them get close to him.

Dorothy was disappointed that, in her marriage, Jack was a "no-show" when it came to child rearing, managing the household, and attending social gatherings when he would fail to keep his promise to meet her. The family's tone and activities revolved around Jack's moods and whims. Everybody postponed their plans, hoping that by chance they would be able to grab some time with him. The children learned that they could have special times with their dad by going to his law office with him on Saturday mornings and playing in an adjacent room while Jack worked. Dorothy even went back to school to become a paralegal and took a job in Jack's office, working alongside her husband "just to nab some time with him." On those rare occasions when Jack tried to take an active role in his family, he said he felt rebuffed by his wife, who felt that he was intruding on her turf.

Jack, who is still very invested in his work as an attorney, recently went to his physician because of stress-related health problems and was told that the best antidote to his stress would be long weekends and vacations. On these vacations, Jack lugged his legal files across the country. Dorothy complained that he continued to work on their trips, and it was very lonely for her to visit the museums while Jack stayed in the hotel working. Even when they took those long weekends at their mountain retreat, Jack maintained frequent contact with the other attorneys in his law firm in the city.

To fully understand what is happening in the Smith family or any family, social scientists have historically focused on individual family members, such as adults' parenting behaviors and children's responses to parenting. More recently, a complete understanding of the Smiths and families like them has expanded to include a systems perspective of family functioning. Contemporary family systems theory is derived from *general systems theory*, a way of thinking about the world in which objects are interrelated with one another (Whitchurch & Constantine, 1993). This chapter will introduce the basic concepts of the family systems perspective and will examine how the most important human systems, including family, work, neighborhood, school, and the larger social and cultural systems that shape lives, are very closely connected, interrelated, and interdependent (Gacic, 1986). In later chapters, the application of family systems concepts to alcoholic families will give you a more complete understanding of the complexity of alcoholic families. Applying a systems approach to alcoholism acknowledges that alcoholism is not an isolated phenomenon but is integrally and inseparably related to the functioning of the family system and social systems that form the "context" of the family (Gacic, 1986).

Family Systems Perspective:
Core Assumptions and Concepts

Interrelatedness

General systems theory defines a system as a set of elements standing in interrelation among themselves and with the environment. When applied to the family, these elements include not only individual family members but the interrelationships among the members. For example, the Smiths, as a family, are composed of more than their five individual members. The Smith family is also made up of the relationships that exist between Jack and Dorothy as spouses, between each parent and each child, and between each pair of siblings. A pictorial representation of the Smith family would feature figures representing its five individual members, as well as multiple arrows criss-crossing among family members, representing family interactions and interrelationships (see Figure 1.1).

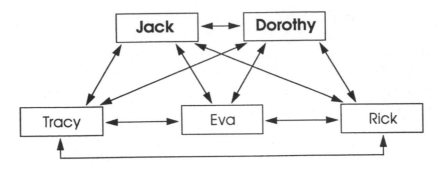

Figure 1.1: Composition of the Smith family system

Emergent Properties

As a result of these interactions and interrelationships, properties or characteristics of the family emerge. The concept of emergent properties may be illustrated by the example of a cake, which includes multiple individual ingredients (flour, eggs, sugar, cocoa) but whose "cakeness" (flavor, texture, degree of appeal) can only emerge as a result of the interaction of these ingredients produced by the dynamics of temperature/energy and time. These *emergent properties* develop only at the system level of the family and are a function of the dynamics of the family system, such as the degree of cooperativeness, efficiency, or cohesion of a particular family. Within a family, the individual ingredients are comparable to individual family members and their characteristics. The dynamics of family interactions and relationships can be compared to the energy of heat; time required for baking can be compared to the developmental processes of the family over time; and the emergent family properties are the family's unique cakeness. The unique properties of the Smith family would emerge as a function of the blending of the characteristics of its individual members: Jack's preoccupation with work, Dorothy's loneliness and resentment, and the children's anger toward their father and their longing to be closer to him, as well as the underlying love and caring felt by family members for each other in spite of their problems. Over time, the interactions and interrelationships within the family will generate the energy necessary for these characteristics to interact, and the unique "flavor" of the Smith family will emerge. These emergent properties might include a family focus on Jack and a degree of ongoing tension in the family associated with his preoccupation with his work.

Assumptions of the
Family Systems Perspective

The family systems perspective is grounded in two fundamental assumptions. First, a family must be understood as a whole (Anderson & Sabatelli, 1993; Isaacson, 1991; Whitchurch & Constantine, 1993). A family is more than the sum of its parts, and so family functioning cannot be comprehended by examining its individual members in isolation from each other. Because family members' behavior is actually interlocking (Isaacson, 1991), an understanding of any family must include the interactional dynamics among family members, as well as the circularity patterns and the emergent properties of the family. For example, the family dynamics generated by Dorothy Smith's resentment of her husband Jack's absence from involvement in the family can be more completely understood if you also take into account that Jack experiences feelings of rejection when he does try to participate more actively in the family. This pattern of interaction sets Jack and Dorothy up for the perpetuation of Jack's uninvolvement and Dorothy's feelings of resentment.

Second, family systems are assumed to have the ability to be self-reflexive. That is, families have the potential ability to "see the forest *and* the trees": to "step back" and examine their systems, as an outsider might, in order to increase their self-awareness, set goals, and organize goal-directed behavior. Communication among family members facilitates the family's ability to be self-reflexive.

Interdependence of the Family

The members of a family are interdependent, held together in the family system by their relationships. As a result, family members' behaviors exhibit mutual influence, meaning that what happens with one part of the family system affects every other member of that system. One aspect of this interdependence is circularity (Robinson, in press). Over the course of time, family members develop certain behaviors in response to each other. For example, Jack Smith's intense involvement with his work affects his wife and children by creating their feelings of isolation from him. Dorothy may respond to Jack's career commitment with complaints and efforts to influence him to work less. Circularity may occur when Jack, in turn, retorts that "I might spend more time at home if you complained less."

Although all members exert influence within the family, not all members exert equal influence. A kind of layering exists within the organization of each family system, resulting in a hierarchy of power and influence among family members. Although Jack's wife and children may be able to influence him to some degree to join them in more family activities, the power to make that change is ultimately in Jack's own hands.

Family Systems Concepts

Family Boundaries

Boundaries define the family system and represent the point at which the system interfaces with other systems. Within the family, internal boundaries delineate subsystems, such as the marital or parental subsystem. In Figure 1.2, the line around Jack and Dorothy indicates the marital subsystem, and the line around Tracy, Eva, and Rick indicates the sibling subsystem. Internal boundaries can also delineate alliances and coalitions. An alliance is a subsystem based on some common interest that is not shared by other family members, whereas a coalition is characterized by one member of a family siding with a second member against a third. Within the Smith family, Dorothy and the children may be perceived as forming a coalition against Jack, in their disapproval of his involvement with his work at the expense of his participation in the family. (In Figure 1.2, this coalition is represented by the line encircling Dorothy, Tracy, Eva, and Rick, and excluding only Jack.)

The external boundary around a family delineates family membership: who is considered to be "in" the family and who is not. In some sense, Jack may be considered to be outside this external boundary, especially at times when his wife and children perceive him as being particularly disengaged from them. A family's external boundary also marks the point at which it interacts and shares information with its environment. For example, information considered as private, such as family secrets, will generally not cross this boundary. The dark line surrounding the entire Smith family in Figure 1.2 suggests that a substantial external boundary prevents the Smiths' private "family business" from being shared with outsiders.

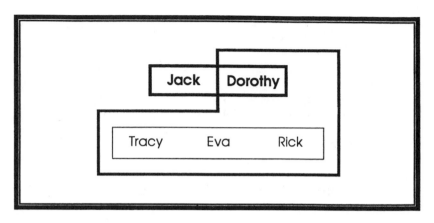

Figure 1.2: Smith family systems and subsystems

Family Change

Family systems are also characterized by their tendency to change or to stay the same by resisting change. A systems approach sees family change as processed by the entire family system, using intrafamily processes of feedback and control (Anderson & Sabatelli, 1993). Feedback loops within the family occur when some disturbance calls for a change in family structure or functioning. Information (the disturbance or call for change) moves from one point in the family system through other parts of the system, and then loops back to its point of origin (see Figure 1.3). For example, in the Smith family, Tracy may express a need for more privacy and ask for the option of closing and/or locking her bedroom door whenever she wishes. As this call for change moves through and is processed by the rest of the family system, Tracy's parents, Jack and Dorothy, may discuss whether or not they can concede to this request, and Tracy's brother Rick may tease his sister about her "private life," or express his own desire for the same right. Eventually, the loop will come back to its point of origin, the daughter, in the form of feedback: change or no change in the degree of privacy afforded her. For example, family members may respect her need by knocking on her door and waiting for a reply, or they may resent the barrier and pound on the door until it is opened.

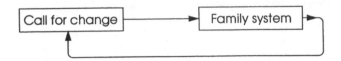

Feedback returns to point of origin, resulting in
change (Positive Feedback Loop) or no change (Negative Feedback Loop).

Figure 1.3: Feedback loop

Negative feedback loops act to maintain equilibrium within the family by ensuring that the system does not deviate too far from its current state of functioning. This is common, because families tend to establish and maintain patterns of interaction. In the Smith family, those patterns might include Dorothy's complaining to Jack, "I wouldn't complain so much if you were home more often" and Jack's responding, "Why should I want to be home more when you complain all the time?" This interaction likely will result in Jack's continuing to spend too little time at home, and Dorothy's continued unhappiness with the situation.

Positive feedback loops, on the other hand, result in a change in the structure or functioning of the family system. Any feedback in itself is not positive or negative, but its quality depends on how that change affects the family system. For example, allowing Tracy more privacy may or may not be beneficial to the family, depending on the degree to which it strengthens or weakens family functioning. It may be that affording the daughter more privacy may strengthen her feelings of being valued and respected by her family and thus diminish her need to demand respect in more indirect "acting-out" ways, thus enhancing general family functioning. If, on the other hand, Tracy uses her increased level of privacy to disengage or disconnect from her family, family functioning is likely to be adversely affected. In either case, a positive feedback loop has been completed, because change has occurred in the family.

Change in family systems can take two forms: first- and second- order change. When a family makes a first-order change, family members modify their individual behaviors. No positive feedback loop is completed because family structure and functioning stay about the same. For example, Dorothy and her adolescent son, Rick, may experience a conflictual relationship around the issue of Rick's responsibility for contributing to household chores. Dorothy may perceive that Rick is not carrying his share of the load, whereas Jack may often give in to the temptation to let Rick off the hook at home, promising to "take care of it with Mom." "Change" may occur when Dorothy forces Rick into compliance through threatened punishment, such as the loss of access to the family car, but the source of the conflict is not identified or addressed. Second-order change involves an alteration of the family system, such as a reorganization of interactional patterns. If Dorothy and Rick's relationship were examined in the context of their entire family, it might be found that strengthening the marital/parental subsystem in order to create more consistent parenting patterns would reduce the conflict between parent and child. First-order changes are more subject to relapse, whereas second-order changes are more likely to endure because the actual structure of the system has been strengthened (Anderson & Sabatelli, 1993).

Looking Within the Family

What Is Family Functioning?

Family, as viewed from a systems perspective, comprises a group of interdependent individuals who share a sense of history, experience a degree of emotional bonding, and devise strategies for meeting the needs of individual family members and the family as a whole (Anderson & Sabatelli, 1993). As these needs change at different stages in the family's lifespan, strategies to meet these needs also must change. Within the Smith family, for example, Tracy's request for more privacy represents a normal developmental need for increased autonomy and requires the family to assess how it can best meet Tracy's need.

The goals of individual family members and the family as a whole can be placed in two primary categories: (1) the survival of the family and (2) the growth and development of its individual members (Anderson & Sabatelli, 1993). Families reach these goals through the achievement of four major tasks: (1) identity tasks, (2) boundary tasks, (3) physical maintenance of the family, and (4) management of the family's emotional climate. Although these tasks are generally common to most families, the particular strategies used to achieve these tasks differ among families and reflect each family's uniqueness.

One index of how well a particular family is functioning is how well it performs the four tasks necessary to ensure its goals of survival and growth; that is, if the family is achieving its goals, it is "getting the job done," regardless of differences in how this process "looks" in different families. A family with two parents, one child, and ample economic resources, for example, will probably develop strategies for meeting family members' needs that look very different from the strategies developed by a single parent with three children and limited economic resources. Both families, however, may be accomplishing their family tasks equally well.

Although strategies differ among families, most families use rules to carry out their tasks. Rules define what is and is not acceptable in a family and reflect each family's identity. Some family rules are specific to particular family tasks, but they could include "we all pitch in to get tasks done," "we negotiate how we accomplish tasks," and "what Mom says goes." Rules may be overt (i.e., expressed openly) or covert (i.e., never openly stated but well understood). Over time, rules are influenced by metarules, or rules about rules. Metarules delineate how rules operate, which rules are more important, and the exceptions to rules. For instance, a rule within the Smith family might be "curfew is midnight on weekends," whereas a metarule within the same family could be that Dad will grant an extension if approached at the right time in the right way.

Family Identity Task

The identity task of the family is twofold: the development of a family identity and individual development of family members' identities. First, by developing a family identity, the family organizes how it thinks of itself as a family. This is often accomplished through the development of family themes that reflect the family's distinctive characteristics, such as values, ethnicity, and manner of relating to each other and to others outside the family. Family themes may have their roots in family of origin, religious beliefs, or ethnic origins, and they may be expressed by family members in statements such as "Our family is very (close, resilient, religious, disorganized, traditional, etc.)." The Smith family themes, for example, might be based on traditional gender roles and the importance of success and economic security, as indicated in

Jack Smith's investment in his career and his wife's picking up the slack at home and in the family.

Families use their themes to guide their identity development. Family members choose behaviors that fit these self-perceptions, and so themes are perpetuated. Rick, for example, may follow up on the Smith family's themes of success and hard work by choosing behaviors contributing to his development of a traditional male gender identity: assuming the family provider role and achieving economic success as an adult.

The second component of the family identity task is the socialization of individual personal identities of family members. Interaction of family members helps each member learn about his or her self. These interactions include parental messages to children, such as "You are so (smart, stubborn, etc.)." These messages guide family members' choice of behaviors. Behaviors are chosen that fit the family's perceptions and expectations, and so identities are reinforced and perpetuated. For example, the Smith family's expectations may be that children will be self-sufficient individuals, and so children will be more likely to behave in autonomous ways. Alternatively, children may be assigned roles that support the family's functioning and contribute to identities children are likely to carry forward into adulthood. The Smiths' third child, Eva, exemplified this process when she became defiant and contentious during her high school years. Eva, by taking on and acting out the family's frustrations through her own noncompliance, shifted the focus from Dad's absence at home to herself. Although Eva's behavior was only a symptom of her family's problems, she was viewed during this time as a "problem child" and began to develop a sense of her own identity around being a troublemaker.

Family Boundary Tasks

Boundary tasks are the second category of family tasks that contribute to the survival of the family and individual development of family members. Family boundaries can be classified as external or internal and fall along a continuum of permeability, depending on how freely and easily information crosses the boundaries. A rigid boundary may be conceptualized as a thick, dark line with no breaks. A permeable boundary may be conceptualized as a thin, broken line that could be easily traversed. The establishment of external boundaries defines fam-

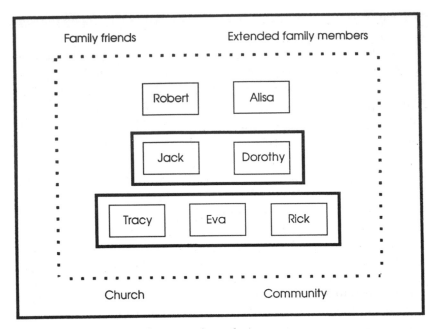

Figure 1.4: Smith family system boundaries

ily membership, that is, who is in the family (including nonbiological kin) and who is outside the family. External boundaries also define the family's relationship to systems outside the family, particularly the flow of information between the family and external systems, such as community, church, and school. As mentioned earlier, the Smith family may be perceived as having a somewhat rigid external boundary in the sense that very little private family information is shared with others outside the family. In other ways, however, the boundary surrounding the Smiths is somewhat permeable (see Figure 1.4). For example, two long-term friends, Robert and Alisa, who are not biologically related to the Smiths, are nonetheless considered to be "part of the family." Similarly, when the children lived at home, they knew that their mom would not mind their bringing friends home for dinner unexpectedly. Also, during the years when Jack was most involved with his career, Dorothy frequently took advantage of community resources and family friends to provide care and activities for the young children.

Families also establish internal boundaries. Internal boundaries exist around individual family members and around family subsystems, such as the marital dyad (Jack and Dorothy Smith) or the sibling sub-system (Rick, Tracy, and Eva). These internal boundaries are depicted in Figure 1.4. These boundaries regulate the flow of information within the family and so affect the degree of privacy and autonomy afforded family members. Examples might include the degree of consideration Dorothy and Jack show for their children's right to not share all per-sonal information with the family, and the respect granted by their chil-dren to Dorothy and Jack's right to protect the privacy and intimacy of their marital relationship.

Maintaining the Physical Environment of the Family

Families also face the task of providing for the basic physical envi-ronment and the physical needs of the family and its members in a way that supports and enhances their well-being and health. The strategies a family uses to achieve this task depend on the resources available to it, such as time, money, and energy. The manner in which a family's physical needs are met is also influenced by the family's values related to the use of its resources and the particular family members who have the power to control how resources are used. For example, in the Smith family, just like other families organized around traditional roles and rules, Jack has been responsible for providing and controlling the finan-cial resources for housing and food for the family, whereas Dorothy has been responsible for providing the time and energy necessary for man-aging the functioning of the household and caring for the children when they were young.

Those families that have enough organization and enough flexibility to allow for needed change and creative ways of thinking about meet-ing this task tend to be the most effective in caring for their families' physical needs. Families that are overorganized in their maintenance strategies may be too rigid to be open to options for alternative ways for meeting the physical needs of the family, such as departing from traditional roles when it better serves the needs of the family. In con-trast, extremely underorganized families may have few or no estab-lished strategies for taking care of the physical needs of the family. In underorganized families there may be no established routine for mak-ing sure the bills are paid or that there is food in the refrigerator. The normal hierarchy of responsibility and authority within the family may be reversed in extremely underorganized families, when children assume the adult role of caring for and ensuring that the physical needs of the family are met. For example, during a brief time in the Smith family when Jack was frequently out of town on business, Dorothy became ill. Rick, their oldest child, took on a "parentified" identity when he assumed much of the responsibility of caring for his two younger sisters, monitoring their homework and bed times. When this type of temporary parentification is called for in families as a form of adaption to temporary situations or circumstances, it remains clear that the ultimate authority still rests with the parent(s). Long-term parentification is discussed in more detail in later chapters.

Managing the Family's Emotional Climate

Management of the family's emotional climate promotes the wellbeing of family members by nurturing family members, building family closeness, and managing conflict within the family. Rules, which may be overt or covert, evolve within each family regarding how the family becomes and stays close and how family members nurture each other. These rules are only "right" or "wrong" depending on how well they help the family experience cohesion, support, and nurturance. The Smiths, for example, do not often openly express affection to each other, but they know that it is just "understood" that they all care for each other and will "be there for each other" whenever needed. Other families may communicate caring and closeness through openly expressed affection, such as hugs and saying "I love you" at the end of the day or when saying goodbye. Both types of families are equally caring and cohesive, although these qualities are expressed in different ways.

Managing the emotional climate within families also entails dealing with conflict. Each family has its own rules regulating the ways in which it responds to conflict. Families whose decision-making processes and power distribution allow the participation of all family members in dealing with conflict promote feelings of worth and acceptance among its members. In addition, conflict management strategies that do not deny conflict as normal in families, that address actual conflictual issues, and that allow for negotiation and compromise facilitate the family's successful management of its emotional climate. It is important to note that although complete control of the family system does not lie with any one member, some members may have more influence than others in determining the behavior of that system, including its response to conflict and its degree of openness to change (Whitchurch & Constantine, 1993). Within the Smith family, no family member is denied the right or opportunity to express his or her position on a conflictual issue. When the Smith children were living at home, opinions on issues such as curfews and allowances would be expressed by Dorothy and the children; however, as husband and father, Jack reserved the right to have the final say on most such issues.

Family Development and Stress

Strategies and rules used to achieve the four family tasks not only differ among families but also change across time. Stress in the family is an occurrence that calls for change or reorganization within the system, reflecting the family's ability to adapt (Anderson & Sabatelli, 1993). All families experience stress, and functional families are able to be flexible in responding to that stress (Isaacson, 1991). For example, developmental changes in the Smith family occurred as the children grew older, became more autonomous, and eventually moved out of the Smith family household. These changes, or stressors, call for modifications in the processes (strategies and rules) the family uses to accomplish its tasks. Rick, Tracy, and Eva each gradually assumed more responsibility within the family and in their own lives and were granted more autonomy by their parents.

In general, families have a drive for equilibrium and constancy in their developed patterns of functioning and so tend to resist change. But when the need for change reaches a critical point and is greater than the need for constancy, how families respond to the crisis is an indicator of their effectiveness. A typical example of developmental change in families that calls for change is parents' need to find the best balance between holding on to and letting go of their adolescent and teenage children. As mentioned earlier, when Tracy Smith expressed her need for more personal privacy, her parents and siblings had the opportunity to respond in a way that acknowledged this need for change as a function of the developmental stage of Tracy, as an adolescent, and of the Smith family, as a family with growing children.

Looking Beyond the Family

Just as there are subsystems embedded within the family system, the family system is embedded within the larger, overarching system of our culture: the suprasystem. Looking at the family in the context of its suprasystem allows us to ask questions about the family's interaction with its external environment and to examine the ways these inter-actions affect the family's functioning. For example, families may be better understood if they are examined in relation to their racial or eth-nic subcultures, their extended family of origin, or their religious community.

A family system is separated from its suprasystem by an external boundary. Rigid external boundaries allow very little interaction be-tween the family and its environment, whereas more permeable bound-aries permit greater freedom of interaction between the family and oth-ers on the outside. During the Smith children's school years, Jack was very involved in the formation of his law career, and Dorothy tapped re-sources outside of the family as support in raising her children. She participated in a mothers' morning-out group, sharing child care with several other mothers in the neighborhood. The children regularly at-tended story times at the public library and participated in church ac-tivities throughout childhood and adolescence. The children often spent Sunday afternoons at their grandparents', allowing Dorothy time to herself while Jack was at the office catching up on work. Thus, the Smith family was surrounded during this time by a quite permeable boundary, allowing family members, especially Dorothy and the chil-dren, to access valuable social support from its suprasystem: neighbors, friends, extended family, church, and community.

Summary

Over the last two decades, family practitioners have increasingly chosen the family systems perspective to guide their work with fami-lies. Interest in the family systems viewpoint is consistent with the growing tendency to approach understanding of human development and human behavior in its context: the context of family, community, and the overarching social patterns and institutions of our culture. This trend reflects the philosophy that individuals do not live or develop in isolation from others with whom they interact and by whom they are influenced. So it is with families. A full understanding of how any family "works" in promoting its own survival and the well-being of its members can only be achieved by exploring the structure and dynamics of that family as a system and the context in which the family exists.

2 A SOCIOHISTORICAL PERSPECTIVE OF ALCOHOLISM IN THE UNITED STATES

Just as each child lives and develops within the context of his or her family system, each family lives and develops in the context of its suprasystem, the overarching social patterns of our culture. As we discussed in Chapter 1, an understanding of the dynamics of the family system can guide our work with children of alcoholic families. Similarly, an understanding of the values, attitudes, and beliefs surrounding alcohol use and abuse in our culture can contribute to our understanding of these families.

Since the founding of our nation, alcohol has played an integral role in American culture. Over the course of our history and into the present, the consumption of alcohol has constituted an important part of the celebration of special occasions such as religious ceremonies, holiday seasons, births, and marriages, as well as recreational periods such as weekends and vacations. In these contexts, alcohol is generally viewed as beneficial to our society in that it promotes a sense of unity and community. Since the very early beginnings of the American culture, however, alcohol also has been perceived as a double-edged sword to society. Alcohol has been and continues to be consumed in excess by many Americans, with consequent harmful effects to the individual, the individual's family, and the members of society.

A sociohistorical perspective of alcohol use and abuse proposes that variations in alcohol usage and related problems in society are connected to other characteristics of that society. These sociocultural characteristics influence patterns of alcohol use and abuse at any point in time, and because characteristics of any society are never static, these influences vary over time and are reflected in variations in the patterns of alcohol use.

The question of how people have used alcohol over the course of history has been explored by sociologists and anthropologists. Studies of drinking behavior in diverse cultures indicate that cultural characteristics are the most powerful determinants of whether or not alcohol consumption eventuates in alcoholism (Levin, 1995). The assumptions and values of a culture related to heavy drinking constitute the culturally determined meaning of heavy drinking in that culture. These societal assumptions and values are internalized by the members of that culture and consequently influence their drinking practices.

An understanding of "how Americans drink" must include an understanding of the relationship between characteristics of our society and the alcohol consumption patterns of the members of our society. The purpose of this chapter is twofold. An overview of trends of alcohol use and misuse in the United States since the founding of our country will be presented. Concomitant attitudes and values toward alcohol consumption will also be noted, and the suggested relationship between attitudes, values, and rates of use and abuse of alcohol will be addressed. The value of this information lies in its potential basis for inferences concerning the cause of alcohol-related problems in our society and consequently for prevention and control of alcohol-related problems.

Alcohol use and abuse in the United States is multidetermined. Many factors, within society as well as within the individual, influence patterns of alcohol consumption. An examination of trends of alcohol consumption across the history of the United States indicates that environmental factors operate on a broadly based scale to influence alcohol use (Connors & Tarbox, 1985). Examples include governmental regulations of alcohol production and sales and social influences such as cultural norms that sanction or prohibit alcohol use and/or abuse. In addition, alcohol consumption is also influenced by individual differences, intrinsic characteristics of the individual that correlate with various patterns of alcohol use and abuse. For example, personality characteristics, unique biochemical or genetic constitutions, and family alcohol use may influence an individual's drinking pattern. (The biosocial perspective of alcohol abuse is more fully discussed in Chapter 8 of this book.) It is important to note that neither factors in the environment nor intrinsic influences predestine any individual's pattern of alcohol consumption. Rather, environmental influences interact with individual characteristics to determine how great an influence these factors have on the drinking patterns of each person within the culture.

History of Alcohol Use and Abuse and Concurrent Sociological Factors

Alcohol consumption has been an integral part of American life since the inception of our society. Colonists brought alcohol to America, and colonial Americans adopted drinking practices from Europe. Customs and attitudes supporting consumption of alcohol were evidenced in the popularity of the tavern, which was the center of town politics, business, trade, and pleasure and where beer, wine, and distilled spirits were consumed frequently and in considerable quantity (Maisto, Galizio, & Connors, 1991). Drinking in taverns was very much a part of colonial life, and positive attitudes toward alcohol saw it as meeting physical, social, and psychological needs.

During the era of the American Revolution, most Americans drank alcoholic beverages and considered them to be healthy and beneficial. Even moralistic Puritan ministers considered alcohol as "the Good Creature of God." Drunkenness was denounced as misuse, but blame for drunkenness was placed on the sinner, not the alcohol (Ray & Ksir, 1996).

Soon after the Revolution, the perspective of alcohol as the cause of serious problems began to develop. This was the basis of a perspective still existing in American culture today, which views alcohol as an active source of evil, damaging everything it touches. The Temperance movement began to emerge from this perspective around the turn of the century. Temperance refers to the idea that people should drink no distilled spirits and should drink wine and beer only in moderation. Citizens took pledges to this effect.

In the late 1800s, important changes began to occur in the drinking patterns of Americans and in societal attitudes and values about alcohol use and abuse. Per capita consumption soared, society was moving toward urbanization and industrialization, and the negative consequences of heavy drinking became more evident. With the advent of artificial refrigeration and preservatives, the number of breweries increased. Increased consumption of beer was fed by the wave of European immigrants entering the country at this time, and drunken behavior became associated with these immigrants. Increased consumption of distilled spirits also made for more socially disruptive drinking. As drinking became more socially disruptive, it became less socially acceptable, and people began to speak out against alcohol consumption.

At the turn of the century, increased opposition to drinking arose, and Temperance advocates began to call for abstinence from all alcoholic beverages. Political and health concerns were interwoven with a middle-class, Protestant, evangelical concern that the "good and true life" was being undermined by ethnic groups with a lower standard of morality. The tavern or saloon became the focal scapegoat of the Temperance movement and was blamed for social ills such as thievery, prostitution, gambling, and political corruption. Consequently, pressure grew to prohibit the sale of alcohol altogether. The "captains of industry" of the late 19th century, including Rockefeller, Carnegie, and Ford, were foremost among those who supported total abstinence from alcohol because they believed abstinent employees would be better employees (Maisto et al., 1991). With the approach of World War I, the anti-alcohol drive had gained considerable financial, social, and political power. As a result, state Prohibition began in 1850, wherein state laws prohibited all sales of alcoholic beverages. By 1917, 64% of the population lived in "dry" territory, and 2 years later, national Prohibition was enacted by law (Ray & Ksir, 1996).

Prohibition, however, never had the general public support that forbidding the use of alcohol has had in some Moslem countries, and it did not result in an alcohol-free society. People continued to drink legally from readily available patented medicines containing alcohol, called tonics and stimulants. People also continued to drink illegally in private clubs and speakeasies. It became clear that it was not going to be easy to enforce Prohibition for the large minority who were violating the law. In fact, organized crime became more organized and profitable as a result of Prohibition, and drinking was assigned a kind of "allure of the forbidden," glamorizing gangsters and bootleggers. Also, there was concern among the general public that the widespread violation of Prohibition laws created a sense of lawlessness and weakened respect for law and order.

Although Prohibition did not eliminate consumption of alcohol, it did appear to reduce overall alcohol consumption. Hospital admissions for alcoholism and alcohol-related deaths declined. At its best, legal prohibition of alcohol reduced availability, consumption, and related problems. At its worst, Prohibition encouraged organized crime and created expensive enforcement efforts. The repeal of Prohibition in 1933 was actually more a function of economic and legal practicality than of any significant change in attitudes and values about alcohol consumption (Ray & Ksir, 1996).

After the repeal of Prohibition, each state had its own means of regulating the sale and consumption of alcohol. Most states allowed at least the sale of beer, reflecting the pre-Prohibition perspective that beer was a safer alcoholic beverage than distilled spirits. Alcohol sales and consumption increased rapidly from 1935 to 1945, when per capita consumption returned to pre-Prohibition levels.

Alcohol consumption rates began to increase steadily again in the 1970s, when many states lowered the legal drinking age from 21 to 18 or 19 years of age. This change likely reflected U.S. involvement in the Vietnam war, and the philosophy that "if our boys are old enough to fight for this country, they are old enough to drink." However, per capita consumption rates began to increase steadily again, and concerns over young people dying in alcohol-related accidents resulted in Congress authorizing the Transportation Department to withhold federal highway funds from any states with a legal drinking age under 21. Consequently, by 1988, 21 was the uniform drinking age across all states.

The early 1980s brought a reversal of trends. A growing emphasis on health, fitness, and nutrition in our culture influenced changes in social attitudes about drinking and an increased awareness of the negative consequences of alcohol. In addition, tighter governmental controls resulted in limitations on the use of alcohol and a slight decline in per capita consumption (Maisto et al., 1991).

Alcohol Use and Abuse in Contemporary American Culture: Who Drinks and Why?

Since the repeal of Prohibition, drinking has become the norm in most American subcultures. Studies indicate that most Americans drink at least once a year (although it is important to note that 10% of the population drinks half the alcohol consumed each year).

Sociological characteristics, such as gender, age, geographic region, and socioeconomic status, have been found to be powerful indicators of drinking practices. For example, those Americans most likely to be drinkers are men of all ages more than women, young and early middle-aged people more than late middle-aged and elderly, urban more than rural, secular oriented more than religious, single more than married, better educated more than less educated, and economically better off more than the poor. Members of our culture who are most likely to be heavy or problem drinkers include men ages 45 to 49, blue-collar workers, men who have completed high school but not college, residents of the largest cities, and men and women with no religious affiliation.

The above sociological profiles of those who use and abuse alcohol in our society are based on statistical generalizations (Levin, 1995). It is important to note that people of all backgrounds become addicted to alcohol. Groups who are found to have relatively low rates of alcohol-related problems may in fact be underidentified because they have the means to protect their problem drinkers from the consequences of their drinking. In addition, as more and more Americans are assimilated into the common middle-class structure, as regional differences blur, and as sex roles become less rigid, characteristics such as gender, place of residence, and socioeconomic status are likely to become less predictive of the use and misuse of alcohol. For example, although overall rates of alcohol consumption now appear to be stable, very recent studies show an increase in drinking in males and females in their 20s and among women ages 35 to 40 (Levin, 1995).

Why Do Americans Drink?

Americans use alcohol in different ways and for different purposes (Levin, 1995). For example, some individuals drink to induce particular feelings, such as relaxation, social ease, or drunkenness, without regard for effect on others (Levin, 1995). This may be thought of as instrumental or utilitarian drinking in that it is devoted to personal ends and individual self-gratification, whether or not it takes place within a group.

For other drinkers, alcohol holds symbolic meanings. For example, alcohol may symbolize a source of power for some, as is implied in much of the contemporary alcohol advertising, which commonly portrays alcohol consumption as part of the lives of the wealthy and glamorous. For others, drinking may hold religious meaning, symbolizing communion with the deity.

Alcohol consumption can also serve the purpose of social integration. Socially integrative drinking is done with a convivial attitude, as in sharing drinks at parties and celebrations. In our culture, socially integrative drinking is seen as a means of enhancing one's feelings of identification and union with others and so is socially sanctioned.

Why Do Americans "Problem-Drink"?

There is no universal, cross-cultural, absolute distinction between alcohol use and abuse. Guidelines for drinking behaviors that are sanctioned and those that are prohibited are expressed in the norms each society establishes for its members. In this way, the boundary between acceptable drinking and problem-drinking practices is established by each culture according to its distinctive values and attitudes about alcohol consumption. Within any particular culture, those members whose drinking patterns do not fit that culture's norms for acceptable drinking behavior are considered "problem-drinkers" or alcoholics. To bring our sociohistorical understanding of alcohol use and misuse in our own culture into the present, it is important to examine the contemporary norms that influence how members of our culture drink. It is also critical to consider the factors that may influence members of our culture to deviate from those norms.

Norms Surrounding Alcohol Use

Clear, consistent norms act as a form of social support and social control. In early interdependent settled communities in our culture, where people had to account for their behavior and provide for them-

selves by growing their own crops, drinking was usually well controlled by structured social systems that specified social rights and obligations (Ray & Ksir, 1996). Still today, lower rates of drinking seem to
correlate with learning to drink in a situation of strong social control in
which moderation is the social norm. For example, there are few abstainers *or* problem drinkers among Jewish Americans, who are socialized to drink in moderation primarily with the family (an example of
socially integrative drinking) and on ceremonial occasions (an example
of symbolic drinking in a religious context).

Ambivalent Societal Attitudes
Toward Alcohol Consumption

In our contemporary culture, however, norms regarding acceptable
patterns of alcohol consumption are not always clear and consistent. As
is the case for many Western societies, we are experiencing rapid social
change, with concomitant confusion around guidelines for the appropriate use of alcohol. Mixed messages are given to members of our culture about where the line is drawn between alcohol use and abuse.
There is considerable ambivalence about alcohol consumption in our
culture, and this ambivalence makes the norm of moderation less
powerful.

Legally, this ambivalence is reflected by the widely disparate laws
different states use to try to control the sale and use of alcohol. Even
within individual states, some counties prohibit the sale of all alcoholic
beverages, whereas others do not. Perhaps even more important, as a
culture we hold very ambivalent values and attitudes regarding alcohol. We recognize the potential problems associated with alcohol, and
at times, we have even tried to impose legal prohibition. However, we
also support a flourishing alcoholic beverage industry and advertise
alcohol in glamorous and seductive ways (Poley, Lea, & Vibe, 1979). On
one hand, there are currently groups advocating a mandatory ban on
the broadcast of beer and wine advertisements on radio and television.
On the other hand, opponents contend that this ban violates Americans' right to free speech (Ray & Ksir, 1996). Ambivalence also remains
in public opinion, reflected in the common truism, "Everybody enjoys
a drink, nobody enjoys a drunk" (Maisto et al., 1991). And who among
us has not seen behavior that is typically considered unacceptable for-
given or at least excused because the individual "had a few too many"?

Ambivalence toward alcohol is also reflected in the models that members of our society employ to conceptualize and understand alcohol abuse in our culture. The early moralistic perspective saw alcohol misuse as a character flaw, reflecting a lack of morality and willpower on the part of the individual. Vestiges of the moralistic perspective still exist and are considered by many to have a legitimate place in our response to alcohol misuse. Those who perceive alcohol abuse as a moral weakness consider legal and punitive measures as well as religious recourse of seeking help from a higher power as solutions to alcoholism (Poley et al., 1979).

In contrast, many members of contemporary American society regard alcoholism as a disease process because it destroys physical and mental health as well as families. Understanding alcohol abuse as a clearly identified physical process changes the emphasis from moralistic to medical and shifts societal efforts to deal with alcohol-related problems from punitive and moralistic approaches toward an emphasis on treatment. A Gallup poll in the late 1980s revealed that over 90% of the American public believe alcohol dependence is a disease. This is also the dominant position among treatment professionals and Alcoholics Anonymous.

It is interesting to consider what a medical or disease model of alcoholism reflects about our society's attitude toward alcohol use and abuse. This perspective proposes a philosophical question: By considering people with alcohol-related problems as having a disease, do we imply that they are absolved of responsibility for their own behavior? Those who support this model would respond that the behavior of alcohol abuse is the result of the disease process and so should not be punished. In contrast, those who support the moralistic perspective stand for the belief that alcohol abuse is a learned and voluntary behavior and thus can be "unlearned," particularly when the abuser is motivated by negative consequences such as legal repercussions (Maisto et al., 1991; Poley et al., 1979).

Clearly, social norms are powerful influences in controlling individual and group behavior within our culture. Social norms are strongest in their influence, however, when they are clear and consistent in their messages regarding which behaviors are sanctioned and which are prohibited. The ambivalent attitudes about alcohol that coexist in our society constitute one contribution to alcohol abuse, in that ambivalent norms can be similar to permissive norms in their resulting in higher levels of problem drinking and alcoholism.

Relatedly, internalized social norms or cultural controls that inhibit the abuse of alcohol among members of our culture can break down in the face of other influences. Characteristics of the sociocultural environment can precipitate deviation from the norms of sanctioned drinking behavior.

What are the dynamics of American culture that may put members of our society at an increased risk for the misuse of alcohol? Ours is a culture built on an individualistic perspective of achievement and success. This perspective is grounded in the frontier philosophy of the Old West: set out, stake your claim, and make good by virtue of sheer determination and hard labor. The contemporary version of this perspective contends that any individual who wants it enough and works hard enough is potentially able to succeed. Success in our culture is most often measured in the accumulation of wealth, material goods, prestige, and status.

The individualistic perspective puts an enormous amount of pressure on members of our culture to "become someone/something," even at the expense of their own physical and psychological well-being. This pressure creates anxiety, and sociologists propose that the greater the anxiety and tension in a culture, the higher the rates of problem drinking will be as a means of tension reduction. In our culture, alcohol is widely marketed as a readily available means of reducing tension and anxiety. Ours is a society that emphasizes consumerism, immediate gratification, and a pain-free, pleasurable life (Talashek, Gerace, & Starr, 1994). We very casually sanction the idea of "having a drink to wind down" from a hard day or having a few drinks on the weekend to relax after a particularly stressful week. These attitudes can predispose members of our culture to problem drinking and alcoholism. There is thus a relationship between the high levels of anxiety experienced by many members of our fast-paced, high-pressure culture and heavy drinking patterns. In fact, stress indicators in our culture, including business failures, divorces, abortions, disasters, unemployment, and high school dropout rates, have been found to be significantly associated with drinking norms of heavy drinking and alcohol-related arrests (Ray & Ksir, 1996).

A marked discrepancy between the goals and ideals of a culture and the ability of that culture's members to achieve those objectives may be a precipitating factor in alcoholism (Poley et al., 1979). The individual-istic perspective of achievement and success does not take into account the impediments intrinsic to our culture that stand in the way of many individuals' opportunity to achieve the "American dream." Sociocul-tural barriers such as oppression and discrimination based on race, gender, socioeconomic level, and sexual orientation restrict many Americans' opportunities and resources for realizing the goals and ide-als of our culture. When people are not able to live up to the individu-alistic national dream, frustration, anxiety, and guilt set in. Consequent depression can result in a devaluation of one's own culture, and thus a devaluation of the culture's norms. So what if heavy drinking is "frowned upon"? Alternate sources of feelings of pleasure and satisfac-tion may not be available, but cheap spirits are. Alcohol misuse then becomes a passive expression of frustration, even rage, and a means of self-medication (Levin, 1995). This is a kind of relief or escape drinking, for example, among individuals living in extreme poverty who may use alcohol as a reprieve from feelings of powerlessness and failure.

Conclusion

Alcohol consumption remains a significant part of our culture and may even be considered part of our national identity. Alcohol use has become part of the common experience of children and adults alike, either directly or indirectly. Virtually every adolescent and adult in the United States today is exposed each day to the opportunity to use alco-hol. One assumption held by the general public is that because of the widespread familiarity with alcohol in our culture, we can be relaxed about its use (Poley et al., 1979). Handling the benefits of the pleasur-able qualities of alcohol (e.g., its taste and psychological effects) respon-sibly is considered to be one of the tasks imposed on a free society. However, alcohol use and misuse is a social problem because it affects a substantial number of people in ways considered undesirable by so-ciety in general.

Concern about alcohol use became more common in the 1980s and continues into the turn of the century (Maisto et al., 1991). A definite trend has been noted: The greater the per capita consumption of alco-hol, the greater will be the problems of alcohol dependency, crime, and accidents related to alcohol. The effects of alcohol abuse and alcoholism in lost production, health care costs, motor vehicle accidents, fire losses, and crime result in an estimated social economic cost of $43 billion to $60 billion, more than the combined social cost estimates for cancer, respiratory disease, and endocrine, nutritional, and metabolic diseases (Maisto, Galizio, & Carey, 1985). These costs, of course, do not account for the costs that are more difficult to assess: the human suffering associated with alcoholism.

As a country, we have much to gain from a better understanding of the development and maintenance of our alcohol use and abuse. Collective social awareness and understanding of the dynamics of alcoholism can become the basis of policy decisions and consequent action. In the meantime, practitioners must focus on identifying and helping children who daily are paying the price of human suffering associated with living with alcoholism in their families.

3 LIVING AND SURVIVING IN AN ALCOHOLIC HOME

CASE 3.1

Flames engulfed our tiny wood frame house. I was five years old. I remember standing, paralyzed by fear, as the fire roared and swelled. My older sister and I huddled together in terror as neighbors worked frantically to retrieve household belongings from the raging inferno. A gas kitchen stove had exploded, I heard someone say. Minutes before, I had witnessed flames leaping up the kitchen wall and my mother's sharp demands for me to hurry for sand as she desperately tried to douse them. The fire continued to rage out of control until our house burned to the ground. In many ways, that fire symbolized my entire childhood. The volatility, rage, and chaos of the burning house were a prelude to what was to come in the next five years as my father became progressively sicker from the disease of alcoholism.

Within two years, my hardworking and resourceful father had managed to finance the rebuilding of that house on the same plot of land where it had burned. But the wonderful memories in the old house burned along with our personal belongings. My dad began to drink outside the house at first. Then he began hiding beer and liquor bottles around the house. Eventually, he started drinking out in the open at home, despite my mother's bitter protests, and finally staying out drinking all night.

On weekends, my little sister and I waited for our father outside the movie theater as the marquee darkened, the sidewalks emptied of people, and the street traffic hushed. Underneath the big-screen excitement of James Dean and Marilyn Monroe, a ten-year-old boy's worst fear had come true. Dad had abandoned us once again. We either walked the three-mile trek in the dark or the police took us home. I preferred the walk because riding in the patrol car scared and embarrassed me. I always felt like I had done something wrong, and I didn't want neighbors and friends to see the officers pull up in front of my house. Many repetitions of these nights forced me into the caretaker role of my younger sister. Sometimes she would cry and, although I wanted to, I had to make her think I was in charge. I was scared and mad because of the cold and dark, empty streets. My feelings of abandonment were expressed through anger that camouflaged deeper emotions of hurt and rejection.

Saturdays would be different, we convinced ourselves, because that was the day we always went into town to buy things. By the time we would get inside the department stores to try on outfits or shop for special things, Dad would be stumbling and slurring his words. The stares from clerks and other shoppers would embarrass me so badly that I wanted to disappear. At restaurants, he would humiliate us by loud and obnoxious behaviors. He would insult our waiters, knock over glasses of water, or drag his coat sleeve through his rice and gravy. I was embarrassed by the way he behaved and was afraid people wouldn't like me because of it. He seemed to care more for his bottle than he did for his family. That made my sense of self-worth nosedive. I reasoned that if he couldn't remember to pick me up at the movies, then I must not be very important. I became shy and withdrawn and felt all alone. I bottled my feelings up inside and never let anybody know how badly I felt.

Things got progressively worse between my parents. They had explosive arguments and violent physical fights. That's when I took center stage, trying to stabilize an out-of-control family. I refereed verbal bouts that lasted for hours, hoping and praying they wouldn't hurt or kill one another. My house was an arsenal of weapons. Kitchen knives, dishes, frying pans, knickknacks, mirrors, pictures off the wall, hair brushes, even furniture were heaved, thrown, slung, and slammed during weekly angry outbursts between my parents. It became routine for me to stand between my father's threatening fist and defiant stare and my mother's raised arm. I tried to conceal the family battle from neighbors by closing doors and windows and drawing all the curtains in the house. I cleared tables of fragile figurines, hid breakable items, and removed wall hangings to prevent their destruction during the domestic war.

Sweeping up shattered glass, plastic, and debris became a weekly ritual in the aftermath. My sisters and I were left to survive as best we could on our own in a world we didn't understand. Our house became a battleground, and we became the spoils of war. I became ringmaster of our family circus—the protector, the peacemaker, the referee, the family hero—in short, the one who ran the show. Although I couldn't stop the violence, I could control the scenario so that neighbors wouldn't see, the house wouldn't be destroyed, and no one would be killed or sent to the hospital or prison. It was a role no ten-year-old child would choose; it was one I took by default, out of necessity, out of a will to survive.

I continued to carry my role of ringmaster into adulthood, although I no longer lived in a chaotic family. After years of seeing my parents out of control, I began to deplore any situation in which people could not control themselves. I learned very early to always be in control. As a grownup, the need to control everything and everyone around me became an obsession. Things had to be done my way or not at all. But the old survival skills that saved me as a child no longer worked as an adult and caused me many problems in my interpersonal relationships at work, at home, and at play. I carried my ringmaster role into my work and became a workaholic. I received my self-worth from work, and it became my life. Through years of hard self-inventory and the help of Al-Anon and Adult Children of Alcoholics Groups, I gained insight into my inner feelings and perceptions. I realized that I didn't have to continue on the same self-destructive course of my alcoholic upbringing. Using my childhood background as a transformational experience from which to learn, I began to reinterpret my life in a much more positive and constructive way. As a recovering adult child of an alcoholic, I have discovered, through extensive personal inventory and hard work, that life can be quite satisfying.

— *Bryan Robinson*

Many politicians, writers, comedians, and entertainers (for example, Bill Clinton, Carol Burnett, Jonathan Winters, Chuck Norris, and Suzanne Somers) are children of alcoholics; the shorthand term is COA. Many COAs discover that, as adults, they are reliving the same destructive patterns of their families of origin. Anywhere from 40 to 50 percent become alcoholics themselves; others develop eating disorders or become workaholics, as Bryan did. One reason for this is that COAs do not know what a healthy family is supposed to be like. They do not know what normal is. Because of their early wretched family life, they develop unrealistic expectations of the ways families function. Many times they develop a fairy tale image, and when the dream isn't fulfilled, they feel like they have failed.

As a child, Bryan's vision of what a family should be like came from the television shows he watched, *Leave It to Beaver* and *Father Knows Best*. He dreamed of living in a beautiful house like the Cleavers or the Andersons on a quiet and shady, tree-lined street. There would be peace and tranquility, and everyone would smile and talk instead of frown or yell. He would live happily ever after. Needless to say, these unrealistic expectations are sources of trouble in adulthood for anyone who expects their families to be so perfect.

As you can tell from Bryan's story, the drinking parent is not the only family member who suffers from alcoholism. Children are the innocent, unseen victims. They suffer slowly and methodically every day they live in a chemically dependent family. The longer they live in the disease, the stronger the grip it takes and the longer and more difficult the reversal process. Although for years, treatment efforts were directed exclusively at the alcoholic parent and spouse, there is growing recognition that the entire family system is affected by the disease and that all family members need treatment. Still, children of alcoholic parents continue to be the most neglected family members in terms of diagnosis and treatment.

The codependency operating in alcoholic families hampers children's efforts to separate from their parents and grow into mature, individual human beings. The sooner practitioners can recognize the problem and intervene, the quicker these negative effects can be circumvented. For intervention to be effective, however, practitioners must fully understand the family disease concept of alcoholism.

Alcoholism as a Family Disease

Alcoholism is a family disease—one that affects every member of the family system in a devastating way. Thinking of the family unit as a system helps to better explain the family disease concept. Suppose we wanted to know how the cardiovascular system works (Flake-Hobson, Robinson, & Skeen, 1983). We might go to a medical laboratory, locate a heart and the attached blood vessels, then carefully dissect and study them. In this way, we would learn something about the basic structure of the cardiovascular system, that the heart has four chambers and a number of valves. But we would still not know how these chambers and valves work because the heart would not be functioning. Only by studying the cardiovascular system while it is functioning in a living person would we see how the chambers and valves pump blood through the body. We cannot know what happens to the heart when a person is running, for example, without seeing the cardiovascular system in relationship to the whole body system. This holistic approach informs me that, while running, the muscles of the body require more oxygen than they do at rest, and the heart beats faster to supply oxygen. In other words, the total body system is affected by the running and must change to adjust to it.

The same is true of an alcoholic family. No family member can be understood in isolation from the other members of that family system. No particular family dynamic can be understood in isolation from the dynamics of the entire family system. The family must be seen as a composite because each member, as part of a functioning system, is interdependent on the other members. Practitioners cannot understand fully what happens to a child of an alcoholic parent without understanding the interworkings of that child's entire family system.

A family system will always try to maintain a sense of equilibrium. As the family works together to run smoothly, any change in one part of the family system will necessitate changes in the other parts of the system. The behavior of any one member of the family will affect all of the other family members. When such changes occur, some shift in family structure and/or functioning must occur in order for the family to regain its equilibrium. In alcoholic families, the alcoholic's drastic behavior changes create disturbances within the family and threaten to throw the family's sense of balance out of kilter. Other family members must then alter how they function in the family in order to accommodate these changes and to keep the family system running in a viable way.

Alcoholism does not burst into the family as a heart attack would; rather it creeps slowly and silently until the time when it is finally detected and then, hopefully, faced by the family. But, by that time, it has left a mark on each family member. (Bowles, 1968, p. 1062)

Janet is a case in point. As she continued her alcoholic binges, Janet became dependent upon other family members to assume her former responsibilities, which helped glue the family together. She doesn't show up for work; laundry doesn't get done; and meals are unprepared. Husband Sam began putting her to bed when she collapsed in the living room, he called Janet's boss and told him she had the flu, and he straightened the previous night's mess before the kids came downstairs in the morning. As Sam scurried out the door late for work, he told his oldest son, Jamey, to let Mom sleep and to help out by cooking breakfast and getting baby sister off to school, like a big boy.

As his mom's drinking continued, ten-year-old Jamey was cooking all the meals, doing the laundry, and essentially rearing baby sister while Dad took care of Mom. The whole family system had shifted to compensate for the instability of Mom's alcoholism. The family's structure had shifted in that Jamey was now assuming a parental role. The family's functioning had also shifted as everyone organized their lives around picking up the slack for Mom. Because of the denial that is such an integral part of alcoholism, members do not know that the disease is eating insidiously away at the family's fabric. Everyone covers for Mom to protect the family secret, and they cannot recognize the disease for what it is.

As alcoholism progresses, the whole family becomes progressively sicker, too. Everything revolves around the dependent parent, whose behavior dictates how other family members interact inside and outside the family. Each family member adapts to the dependent's behavior by developing behaviors that cause the least amount of personal stress and tension within the family. The functioning of all family members continues to shift to compensate for the insidious illness.

Because parental alcoholism is a secret both within and outside the family, children are made partners in the family's denial that a parent is drinking. COAs survive by hiding their parents' problems, pretending everything is normal, and trying to avoid being discovered (Knight, 1993). It is in response to the disease of alcoholism that family members unconsciously play a role that counterbalances the alcoholic's behavior, sustains some degree of equilibrium in the family's structure and functioning, and keeps the family going.

Identity Development and
Survival Roles in Alcoholic Families

One of the most important tasks of families is the identity task, which involves both the development of a family identity and the development of the identities of individual family members. Information about family identities can generally be discovered by asking family members what their family is like. Responses tend to reflect how the family thinks of itself, unique characteristics of the family, and family themes that represent the ways family members generally relate to each other and to others outside the family. Because an alcoholic family system is always organized around the behaviors and demands of the person who drinks, family identity also revolves around the alcoholism. Family secrecy is a central theme in alcoholic families. Because alcoholic families perceive themselves as very private, a rigid external boundary is likely to exist around the family, limiting interaction with outsiders. For example, a rigid external boundary may separate immediate family members (parents and children) from extended family (grandparents, aunts, uncles, and cousins). This rigid boundary not only would keep extended family members outside of the family (sharing few or no activities) but also would prohibit their acquiring knowledge about the alcoholism in the family. Children may not be allowed to invite friends over, and parents are not likely to be involved in extracurricular activities at school and in the community. Given these circumstances, when the child of an alcoholic family is asked what his or her family is like, he or she is not likely to feel comfortable answering openly and honestly. However, the child would be quite likely to privately think of descriptors such as *crazy, confusing, lonely, scary, sad,* all reflecting characteristics that dominate alcoholic family identities.

The second part of the family identity task is the development of individual family members' identities. Through interacting with parents and siblings, children learn about themselves, what they are like, and who they are in relation to others. Parents actually "tell" children who they are and who they will become through the expression of perceptions and expectations. For example, independence becomes part of a child's individual identity when he hears in his family that "You have to look out for yourself in this world." Similarly, a child learns to perceive herself as competent when she is told, "You can accomplish whatever you set your mind to" or develops self-doubt when she hears, "What's the matter with you? You can never do anything right!" In an alcoholic family, parental messages to children are often ambiguous and inconsistent. When a parent is drinking, he may berate the child in an effort to shift the focus from his or her own behavior, contributing very negative messages to the child's identity development. Alternatively, when the alcoholic parent is sober, feelings of guilt, remorse, and love may prompt him or her to interact with the child in positive, affirming ways. The development of an individual identity grounded in family experience can therefore be a very confusing and difficult task for children of alcoholic families, and many of these children grow into adulthood without a clear idea of who they are.

Families also participate in the development of their children's identities by assigning them roles that support the family's functioning. Every child in an alcoholic home takes on some role or combination of roles simply to survive. These roles, although they appear to function effectively in childhood, shape children's identities and become a noose around the children's necks as they grow into adulthood (see Table 3.1). These roles, each different from the other, all serve the same purpose: to disguise the disease of alcoholism. Even parents have difficulty detecting the disease because they get sidetracked by the roles family members play. The roles distract and protect parents and children from the real problems and feelings hidden behind the facade. Mom drinks, household patterns are disrupted, children click into their assigned roles, and the family is able to carry on with some semblance of continuity. This pattern of circularity serves as a communal protection system so that the family can continue to function and each member can achieve some security and stability. Meanwhile, the disease continues its masquerade.

The chief enabler in an alcoholic family can be the alcoholic's spouse, parent, or child. As her disease progresses, Janet becomes more dependent upon Sam, who is the enabler in this case. The duties and obligations of the dependent are transferred to the enabler, whose role is to provide responsibility within the family system. The enabler smooths out the rough edges created by the dependent's drinking and makes

TABLE 3.1. The Survival Roles and Settings of Children of Alcoholics

Home	School	Work	Social Settings
Hero (responsible child)	Class star	Workaholic	Social good girl/ good girl
Scapegoat (acting-out child)	Problem child	Troublemaker	Social misfit
Lost child (adjuster)	Class isolate	Loner	Social recluse
Mascot	Class clown	Practical joker	Stand-up comic

SOURCE: Adapted from Wegscheider (1976) and Black (1982).

everything appear OK on the surface. Sam, for instance, put Janet to bed when she passed out, cleaned up her mess, lied to her boss, and instructed the children to assume their mother's duties. As Sam protected his wife and compensated for her loss of control, he in effect enabled her disease to continue. For this reason, the nonalcoholic parent is often referred to as the codependent.

The enabler role relates to the family task of maintaining the physical environment of the family. When alcoholism dominates the dynamics of the family, routines related to daily maintenance tasks like paying bills, washing clothes, and getting meals on the table become difficult to sustain. The family then becomes very underorganized or even chaotic, resulting in little predictability or consistency around issues such as management of finances, schedules, and meals, and each member just tries to get by each day as best he or she can. It is at this point that a family member often assumes the role of enabler and assumes double duty in order to reestablish some degree of order and routine in the household. The nonalcoholic parent in the family may overfunction in making sure the physical needs of family members are met to compensate for the underfunctioning of the alcoholic parent. Frequently a child, especially the oldest child in the family, assumes this role. The parent-child hierarchy then flip-flops as the child learns to use the washing machine, get younger siblings off to school, make excuses to bill collectors on the phone, and heat a can of soup for breakfast. In all families, there are times when children may need to pitch in more than is customary in order to temporarily adapt to unusual family circumstances. However, when this behavior becomes an ongoing pattern, parentification occurs, and the normal hierarchy of responsibility and authority within the family is reversed as children assume the adult role and responsibility for ensuring that the physical and emotional needs of family members are met (Chase, 1998). Parentified children take on an intense sense of responsibility for their alcoholic parent's well-being. Later in life, when it is developmentally appropriate and healthy for children to individuate from parents and to assume a sense of separateness and autonomy, parentified children find it extremely difficult to "let go" of the intense connections of childhood.

The Family Hero

There is a family hero in every alcoholic home. The hero is usually the oldest child, who feels responsible for the family pain and works hard to make things better. The family hero role may overlap with that of the chief enabler. Family heroes are ten years old going on thirty-five and are determined to prove to the world that everything is normal at home. Their job as children is to perform so well that others have to think that things are OK for them to be functioning so effectively. Heroes provide self-worth to the family, yet underneath the facade, deep-seated feelings of inadequacy and poor self-esteem predominate. In the case of Janet's family, Jamey was fast on his way to becoming the family hero.

At school, heroes excel in academics, athletics, or both. Parents often think these kids have miraculously survived the alcoholism because they appear to be resilient and to be independent of the need for help. Outwardly, they appear to have it all. They may be the most attentive, the most dependable, the smartest, and the most popular children in school. They follow the rules, always finish their schoolwork in the allotted time, and often are leaders in school government and extracurricular activities. They can be the president of the student council, the star quarterback, or the homecoming queen. Because achievement and competition are so highly valued in our society, family heroes usually go unnoticed and in fact are rewarded for their super achievements. This is not to say, however, that all successful or competent children are COAs. It is the overdeveloped sense of accomplishment, responsibility, and perfectionism that parents must look for. These kids are another example of parentified children. They never know what it is like to play and relax, and they become serious little adults. Their childhoods are filled with serious issues (such as "I wonder if Mom will be OK while I'm at school today") that are usually reserved for adulthood. While COAs dwell on their parent's drinking and welfare, their friends are playing and enjoying the carefree world of childhood.

Nina, one of two siblings in a COA treatment group, took care of everything around her house because her single mother was an active alcoholic. Nina had been making breakfast for herself and her little sister and getting them both off to school each morning ever since she could remember. She had great difficulty benefiting from the program because she forfeited her own needs in favor of her six-year-old sister. Her sister clung to her during group, and Nina spent most of her time parenting and protecting her sister. During fun activities, she reprimanded her for "acting silly" or "going the wrong way in a game." She was always on the lookout and chastised her for such minor infractions as taking two crackers at snack time, instead of one. She could not relax and play or enjoy the art and puppets because she felt it was her duty to keep everything on an even keel. Nina was always on guard. Once, when another child complimented her sister's painting, Nina snapped, "Don't make fun of her picture!" Dismayed, the other child became angry and hurt. Nina was merely protecting her sister from what she thought had been a criticism of her. She spent enormous amounts of energy trying to control and change her sister. She once explained why she did not laugh or play at home: "Sometimes you don't play around an alcoholic because like my mom, she'll think you're laughing at her, and she'll knock your head off."

Once they grow up and enter the workforce, family heroes encounter the greatest difficulty with their roles. They often become compulsive workers and frequently work addicted. They become highly successful in their chosen careers and, like the corporate executive, quickly climb the ladder of success. But they pay a huge price for their overdeveloped sense of responsibility and accomplishment. Obsessed with the need to control and manage people and things around them, heroes put their own feelings and needs on hold. Socially, they have difficulty being intimate and expressing their feelings to another person. Unable to express or identify emotions, heroes find it difficult to trust other people. They may have few or no friends and immerse themselves in their jobs to fulfill relationship needs. Heroes beat their heads against an imaginary wall to change other people and situations that are beyond their control. They become resentful and bitter adults because their childhoods have passed them by. They become uptight, rigid, and inflexible and panic in spontaneous and unpredictable situations.

The Scapegoat

Harley was the scapegoat—the family's target for their problems and frustrations. Following behind the family hero was such an insurmountable task that Harley learned he could not compete with the older sibling. He took attention off the family by internalizing family frustrations and getting into trouble. Scapegoats express their inner pain by causing trouble at home and at school. Delinquency, unplanned pregnancies, and substance abuse are a few ways their pain is transformed and released as anger. They get into fights, get into trouble with the legal system, use drugs, or run away from home. By acting out his family's pain, Harley, and not the family, becomes the focus of the problem.

Generally, in a group setting, the scapegoat will be the most disruptive and the one child that teachers never forget. Unlike family heroes, who are remembered for good things, scapegoats are remembered for the bad.

Scapegoats are the ultimate test of a parent's patience. Eleven-year-old Harley was usually coming off the walls within five minutes of his arrival at the COA group—pushing and shoving other children and acting out in various ways. Harley had no doors on the inside of his house. His father had removed the doors from their hinges so that the children could not take refuge in their rooms. Harley said his father hit him, slapped him around, and yelled at him all the time. One Christmas morning, Harley said, his father, in a drunken rage, chased him out of the house with a stick. Shirtless and shoeless, the child ran in the snow to a neighbor's house where he waited for his father to calm down. "We never get any sleep around my house," Harley complained. "My dad comes in at three in the morning, waking everybody up, pulls us out of bed and makes us look at a car he just overhauled or something he just made." Harley was able to verbalize his feelings of anger and fear toward his alcoholic father and to express them in a finger painting. Ordinarily, these feelings are masked by the destructive Harley with whom most people are more familiar. After working with him for a period of time, it was discovered that underneath his anger, Harley was a very sensitive child.

In the work world, scapegoats can never seem to do anything right. They constantly fail because of self-sabotage. Rather than following company rules, they may take shortcuts and get into trouble with the boss. Unable to get along with others, they involve themselves in destructive squabbles with coworkers. Alcohol and substance abuse may interfere with their job success.

Socially, they are misfits who have difficulty fitting in. Scapegoats have difficulty functioning in social situations and receive social disapproval because they behave in socially unacceptable ways. As a result of their poor social skills, they become outcasts. Outwardly social jerks, scapegoats are inwardly lonely, hurt, afraid, and angry.

The Lost Child

Six-year-old Sheila had already become the lost child in her family. She was always on the outside of family squabbles, crouched in a corner playing with her doll or lying in her bed staring at the ceiling, daydreaming. Remaining in the background, Sheila never caused an ounce of trouble for the family. Quiet and undemanding, her role was to provide relief for the family. Sheila had isolated herself from the family and lived in a world of hurt and loneliness.

Lost children are often middle children who do not know where they fit in their families or at school. As adults, they do not know their place in the work world and the world at large. They are the unnoticed children—the ones whom nobody sees and nobody remembers. Teachers especially have difficulty remembering these children because they demand neither positive nor negative attention. They are neither troublemakers nor class leaders. Sheila spent her time on the fringes with few family interactions or neighborhood friends. Generally, she was left alone and overlooked by parents, the educational system, and society in general.

Ten years later, at age sixteen, Sheila seemed cut off from the COA group and spent as much time as she could by herself on the sidelines. As we talked about feelings when a parent drinks, Sheila remained quiet and listened attentively to the other children but never uttered a sound. Given a chance to speak, Sheila said it made her angry when her mother drank. Although she said she was angry, she did not sound angry and had difficulty expressing it. Her verbalization of anger was emotionless—so deep down that she could not tap into it. She told of a time her drunk mother smashed her tennis racket into a million pieces. Her father was furious because he paid so much for the racket in hopes of bringing his daughter out of her shell. Sheila's mother denied any wrongdoing and blamed it on her daughter. Ultimately, Sheila's father believed her mother's version of the story and punished the child not only for vandalizing, but also for lying to him. The well-intentioned act of purchasing the tennis racket backfired to send Sheila further into her shell. Lost children deal with their feelings by locking them away inside so deeply that they are hard to retrieve. Sometimes they turn their anger inward and hurt themselves through suicide or drug abuse.

At work, lost children keep to themselves. They are always on the outside looking in. They say little and prefer to work alone. They may have difficulty being team players. They always do as they are told and never make waves. Coworkers eventually begin to leave them alone and often forget to include them in group activities. Employers may overlook them at raise and promotion time.

Sometimes they can be social wallflowers and spend their leisure time outside of large groups. They may have few friends and few long-term relationships. They prefer activities they can do alone or with few people. Outwardly shy and withdrawn, lost children feel lonely, hurt, and inadequate.

The Mascot

Nine-year-old Jack was the family mascot. He took the spotlight off the family's problem and put it on himself by cutting up, being cute, and acting silly. His role was to lighten the family's burden by diversion through humor and fun. Jack's jovial nature was clearly a cover-up for the opposite feelings of fear and sadness that he encountered from his alcoholic father's daily verbal and physical abuses.

Mascots tend to be youngest children, often called the baby of the family. They make light of serious situations and try to keep the tone upbeat, everybody happy, and nothing too serious. Mascots are perhaps the most difficult children to reach because they have an impenetrable veil of laughter. Jack was the class clown, the center of attention, who would go to any extreme for a laugh. He was the child who was not a serious problem but whose nonalcoholic mother labeled a "nuisance." His clowning around was disruptive at times, and Mom found herself constantly saying to him, "settle down" or "buckle down and get serious" or "this is no laughing matter."

One night in the COA group, Jack made a joke of the time when he was small that his alcoholic father threw him against a wall. Despite the fact that he suffered a broken leg, Jack giggled through the entire story. He talked of how his drunken father embarrassed him in front of his friends who, in turn, made fun of his father when he was drunk. The only way Jack could talk about the ordeals was to pretend that he was unafraid and unbothered by them. The group leader told him that getting smashed against a wall must have been a very scary and painful thing and that most people wouldn't think that it was funny. When asked if he laughed when it happened, his smile vanished and he whispered under his breath, "No, I cried." Practitioners and teachers need to know that the class clown who cuts up and laughs on the outside may be crying on the inside.

At work, mascots are considered practical jokers, the company buffoons. Everyone enjoys being around them because they keep everyone laughing, but nobody takes them seriously. They may even be viewed with suspicion by their employers. Jack's employer, for example, might wonder if he takes his work seriously or if he is reliable enough to make important decisions and handle responsibilities. Other family mascots turn their family roles into successes. Carol Burnett and Jonathan Winters clowned their way from alcoholic homes to fame and fortune by becoming comedians in the entertainment industry.

Socially, mascots are the life of the party, and everyone clusters around them. Like stand-up comics, they are always full of wisecracks and jokes to entertain others. Underneath, however, mascots have difficulty handling stress. They are sad, afraid, insecure, and alone. Their role as court jester also keeps them out of serious and committed relationships. Chemical dependency is often their substitute for intimacy.

Tips for Practitioners

The four survival roles are often called "false selves" (Wood, 1982, 1987). They represent an unconscious attempt by children to deal with their parents' failure to parent and to conceal and protect important aspects of inner reality. The false selves of superiority (hero), aggression (scapegoat), withdrawal (lost child), and wit (mascot) overtly contradict and deny the real covert feelings of vulnerability, need, and damaged self-esteem. The survival roles that COAs play become a rigid part of their personalities and serve as roadblocks to their recovery. Ironically, the roles serve two competing purposes. They provide a means through which children can survive the disease of alcoholism, while simultaneously camouflaging the disease from those in helping positions.

COAs are masters at camouflaging their heartache. Noted authority Claudia Black (1982) has said that children of alcoholic parents offer three unwritten rules very early: Don't talk, don't trust, and don't feel. As a fourteen-year-old boy told me, "When my stepfather comes in drunk. I don't pay him any attention when he talks to me. Now if my mother tells me to go to bed, I'll go."

His sister agreed. "It don't bother me none, because I just ignore it [her stepfather being drunk]." "If he ever touches me, I'll knock him out," the younger brother proclaims.

Even in special groups for COAs, the children's defenses are strong. The hurt and pain are buried so deep inside that it is difficult for them to reach it, and the barriers are hard for counselors to penetrate. So often, practitioners deal with anger, defiance, indifference, or laughter and smiles that camouflage a festering sore. Once they recognize the various roles, however, practitioners can help COAs remove false selves that stand in the way of recovery and help them face who they really are.

Helping the Family Hero

- Be on the lookout for overly competent children who appear to function at their maximum. Make sure that these potential family heroes get as much attention as your other children, who may have an easier time showing their needs or asking for what they need. Helping family heroes balance their lives between work and play is a worthy and realistic goal.
- Insist that these kids do not sacrifice or forgo potential benefits derived from activities, experiences, or interactions because they are too busy putting others' needs before their own.
- Continue to present kids with challenges that match their developmental abilities, but help them learn not to take on too much. Avoid unusually high expectations and burdening these kids with adult-like responsibilities, even when they are eager to accept them.

- Let them know it is OK to relax and do nothing. Reassure them that they do not always have to be producing to please someone else and that it is acceptable to please themselves, which may include doing nothing.
- Validate these kids for *who they are* and not just for *what they do*. Provide unconditional support for them as individuals—not support for what they produce or achieve. Let them know that you accept them regardless of whether they succeed or fail. Value them and hold them in esteem by letting them know they are special even when they are not producing a concrete object.
- Teach them to develop flexibility by building in spontaneous, spur-of-the-moment activities from time to time.
- Encourage them to identify their true feelings and to express them often in conversations or through creative outlets.
- Provide them with guidance when they must make significant and difficult decisions that parents have left up to them, such as how and where to spend their after-school time, whether to go to the prom with a certain date, or which career to choose.
- Encourage them in their successes and enjoy their accomplishments with them, but let them know that it is acceptable for them to fail and that they do not have to be perfect in everything all the time.
- Be there after a big failure or letdown. Help them understand and accept that failing is part of being human.
- Make sure they get a chance to play, relax, and have fun and to enjoy their childhood with other youngsters their age rather than spending their time with adults in adult activities. Welcome laughter, giggling, even silliness by building in funny stories or experiences during the day. The drive to achieve, succeed, and please others causes COAs to miss the experience of childhood. Despite behaviors to the contrary, COAs who are family heroes need adult guidance and supervision and time to play, learn, fantasize, and enjoy the rights of childhood. Childhood lays the bedrock for adult lives. Youngsters who have a chance to be children will become healthier and more well-rounded and are less likely to mourn their losses in adulthood.

Helping the Scapegoat

- Consider the scapegoat's behavior a cry for help and not a personal threat against you.

- Avoid writing scapegoats off, as there is often a tendency to do. These kids tend to be the least liked of the four roles because their sometimes violent, unlawful, and personality-threatening behaviors frequently arouse fear and anger in the adult. Plus, they take the most energy.
- Take a personal inventory of your feelings toward the scapegoat. Give yourself permission to say you have difficulty liking this child, if that is how you honestly feel. Practitioners do not have to like all children the same, but they are obligated to treat all children fairly and help them meet their needs.
- Reverse your behavior toward the scapegoat if you harbor negative attitudes. Sometimes you may be so angry or fearful that you find yourself saying and doing negative things to the scapegoat rather than positive things. Chances are, a change in you will produce a change for the better in the scapegoat.
- Be honest with your feelings. As a practitioner, it can be hard to admit when a child makes you angry. Denying your true feelings only reinforces the dysfunctional denial system in the child's alcoholic family.
- Communicate your feelings to the children. If scapegoats do something to make you mad, let them know it in a caring way. But tell them that you are angry about a specific thing they did, not at them as a person. You are teaching many concepts by using this approach: (1) You are teaching COAs that they do not have to deny their true feelings as they must do at home. (2) You are teaching scapegoats that they can *talk out* their feelings constructively rather than *take them out* on someone else in a destructive way. (3) You are setting an example for mature ways of dealing with strong feelings and directing emotions.
- Avoid being overly strict or punitive with these children and attempt to communicate with the real child underneath.
- Make sure the scapegoat knows what the boundaries are. Spell out clearly for them what the rules and routines are. Reasonable, predictable, yet flexible limits and routines are important to help these children control their own behaviors.
- Take a positive approach by telling them what they are supposed to do and why, not what they are *not* supposed to do. For example, telling a child who is running in the house, "Walk in the house, please. You might fall down and get hurt" gives him the "what" and

"why." But merely telling that child, "Don't run in the house," emphasizes the negative and fails to communicate the message of what it is you want him to do instead.

- Praise the scapegoat for what might seem the most insignificant positive behavior (such as turning in homework, doing one thing you ask, or showing an interest in a lesson even if only for five minutes). These kids need lots of positive attention for behaving appropriately, because most of their feedback from adults tends to be negative.
- Put them in leadership roles in which success can be ensured and give them praise for a job well done. Scapegoats frequently have latent leadership abilities waiting to be tapped.
- Help scapegoats identify and express feelings through various outlets: creative activities, dramatic play, or group discussions.
- Encourage them to vent and direct feelings in appropriate ways. You can show them, for example, that it is OK to vent anger or frustration by pounding clay, kicking a tree, or batting a punching bag. But it is not permissible for them to take it out on another child or adult.
- Provide the child with individual attention through a volunteer, parent, or counselor who can work on a one-to-one basis. Both you and the child may need a breather from each other from time to time.
- Encourage them to take part in rigorous, organized sports that serve as outlets for strong emotions as well as avenues for developing positive social relationships, citizenship, and leadership skills.
- Help other children understand the scapegoat as best you can while simultaneously recognizing their feelings and rights. They should not be forced to interact with the scapegoat if they do not want to.

Helping the Lost Child

- Give them a sense of belonging and make sure they know that they have an important place in the classroom and that they fit in.
- Capitalize on times when the lost child can be integrated into the larger social group. Avoid pressuring the child to be socially gregarious, however, because all kids need some time to be alone.
- Encourage the lost child to venture into pastimes that require social interaction (such as group problem solving, making a collage, paint-

ing a mural, planning a class play) rather than solitude (daydreaming or reading in a quiet corner).

- Display artwork, stories, or other items of interest on bulletin boards to build the child's self-confidence and self-worth.
- Build the child's self-concept by giving praise for the expression of constructive ideas and thoughts.
- Help the child identify and express feelings through safe, non-threatening outlets such as finger painting, woodworking, puppets, dictating stories, music, and other art forms.
- Help the child identify and express feelings through safe, non-threatening outlets such as finger painting, woodworking, puppets, dictating stories, music, and other art forms.
- Present problem-solving activities and ask for help in finding solutions in ways that would let the child feel comfortable. Many lost children hide their exceptional intelligence along with everything else, and parents may never realize the child's potential.
- Construct a sociogram (see Chapter 6) to find out who the lost child would most like to work with in the group and the one who would be a good influence. Pair the lost child with the selected child and assign them a project or activity on which they can work cooperatively.
- Keep a checklist of how many times you interact with the lost child or make positive comments to the child. Check it at the end of the day so that you have an ongoing reminder of how you are doing as well as how the child is progressing.

Helping the Mascot

- Give the mascot lots of individual attention and get to know the child on a one-to-one basis.
- Let the child know that it is OK to be the real person inside and that people will like the child even when he or she is not telling jokes.
- Help mascots open up by winning their trust. Although they may appear happy-go-lucky, they need a lot of nurturing if they are to trust you enough to drop the mask and expose the true self.
- Use storytelling as a vehicle to let the child know that real feelings are OK. A made-up story about a child who is always laughing on the outside but is crying on the inside can communicate a message to the child in a nonthreatening way.

- Use puppets to act out the clown but also describe the sadness the clown feels inside. Then let the child use the puppets to act out a similar role.
- Mirror back to the child appropriate reactions and emotions that match the event. Indicate that we laugh at funny things, for example, but we cry about sad things and we get mad when someone hurts us. If a child laughs when someone is hurt, define the situation for the child and express the feeling in your matter-of-fact voice tone: "That wasn't funny when John fell down. He hurt his leg, and it was very painful for him."
- Let older children keep a daily or weekly journal and assure them that no one will see it but you. Tell them they can talk to you about it at any time.

Hope for COAs

Alcoholism is widespread in our society and is one of the most menacing medical and social problems in existence. The natural focus for treatment has been the alcoholic and spouse, while the children have been neglected. The problems in chemically dependent homes cannot be resolved when treatment is provided only for the parents. In most cases, there is also a child who suffers quietly and desperately. Kids are the invisible victims of a ravaging illness. One of the biggest myths about alcoholism is that, once the alcoholic adult stops drinking, everything at home will be OK, too. If Dad stops drinking, he and Mom will start to get along again, and the kids will readjust automatically. Their school grades will improve, they will get along with their teachers and friends, and everybody will live happily ever after. This scenario is truly a myth. Alcoholic family systems have developed and maintained distinct and entrenched ways of functioning, just to survive. Removing the alcohol from the family does not automatically result in the family's becoming aware and capable of alternate, healthier ways of functioning. Just as these families have learned how to survive as an alcoholic family system, they must learn new ways to function as a nonalcoholic family system.

Millions of children who live in alcoholic homes—even for a short period of time—can become trapped in what has been called an infinite loop of self-destructive behavior patterns (Wood, 1987). For example, many children learn to take control of everything around them to keep their world from coming unglued when their alcoholic parent drinks. Ironically, these acts of self-sabotage bring some sense of predictability to their chaotic families and emotions and help COAs survive the disease of alcoholism.

Although the survival roles provide temporary relief from the disease, there comes a point, usually in adulthood, when these roles become obsolete. They no longer provide the payoff they yielded in childhood and, in fact, work against the COA. The dysfunctional nature of the roles becomes ever more obvious. Adult heroes lose themselves in work and have difficulty being intimate and being in relationships with others. The scapegoats get into all sorts of trouble, become social outcasts, and are shunned by others. Lost children become social recluses and withdraw from people and social situations. Mascots are considered a joke—not to be taken seriously. Many COAs may play more than one role. A composite of two, three, or even all four of the roles may dominate the personalities of some of these children.

After many years of comfort in playing the various roles, COAs have difficulty discarding what has become an integral part of their identities. As adults, they are confronted with the pain and confusion of behaviors that no longer serve their original survival function. Instead, carried into adulthood, the roles contribute to their demise. In their anxiety and confusion, COAs often attempt to cope with their dilemma through alcohol and other drugs, work, food, sex, and other compulsive forms of behavior (see Chapter 5).

The best time for parental intervention is in childhood before the behavior patterns become overly rigid. Hope for breaking the patterns lies in those practitioners who interact daily with COAs. A mainstream understanding of alcoholism as a family disease will enable them to help COAs by working through existing systems and by using the tools and assets already at their disposal. Regardless of whether the practitioners are in the business of alcohol rehabilitation, they have a responsibility to the huge and generally neglected and vulnerable population of children from alcoholic homes. By understanding the disease and how kids are affected by it, teachers, counselors, school administrators, social workers, and other professionals can make a difference in the child's recovery.

4 PSYCHOLOGICAL ADJUSTMENT OF CHILDREN OF ALCOHOLICS

CASE 4.1

As I was getting ready for bed, my mom told me to sleep on the outside of my bedcovers so she wouldn't have to make up the bed. I did what she told me to do. But when my dad came into my room the next morning, he was upset that I slept on top instead of underneath the sheets. I told him what Mom had said, but when he asked her about it, she lied. She denied saying anything like that to me. She was afraid of what Dad would say and do. He didn't say anything to her because he believed her. But he beat me with a belt. Now I don't know who to listen to.

— Rex, age eleven

My mom bought me a $600 set of drums. One night my grand-mother got drunk and slashed them with a knife. They were brand new, too. Naturally, my mom was mad, and so was I. I told her Grandmother did it, but Grandmother said I was lying and blamed it on me. Mom believed her and punished me for some-thing I didn't do. I hate Grandmother for that, and I hate my dad more and more as he starts to be like his bitch wife and for leaving me behind with them. He can take everything he bought me and shove it up his ass (especially the jeep). I wish I had never been born.

— *Rick, age sixteen*

My mother was always drunk, and she beat me from the time I was four years old. While she hit me, she'd say, "You're a good little girl." How could I believe that? I remember she was on the couch and sandwiched me between her feet, and the coffee table pushing me hard against it with her feet and the whole time she was telling me one thing and doing another. I remember thinking, "Well, why are you doing that if you think I'm a good girl?"

— *Deidre, age twenty-one*

Betrayal, deception, lies, mixed messages. Sounds like a James Bond thriller, but unfortunately, it is much less glamorous than that. These are some of the interactions that occur between alcoholic parents and their children. The opening cases are real-life examples of the kinds of mixed messages children get. In the last chapter, we discussed how COAs develop survival roles in response to the disease of alcoholism. In this chapter, we will take you beneath the false selves and examine the profound impact on COAs' psychological development. All kids experience fear, anger, confusion, guilt, embarrassment, and shame. The depth, intensity, and frequency with which COAs experience these emotions are greater than most children. Their feelings, personalities, and behaviors are molded more by the fact of alcoholism than by any other (National Institute on Alcohol Abuse and Alcoholism, 1981). Parental drinking becomes the major driving force in their young lives, and everything revolves around it. Living with an alcoholic parent, it should come as no surprise, can severely damage a child's psychological makeup.

The lives of COAs can be compared with those of psychologically wounded war veterans. Posttraumatic stress disorder (PTSD) occurs when veterans have problems readjusting to civilian life. Like the stress soldiers experience in battle, the stress of life as a COA lies outside the

range of normal human experiences. Symptoms identical to PTSD stalk
children into adulthood until they seek the help of understanding that
their childhoods were not normal or healthy.

Psychological Battleground

> I used to run those battle lines
> Trying to smooth over what got said,
> Trying to get a medal,
> Trying to get some shrapnel in my head.
> Thought it was my duty to plead and to implore—
> I took it all in childhood
> But I can't take it no more,
> 'Cause I caught too much crossfire
> In your covert war.

—David Wilcox, Covert War
© 1991, Irving Music, Inc., and
Midnight Ocean Bonfire Music (BMI).
All rights reserved. International copyright secured.

Although all children must wrestle with some degree of psychological adjustment as they grow up, the slings and arrows of everyday
life carry a sharper sting in alcoholic families, as reflected in the lyrics
of the above ballad. The presence of family conflict, for example, leads
to incredible psychological stress and strains on its members. The analogy of an alcoholic home to a psychological battleground is often used.
In some ways, it is a fight for survival where it is every man, woman,
and child for him- or herself. Children frequently are forced to choose
sides against one parent. Sometimes battle lines are drawn between
adults and children, and the wounds are swift and sweeping. Ross
grumbled that his mother always sides with his drinking father—even
when she knows his dad is wrong. Ross sees this as betrayal and inter-
nally draws the battle lines: "Me against them." Through walls of anger, he distanced himself from both his parents. Other kids complain
that their parents use them as their confidants and try to turn them
against the other parent.

Because everyone who lives in it is affected by alcoholism, it is not
unusual for COAs to bemoan that the nonalcoholic parent is harder to

get along with than the alcoholic. One night, ten-year-old Carlos interrupted the COA group. "I want to know something," he demanded. "Why is my mother so cranky all the time? She's always on me about something—always trying to pick a fight, and she doesn't even drink."

"Does this sound familiar to anyone else?" the group was asked. A resounding affirmation from the other children brought a sigh of relief from Carlos, who learned that he was not alone. Discussing the cranky codependent parent also helped the children understand that it is part of the disease.

Codependent parents often become ill-tempered from battle fatigue. Interviews with nondrinking parents reveal that they feel worried, nervous, and tense because of their spouse's alcoholic behaviors and inadvertently transfer these emotions to their children. Irritable from their own tensions, they often find themselves getting upset with their kids over minor incidents. Wives of alcoholic men are also more prone to develop high levels of depression, so many children live with two dysfunctional parents: one unable to parent due to alcohol abuse, and the other unable to provide a psychological buffer, or even to adequately parent, due to intense depression (Tubman, 1993). Some parents try to hide their distraught feelings from their children by suppressing their own problems and attending to their children's needs. Inevitably, this leads to snapping and other temper outbursts that children do not understand (Wilson & Orford, 1978). The inability of the nonalcoholic parent to provide a psychological buffer between the child and the alcoholic parent has important implications for the psychosocial development of children in alcoholic families. A divided family where children lack a close relationship with at least one parent has been found to be a far more powerful predictor of adjustment problems for children than alcoholism itself (Braithwaite & Devine, 1993). Typically, interventions in alcoholic families are directed either at the alcoholic's drinking behavior and/or protecting the child from harmful consequences of that behavior. It is important, however, for practitioners to recognize that interventions can also focus on strengthening the ability and resources of the nonalcoholic parent to effectively care for him- or herself and consequently be more capable of effectively parenting the children in the family.

Codependent parents struggle furiously to make everything appear normal and to keep things functioning as they used to be. They become so consumed that sometimes the smallest incident will ignite their temper. The seemingly indifferent attitude they often reflect to their children is "Just do what you want, but don't bother me." Because all the attention revolves around the alcoholic, however, children feel neglected, unwanted, unloved, and unworthy. "I just want to know what I did wrong," was Carlos's refrain.

The codependent parents will go to any extreme, even psychological warfare, to keep peace in the family. Sometimes they compromise their values, tell lies, and sacrifice their children's happiness. On other occasions, as in the case of Rex, codependents lie to avoid the ire of the alcoholic, while subjecting their own children to it. Other times as in the case of Rick, alcoholics lie to protect themselves, at the expense of hurting their loved ones. In the more advanced stages of the disease, alcoholics suffer *blackouts*—memory losses while intoxicated that can never be retrieved. In these cases, parents may actually believe that they are innocent of the charges.

The Development of Denial

One of the four major family tasks is the management of the family's emotional climate. This task includes the strategies families develop to manage conflict, an integral part of all family life. Alcoholic families, however, are more likely to develop conflict-detouring strategies than strategies that productively acknowledge and process conflict.

Denial is the most common means alcoholic families use to manage conflict within the family. Families develop rules, which may be overt or covert, to regulate the ways in which they respond to conflict. In alcoholic families, the covert "don't talk" rule is perhaps the most common. As part of their attempts to smooth over family problems, codependents pretend that everything is OK and insist that the children perceive things that way, too. When children challenge the "don't talk" rule by trying to speak honestly about the alcohol-related problems in their family, the child's reality may be invalidated by codependents' responses: "Your father isn't an alcoholic. He's depressed." Or "Your mother doesn't drink that much."

Denial of alcoholism within the family is also accomplished by the scapegoating strategy. Conflict around the alcohol abuse is detoured by shifting the focus from the alcoholic to the problematic behavior of another family member, usually the child who has been assigned this role. As a result, tension and anxiety around the alcoholism are temporarily reduced. Eventually, of course, alcohol-related stress and conflict within the family reescalates, and the projection process must be repeated.

Ironically, although denial helps families cope and survive their pain, it also helps the disease coexist. As codependent parents deny what their children see before their very eyes, the children become confused and have difficulty trusting their own reality. They begin to repress their suspicions and to minimize their feelings about it: "If Mom says so, then things must not be as bad as I had thought." Children often split the drinking parent into a good half and a bad half and downplay the importance of their emotions about their parent's drinking. By age nine, COAs routinely doubt and deny their own perceptions and those of outsiders who try to convince them that a parent has a drinking problem. They deny and lie to their peers to cover up the painful reality with which they are forced to live:

> They are ashamed of their family secret and isolated by it; they feel anger and guilt; they are taught to deny the existence of the problem itself and their own feelings about it; they feel an intense loyalty that would make any revelation a betrayal; and they feel hopeless. (Deutsch, 1982, p. 96)

They even pass the denial on to younger siblings or other family members. A common denial tactic in COA groups is for older children to invalidate the perceptions of their very young siblings. Older siblings (age ten and up) may censure a younger sibling time and time again for violating the "don't talk" rule by revealing family secrets in groups—even when all the children are from alcoholic homes and confidentiality is ensured. As his younger sister spoke candidly about her innermost feelings about their family life, eleven-year-old Mallory tried several times to silence her with such nonverbal cues as raised eyebrows and hateful looks. When that did not work, he tried verbal warnings and reprimands, finally resorting to physical threats. It is through the development of denial that the alcoholism spreads so that, psychologically, alcoholic families develop different characteristics that distinguish them from nonalcoholic families. There are also long-term

effects on children who grow up in families that use denial to manage
the conflict caused by alcoholism. When conflict is dealt with and not
detoured, children learn that it is a normal part of family life and that
it can be managed, and the wounds caused by conflict heal. However,
when conflict is denied and detoured, children learn that it is something so dark and dangerous that it must be avoided at all costs, and
emotional wounds fester. When families allow all members to participate in processing conflict in a fair and productive way, feelings of
worth and acceptance are engendered among its members. In contrast,
when the reality before children's eyes is refuted in order to protect the
family from dealing with the pain of alcoholism, seeds of self-doubt
and inadequacy are sown. Children of alcoholic families carry into their
adult lives the lessons of their childhood. Because alcoholic families are
governed by denial, the children of these families carry into their adult
relationships the lesson that conflict is not normal and not manageable,
that they are not capable of dealing with it, and that it is to be avoided
at all costs, even that of living a lie.

Psychological Profile of
Alcoholic Families

After studying chemically dependent families, social scientists have
discovered specific patterns of interaction that characterize them differently from chemical-free families. We have known for some time that
the presence of an alcoholic parent severely disrupts family interaction,
which, in turn, interferes with children's developmental processes and
outcomes (Braithwaite & Devine, 1993). Authorities agree that more
conflict and dysfunction occur in alcoholic families than in nonalcoholic ones (Moos & Billings, 1982). More recent research on alcoholic
families has begun to focus on the *how* of this process: the actual mechanisms that may account for the negative relationship between adult alcoholism and childhood emotional and behavioral problems. There are
greater numbers of marital disturbances and reports of unhappiness
and instability (Schulsinger, Knop, Goodwin, Teasdale, & Mikkeisen,
1986). Higher levels of maternal depression and marital conflicts and
lower levels of social support and family functioning occur in families
of alcohol-dependent men (Tubman, 1993). Alcoholic families are less
cohesive, less organized, less oriented toward intellectual or cultural

pursuits, and more conflict ridden (Clair & Genest, 1987). The prevalence of more emotional problems in alcoholic families is attributed to frequent quarrels between parents, lack of care for the children, and the entire family's preoccupation with the alcoholic's irresponsible behaviors (Venugopal, 1985). COAs are raised in more disrupted families characterized by more parental arguments, higher divorce rates, and premature parental and sibling death (Black, Bucky, & Wilder-Padilla, 1986).

In her landmark study of 115 COAs between ages ten and sixteen, Margaret Cork (1969) found most families lacking solidarity and in constant turmoil. None of the teenagers in her interviews rated their families as "normal." Sibling relationships were characterized by considerable tension, fighting, and quarreling—the same kind of fighting that their parents indulged in, which results in progressive damage to all family members. With some of the older COAs in her study, the apparent need to dominate their younger siblings was a result of deep aggressive and frustrated feelings. Cork also reported an abnormal amount of dissension and separation among brothers and sisters at all age levels. Instead of warmth and affection, siblings carried a deep sense of hostility and resentment.

The child-rearing practices of alcoholic fathers, compared to nonalcoholic fathers, are more likely to include ridicule, rejection, harshness, and neglect (Udayakumar, Mohan, Shariff, Sekar, & Eswari, 1984). In a longitudinal, qualitative study of alcoholic father-son dyads, children expressed negative perceptions of their fathers when they were drinking (Seilhamer, Jacob, & Dunn, 1993). One child in this study reported that his father "acts strange, frightens the family, if I move, I get yelled at." Similarly, the attitudes of alcoholic mothers, compared to nonalcoholic mothers, tend to be less accepting, more rejecting, disciplinarian, or overprotecting, and these mothers have a significantly greater degree of conflicting attitudes (Krauthamer, 1979).

Alcoholism has been found to adversely affect parenting behaviors through a reciprocal, transactional process between parent and children (Pelham & Lang, 1993). A parent who abuses alcohol is likely to have skewed perceptions of children's behaviors. Developmentally appropriate behavior for a particular child may be perceived by the intoxicated parent as deliberate acting-out behavior against that parent, resulting in the parent's use of ineffective and inappropriate behavior management strategies. In response to these punitive parenting behaviors, children may actually develop externalizing, deviant behavior patterns. The parent's distress level and alcohol consumption then increase in response to the child's deviant behavior. Together, then, the parent and child engage in a dance of sorts that illustrates the complex ways that parenting skills, interpersonal characteristics, family stressors, and child behavior interact to produce family dysfunction in homes dominated by alcoholism (Pelham & Lang, 1993).

Emotional Wounds

Typically, upbringing in an alcoholic family leaves children with many emotional and sometimes physical wounds. Regardless of parents' motives, effects on the children are the same. They react to their parents with a flood of strong emotions, ranging from rage to despair. Carried throughout childhood and into adulthood, these feelings interfere with fully functioning relationships with friends, spouses, and loved ones.

Anger

Anger is possibly the most common emotion children harbor in reaction to parental alcoholism. When children have learned that expressed anger is wrong, unexpressed anger is often veiled with false smiles. Anger is aroused for many of the reasons already discussed: refusal of a parent to support children during disputes, betrayal, mixed messages, and broken promises. Another common reason for anger is destruction of personal belongings. Over and over again, children tell me they have no sense of personal ownership. Material items, like Rick's drums, are potential targets in violent homes and vulnerable to destruction.

Ten-year-old Carlos said his father got drunk and tore up the house. Among the things destroyed were Carlos's prized cassette tapes, which he had been collecting for months. The child was so angry he went to his school and punched a metal caution sign until he broke one of his knuckles. Children are also angry simply because the alcoholic yells and hits family members. Children usually use the words *mad* and *hate* to express their anger, although feelings of hurt and sadness are layered underneath.

Fear and Anxiety

COAs are kids who are afraid and terrified of what is happening at home. The seesaw existence in chemically dependent families is enough to elicit anxiety. Apprehension and fear become normal reactions for children in unpredictable situations. Coupled with violence and psychological, physical, and sometimes sexual abuse, impending doom is the COA's silent companion. Jane said,

> I lived in constant fear of when my father would get drunk again. Each time it happened it got worse. There were signs that I knew, like when he said he was happy. I knew he was going to go off the deep end because he was not a happy person. Other signs were when he stopped reading the newspaper or when he wore this certain red vest, I knew it was going to happen again.

Most COAs have witnessed parents out of control or violent in some way. Many have been slapped, hit, or thrown around more than once. They may be afraid that Mom will fall asleep with a burning cigarette and burn the house down, worry that someone will be hurt in a nightly brawl, or fear that their friends will find out what is going on. Their peer relationships are often founded on insecurity, anxiety, and lack of trust (Cork, 1969). COAs are also more likely to generalize their anxiety and to develop unreasonable fears for which there is no discernable basis (Haberman, 1966).

Guilt

COAs often blame themselves for causing their parent's drinking. Unaware of the disease concept, they often feel guilty and responsible for a parent's drinking and believe that they can get them to stop. Trina said,

> I thought that if I just tried to take some of the burden off my mom, that she would stop drinking. I thought that if I worked a little harder to keep my room clean, to make good grades, and to help around the house, it would make it easier on her. But it didn't. Nothing changed.

Sadness and Depression

Children call it sadness, and adults call it depression. They are common emotional reactions to parental drinking and to the ensuing family

conflict (Clair & Genest, 1987; Moos & Billings, 1982). As parental alcoholism leads to family disruption, children distance themselves from
the family physically (lost child), psychologically (clown) and/or socially (acting-out child). These coping strategies, however, also serve to
distance children from their major source of nurturance and support in
our society: the family. The resulting lack of psychological security and
safety can then give rise to feelings of depression in COAs (Braithwaite
& Devine, 1993). COAs are more likely than offspring of nonalcoholics
to describe their childhoods as unhappy and their home conditions as
unstable (Callan & Jackson, 1986; Schulsinger et al., 1986). They are also
two times more likely to become depressed than children from nonalcoholic homes, and this depression, as it lingers into adulthood, becomes a lifelong legacy (Black et al., 1986). The good news, however, is
that children from recovering alcoholic homes are less depressed than
children from nonrecovering alcoholic homes (Moos & Billings, 1982).
So when parents get help, things can improve at home. Still, children
from recovering and nonrecovering homes alike need their own separate recovery programs to deal with parental changes and the residue
of unexpressed emotions.

Confusion

Little Molly was a bouncy nine-year-old who swelled with delight
when her mother beckoned her with open arms. "Come here, sweet-
heart, and give me a kiss. Mommy loves you so much!" Expecting to be
comforted in the security and warmth of her mother's arms, Molly was
met instead with a sharp slap across her face and a belligerent repri-
mand, "You are a bad little girl!" Then Molly smelled the alcohol on her
mother's breath. She had been duped again. It was not until the age of
fourteen that Molly put a stop to her mother's seductive abuse. Molly
hit her mother upside the head with all her might and was never struck
again.

Parental inconsistency and unpredictability are hallmarks of alcoholism that propel children into a cyclone of confusion. Alcoholics are
notorious for mood swings and making and breaking promises during
drinking bouts. COAs learn early in life about the Dr. Jekyll/Mr. Hyde
syndrome. COAs realize that they have at least three different parents
—the drinking alcoholic parent, the sober alcoholic parent, and the
nonalcoholic parent. Sometimes when both parents are alcoholic,

COAs must figure out how to get along with multiple personalities. In some ways, this predicament is like living in schizophrenia, where parental mood swings are unpredictable and expectations are inconsistent. Children often find themselves walking on eggshells and desperately trying to second-guess parents in order to do what they want. This is very difficult, especially for preschool children, who are starting to discriminate between right and wrong and who need consistency to trust their abilities to venture out socially, share their feelings, and show affection for others. It is equally difficult for school-age children, who developmentally have learned to think concretely about their world and to understand that things in it can be categorized and ordered. There are ethical morals of good and bad, there are laws of legal and illegal, and there are school rules of right and wrong. But things are not so cut-and-dried at home. The order and rules do not apply. Rules, when they do exist, are switched around daily, just enough to keep children guessing and never knowing what to expect. The lives of COAs become two or three times more complicated than children from nonalcoholic homes. They grow up unsure of what "normal" is and insecure about how to act in different situations.

According to Margaret Cork (1969), 94 percent of the teens in her study reported parental inconsistency as the major problem of alcoholism. Codependent parents also send inconsistent and conflicting messages to their kids, who become confused and angry at their parents for deceiving and betraying them.

Embarrassment and Isolation

Roger always complained in group that the other kids made fun of his dad when he was drunk. This caused great embarrassment for Roger. The threat of embarrassment causes COAs to isolate themselves from their peers at a time when other youngsters are forming and consolidating friendships (Cork, 1969). Their freedom to meet friends and to reciprocate friendships is restricted (Wilson & Orford, 1978). Normal friendships are impaired because children try to hide their parent's drinking or refuse to bring friends home for fear of being embarrassed by a drinking, out-of-control parent. Mac's alcoholic father ordered his friends out of the house. Patti complained that her mom would get drunk and "come on" to her teenage boyfriends. Candace said she did not like her dad to come to school functions because he came to school drunk one day and embarrassed her. On his way out of the classroom, he stumbled and fell in full view of her classmates, who giggled and snickered at him. Such experiences have left Candace so shy and with-drawn that she whispers when she talks. Deidre was taunted by her friends at school:

> My dad's drinking had a big effect on me because I was ashamed. I mean, here I was, I had a crazy dad and kids at school would tease me and say, "Give me some of that stuff your dad takes." And it was awful and I didn't want anybody to come to my house. It had a real bad effect on me. It was torture living with him. He'd stay up all night talking and laugh-ing as if there was some demon in him.

When Deidre was finally taken out of the home and placed with her grandparents, she carried the embarrassment with her:

> I remember I would lie at school when kids and teachers would ask me who I lived with. I'd say my mom, dad, and little brother. I was so ashamed of living with my grandparents because I wanted to live in a normal family like everybody else. And I remember lying so many times.

As a reaction to shame and embarrassment, children often with-draw and isolate themselves from peers. COAs also become more pre-occupied with their thoughts than with those of the outside world (Fine, Yudin, Holmes, & Heinemann, 1976). Many of these kids build a wall around themselves for protection against the alcoholic parent. They insulate their emotions and seal their feelings in a time capsule. Many do not open that time capsule until their thirties or forties. Tragi-cally, some never reopen it.

Grief

"Coming from an alcoholic home makes me want to be totally differ-ent from my alcoholic parents," Deidre said.

> And it makes me want to have a family because I've never had one. I've never considered myself part of a family, and I want to have a family more than anything. I don't think that would be so important to me if I had lived with my parents in a normal life.

Grief is an emotional reaction that most COAs experience on many levels. Missing out on a normal family life will be mourned at one time or another in the child's life. The missed experience of a magical, joyful, and carefree childhood is also a common reason to grieve. Losing a parent to alcohol can be so traumatizing to children that it has been compared to the loss of a loved one through death or divorce (Black, 1987). COAs experience loss on many levels and on a chronic basis at a time in life when they are developing a sense of worth and identity. The grief process, however, is usually not fully felt until adolescence, at which time it only adds to the teenager's confusion. According to Priest (1985), teens experiencing feelings of grief around the loss of a parent are often confused about the cause of their feelings. The parent is physically present, so a grief reaction seems to make no sense to the teenager, and the issue of loss remains unresolved.

Psychological Functioning

Many problems befall children as a result of the stresses and strains of an alcoholic upbringing. Emotionally battered and bruised, many children limp through life, their psychological functioning impaired. Poor self-esteem, lack of feeling in control of their own lives, poor coping skills, and problems in interpersonal relationships all characterize their psychological functioning.

Factors Influencing Psychological Outcomes

The outlook for COAs sounds pretty dismal. But before we continue discussing their psychological functioning, it is important to note that not all COAs fit the pattern described. Some never succumb to these devastations. Research suggests that numerous factors operate singly or interact collectively to produce negative psychological outcomes: sex of child (Werner, 1986); sex of alcoholic parent (Steinhausen, Gobel, & Nestler, 1984; Werner, 1986); age of child (Werner, 1986); family socioeconomic status and whether both parents drink (Parker & Harford, 1987); race (Ackerman, 1987); birth order (Keltner, McIntyre, & Gee, 1986); constitutional factors (Tabakoff et al., 1988); offsetting factors, such as other people or institutions that have positive effects on the child (Ackerman, 1987); and whether or not the parent is a recovering or active alcoholic (Callan & Jackson, 1986; Moos & Billings, 1982).

The psychiatric literature indicates a tendency for children's conduct disorders to correlate with paternal alcoholism and for emotional disorders to correlate with maternal alcoholism, although both types of disorders occur with the same frequency when children have two alcoholic parents (Steinhausen et al., 1984). Children with two alcoholic parents become more aggressive and seriously disturbed than those who have one alcoholic parent or none at all (McKenna & Pickens, 1983). In cases where the alcoholic parent is in recovery, family relations are better than in those where the parent is still drinking. Children of recovering alcoholics, in fact, offered ratings similar to kids from nonalcoholic homes in terms of happiness and togetherness (Callan & Jackson, 1986). They rated their lives as much happier than offspring in households where fathers still drank. The health and psychological functioning of children from recovering homes were also similar to those of kids in nonalcoholic homes (Moos & Billings, 1982).

In contrast, parents in families of relapsed alcoholics reported less cohesion and expressiveness and less emphasis on independence, achievement, and moral-religious, intellectual-cultural, and active-recreational orientation than nonalcoholic families (Moos & Billings, 1982). Children from relapsed homes suffered more depression and anxiety and had more serious physical and mental problems.

The combined effects of coming from low socioeconomic backgrounds and having two alcoholic parents puts kids at even higher risk for alcohol-related problems (Parker & Harford, 1987). Birth order also makes a difference in the child's adjustment. Research indicates that middle and later-born children are more likely to develop psychological problems from living in alcoholic homes than first-borns, who are more resilient (Keltner et al., 1986). During the mid-1980s, social scientists identified and began studying a group of youngsters known as resilient or invulnerable children. Additional factors associated with children who are said to be resilient to the effects of alcoholic parents are described in Box 4.1.

Self-Esteem

The self-esteem of children who grow up with alcoholism is often severely damaged. As part of the intake process in one children's program, clinical staff administer the Rosenberg Self-Esteem Scale. Eyeballing the simple inventory quickly shows how poorly the children

BOX 4.1
Resilient Children of Alcoholic Parents

Early research on child development focused on the identification of risk factors present in a child's life, those characteristics of a child's environment that seem to increase a child's odds of negative developmental outcomes, such as serious emotional problems later in life. These factors include parental alcoholism, addiction, mental illness, domestic violence, and divorce. More recently, it has been suggested that the risk factor perspective itself may put children at a disadvantage, in that it creates expectations that they will fail (Butler, 1997). Subsequently, research has turned to attempting to understand why some children succeed in life in spite of the multiple risk factors in their early environments. What are the factors that enable some children who grow up in dismal family situations, such as alcoholism, to escape the darkness of their past and build a healthy future for themselves?

The psychiatric and social science literature has identified a group of youngsters who, although reared under the most dire circumstances, somehow do remarkably well despite their disadvantaged surroundings. Earlier research identified these children as invulnerable or resilient, while more recent work describes them as transcendent. The most common characteristic of these children is their ability to cope and react to stress in exceptional ways. Despite the fact that these children are reared in such extremely traumatic and stressful surroundings as alcoholic homes, they are described as stress-resistant.

Butler (1997) suggests that resilient children bring to mind metaphors from the physical sciences: children who are "self-righting," who "spring back to their original shape" following the blows of their painful childhoods (p. 25). Resilient children are described as those who "bounce back" after adversity (Wolin & Wolin, 1993). Rubin (1996) characterizes transcendent children as those who fall down seven times and get up eight. Anthony (1978) describes the differences between children who are vulnerable and those who are invulnerable. To explain the effects, he compares children to three kinds of dolls—glass, plastic, and steel. Glass dolls are shattered by the stressful experiences of childhood. Plastic dolls are permanently dented, and steel dolls are invulnerable—resisting the harmful effects of their surroundings. Glass (vulnerable) children break down completely, plastic children sustain some serious injury, and steel (invulnerable) children thrive on the trouble and turmoil in their world.

Resilient children share a number of common characteristics. They have good social skills. They are at ease and make others feel comfortable, too. They are friendly and well liked by classmates and adults. They

(continued)

BOX 4.1 Continued

have positive feelings of self-regard. And they sense a feeling of personal power for influencing events around them (internal locus of control). This contrasts with the feelings of helplessness of vulnerable children. Not only do resilient children feel in control, but they also have an urge to help others needier than themselves. There is a certain sense of detachment from the stressful surroundings. Along with this self-distancing comes a greater sense of independence and a more objective understanding of what's going on around them. They are successful, usually receiving high grades in school. Later on, they become high achievers in their careers. Somehow, their intellectual and creative skills are not destroyed by their misfortunes at home. Most of these children who experience inadequate parenting and early turmoil grow up to be competent adults and appear to suffer little or no psychological damage.

Emmy Werner (1986) followed forty-nine offspring of alcoholic parents over eighteen years. She discovered that some children developed severe psychological disorders, whereas others appeared resilient despite their alcoholic upbringing. Children were judged resilient by their outward appearance through interviews and examination of records showing good grades and no mental or behavioral problems. Resilient children did well in school, at work, and in their social lives, and they had realistic goals and expectations for the future. The characteristics distinguishing resilient children from the vulnerable children (who developed delinquent and mental health coping problems by age 18) included:

- They had more pleasant temperaments during the first year of life.
- They had fewer problems in family relationships during adolescence.
- They reflected a greater sense of well-being, self-esteem, and psychological health.
- They appeared more responsible, more socialized, and caring.
- They were more achievement oriented.

Resilient children sound like carbon copies of the family hero (discussed in Chapter 3). On the surface, these kids appear to be functioning exceptionally well. But professionals must be careful making this interpretation until more is known about this special group of children. We know that the resilience of family heroes is also the source of deeper-seated, concealed problems of inadequacy and poor self-esteem. Many cases of invulnerability may be a disguise for an inner misery that resilient children are compelled to hide. It would behoove practitioners to take caution in labeling children who appear to be resilient. It is important that the helping professions not discount the resilient child simply because he or she appears to be functioning better than the more vulnerable children in a family. Resilient children may, in fact, be in greater need than those who can reveal their vulnerability. The best resource for these invulnerable children can be practitioners who make sure that, while developing their talents and skills, these kids also get a chance to balance their personal lives to the maximum.

Findings from recent research by Lillian Rubin (1996) on adults who have overcome the deficits of traumatic childhoods suggest sociological and psychological factors that may help children in alcoholic homes survive and withstand the pain of their experience. Our genetic predispositions certainly make a difference in how we experience and respond to the world, but that process is mediated by the social and psychological circumstances of our lives. For the men and women studied by Rubin, personal qualities and social conditions made it possible for them to flourish as adults in spite of having grown up in extremely troubled family environments. Rubin identified those conditions in the lives of these individuals who had actually transcended harsh childhoods and forged highly functional and reasonably joyful adult lives out of painful pasts. First, transcendent children are *able to leave their families behind*. In fact, they begin this process at an early age when they position themselves as marginal in the family, observers of family life, "in the family but not of it." The child's ability to understand that the pain and suffering in the family is unjust and is not his or her fault is an important step in overcoming such a past. The cost of this realization is isolation, but the prize is being freed to think and act independently of the family pathology. As expressed by one daughter of an alcoholic mother,

> I think I understood when I was very, very young that I wasn't wholly responsible for all the bad things that were happening to me . . . so I understood that I had to try to keep my distance if I was going to maintain my sanity. Even though our household was crazy, there was quite a lot of freedom because there was so much neglect. So the neglect had its positive side because the freedom taught me very early how to be enormously independent. And that has been one of the very important life skills that has helped me pick myself up and move on.

This disidentification with their dysfunctional families *allows transcendent children to seek and find alternative sources of comfort, belonging, and support.* It may be a teacher, neighbor, or friend who plays an important role in the life of the child. It may be another arena of life, such as school, church, or community involvement, which is removed from the family

(continued)

BOX 4.1 Continued

but gives the child a heightened sense of efficacy and a more autonomous feeling of self.

Individual personal characteristics and psychological resources also contribute to the ability to transcend painful childhoods. Transcendent children are family isolates but still somehow grow up to be what Rubin (1996) calls *adoptable*. They have the gift of being able to attract others who can help them fill in the gaps left by their past. They also have the ability to accept and use what others offer by being willing to risk being open to relationship.

In addition, transcendent children carry into adulthood a *sense of mission*—that is, a need to feel useful and a commitment to something larger than self. This mission is related to gratitude they feel for having escaped the pain of their childhoods and a feeling of motivation to use their past experiences to change the present, for others as well as for themselves.

Transcendent children do not forget the pain of their pasts. They do not deny the harsh reality of their experiences, but they are able to extract constructive meaning from that reality. By being able to separate themselves from their families, to seek sources of meaning and belonging elsewhere, and to perceive their life's meaning as encompassing more than self, transcendent children use the painful experience of their childhood to cultivate the strength necessary to transcend the experience of that childhood and to find their way to satisfying adulthood.

Thus, it is becoming clear that resilience and transcendence are not states of being but processes in which some children engage. For these children, innate individual characteristics interact with external supports to create developmental pathways that are interactive, mutually reinforcing, and reflexive and that lead to more positive outcomes than may have been predicted for children from such painful pasts (Werner & Smith, 1992). An understanding that there are many pathways to resilience can assist practitioners in looking beyond the individual child to the environment and to the potential interaction between the two in identifying ways to help children of alcoholic families transcend the trials of their early years (Butler, 1997; Rubin, 1996).

---

feel about themselves. Social science research corroborates that COAs have more negative self-concepts than non-COAs. One of the first such studies to examine self-esteem reported that fifty-four children of recovering alcoholics had lower self-esteem than fifty-four children of nonalcoholics (McLachlan, Walderman, & Thomas, 1973). COAs, compared with non-COAs, rated their families significantly lower in family harmony and reported a significantly more disturbed relationship with the alcoholic parent. Families in which the alcoholic parent was recovered had family relationships that were significantly improved. Adolescents from both active and recovering homes had lower self-esteem than those from nonalcoholic homes. A later investigation compared fifty-four COAs with 129 peers who were not COAs (DiCicco, Davis, & Orenstein, 1984). Overall, the COAs scored lower in virtually all the self-image measures. In a recent study, elementary and middle school-age COAs reported lower self-esteem than non-COAs (Post & Robinson, 1998).

The COA self-concept encompasses the sum total of all the events that were discussed in this chapter. The cranky, nonalcoholic parent who seems to never have time, the drinking parent who unpredictably switches personalities at the drop of a hat or who promises but never delivers, the child's guilt and self-blame for somehow causing the drinking, the betrayal and hostility that accompany parental alcoholism, the embarrassment in front of friends, and the stigma of the family's image that has been tainted by the drinking parent—all culminate in poor self-worth. When children can no longer separate these events from who they are, they internalize them as humiliation and shame. Children begin to feel that they are not worthy, and shame becomes a part of their self-concept.

But there is a good side to all of this too. As Box 4.1 on resilient children indicates, higher self-esteem was a major distinguishing factor between resilient boys and girls (under age eighteen) and vulnerable children who had serious coping problems by eighteen years of age (Werner, 1986). As more is known about resilient children, perhaps the self-image and the lives of COAs can be further improved. Another positive finding is that the self-esteem of many adult children of alcoholics (ACOAs) is high while others' is low, depending upon whether their situations warranted treatment. ACOAs in treatment had much lower self-worth than non-COAs. But ACOAs not undergoing treatment had as much self-esteem and an even higher capacity for intimate contact than adults from nonalcoholic homes (Barnard & Spoentgen, 1987).

Locus of Control

Control is a big issue for COAs, mainly because they have witnessed one or both parents struggling, without much success, to maintain control and to manage their own lives. Children have *internal locus of control* when they gain a sense of mastery over their difficult alcoholic environment. They believe their own actions determine the positive or negative consequences in their lives. In contrast, children with *external locus of control* do not feel in control of their lives. They believe, instead, that external forces govern their destiny. As a result, they externalize their responsibilities, resign themselves to their circumstances, and succumb to the guides of fate and chance.

Do children from alcoholic homes have control over their lives? Or do they bend and sway at the mercy of their everyday worlds? Generally, research findings indicate that children from chemically dependent homes have greater externality than children from sober ones. Joseph Kern and his research associates, Hassett and Collipp (1981), studied forty children between the ages of eight and thirteen. The researchers administered a test that measured locus of control to half the children, who lived in drinking households, and another half, who resided in sober homes. They concluded from the test results that the COAs in their study were significantly more externally oriented than the comparison group. The COAs felt less personally responsible for and less in control of the events that shaped their daily lives. This feeling of being under the control of others generally leads to a lack of initiative and achievement in maneuvering the world to one's advantage.

Other studies have confirmed that children reared in alcoholic households lack a true sense of control over their lives, compared to children reared in nonalcoholic families (DiCicco et al., 1984; Post & Robinson, 1998; Prewett, Spence, & Chaknis, 1981). Authorities believe this difference in psychological functioning occurs because of deficits in childhood socialization of COAs. Paralyzed from the stresses and strains of an alcoholic upbringing, these children are unable to develop an effective ability to manage their lives. Some experts believe that this factor may even contribute to the high incidence of alcoholism among COAs (Kern et al., 1981). There is a consensus of opinion among researchers that, as a rule, children from alcoholic households believe they have little say and control over their personal lives.

An exception to this rule, however, can be found among resilient children and children living with recovering parents. Children of recovering alcoholics tend to have more internal control and to feel greater affection from their alcoholic fathers than children with active alcoholic fathers. Resilient COAs have scores similar to those of children from nonalcoholic homes on locus of control. They are less likely than children who developed coping problems by eighteen years of age to believe that luck and fate were decisive factors in their lives. Instead, they believe that their own actions determine the positive or negative consequences in their lives (Werner, 1986).

Relationship Problems

Family interaction sets the tone and quality of the kinds of relationships kids will have with others outside their homes. Unfortunately, alcoholic homes provide less than optimal training grounds for healthy human relationships. Positive parental role models are generally missing. Distrust of parents is often generalized to all adults—teachers, counselors, other parents, even the clergy—which leads to resentment toward authority and inability to accept it (Cork, 1969). Sibling relationships are the first important peer interactions children have that prepare them for later relationships with the many types of people they will meet outside the home (Flake-Hobson et al., 1983). The sibling relationships in chemically dependent families are often riddled with conflict and dissension. Consequently, COAs have little success or little experience making friends during their youth. Their friends are scared away by the bizarre behaviors of the alcoholic parent or by actual insults and ridicule (Cork, 1969). Some COAs have no time to spend with friends because of their household obligations.

The battle scars from alcoholic homes make it difficult for COAs to develop intimacy and trusting relationships. So it is understandable that this difficulty spills over into adolescence and adulthood in forming companionships, expressing intimacy, and maintaining viable relationships. Studies of interactions during adolescence reveal that as many as 87 percent of the teens from alcoholic homes had ineffectual peer relationships (Booz-Allen & Hamilton, Inc., 1974). Another 64 percent had trouble forming relationships with the opposite sex because of suspicion and distrust. Deidre, twenty-one years old, carried her distrust of intimate relationships into adulthood:

> My counselor said I made decisions when I was little that I had to make to survive in that situation, but those decisions can ruin the rest of my life. I've got to get rid of them. One thing was that I'm unlovable and I can't trust it when somebody says they love me.

In a study of 409 adult children of alcoholics (ACOAs), the respondents reported significantly less communication with their parents, neighbors, friends the same age, teachers, counselors, and friends' parents than a comparison group of adult children of nonalcoholics (Black et al., 1986). ACOAs cited "problems trusting people" as the biggest factor that distinguished them from adults from nonalcoholic homes.

Tips for Practitioners

Practitioners cannot make the alcoholism in the child's life disappear, and they cannot change the way things are at home. But they can help by first accepting the fact that they—as teachers, counselors, social workers, medical personnel, clergy, and so forth—are just as powerless over the parent's drinking as other family members. No one can stop the drinking except the alcoholic. Once this is understood, professionals will realize their best avenue for helping children adjust is to help them make the best of their home situations and to take care of themselves. Practitioners must remember, however, that each child's home situation is made up of a range of child, parent, family, social network, neighborhood, and community variables that interact to influence the quality of that child's life. None of these pieces of a child's life should be overlooked in assessing ways to help children in alcoholic families best adjust to the circumstances of their lives.

Ordinarily, COAs do not reach out. They do not have emotional resources, and they do not use the social supports around them. They repress their feelings or minimize them (Black, 1987). So it is up to practitioners to make the first move. The following tips will give you a head start in the right direction.

- Use caution with the label *resilient* because it conveys the notion that some COAs do not need special help or attention. No one lives for any length of time in a chemically dependent home without suffering some side effects.
- Be on the lookout for children you would otherwise consider resilient. Always make sure these kids get special attention as would any other child. A close, intimate relationship with just one significant adult makes a big difference in their lives.

- Assure children that alcoholism occurs because of problems their parents have. Help them understand that they are not responsible for their parent's behavior, and they did not cause, cannot control, and cannot cure the disease. This may even help them on the road to understanding that they should not be embarrassed by what parents do because parental behaviors are apart from them.

- Help children gain a sense of mastery over their environment. Give them choices to make and challenges that are developmentally sound and that ensure their ability to manage and control their lives. Teaching autonomy through simple, decision-making processes in the classroom can help break children's fear and dependency. Making choices about which activities they want to engage in during free play (preschoolers), how they choose to spend their time on the playground (school-age children), or what theme they want to write about for an assignment (older children) are simple examples in which you can give children opportunities to make decisions about their lives.

- Establish a one-to-one relationship with the child and communicate on a feeling level. Make a special effort to love the child. Let the child know that he or she is important and worthwhile by smiling, hugging, praising, and paying attention to appropriate behaviors. But avoid being a mother or a father. You cannot replace the alcoholic parent and should not try to do so. Allowing too much dependence on you would be a disservice, because this child must continue to deal with the alcoholism long after he or she has left your services.

- Avoid overprotecting children, always realizing that they must be dealt with patiently and might regress to less mature forms of behavior at times. Set firm, reasonable limits. Even though children might have problems, you should not allow them to "run wild."

- Teach children what families are like by reading children's stories. In situations where family alcoholism is complicated by separation or divorce, children may be dealing with a double whammy. These children need special attention to deal with the hurt not only of drinking but also of splitting up their home. Help COAs and other children from homes of divorce and stepfamilies understand that there are many types of families. COAs especially need to know that there is no perfect family like the Cleavers or the Andersons. This gives them an idea of what normal families are like, because they have never lived in one, and it gives them more realistic and less idealistic images for when they grow up.

- Understand that difficulties in the child's behavior do not necessarily mean that the child has become permanently damaged. If a ten-year-old, for example, has become a serious behavior problem in school, this may simply be a cry for help. The kindness of a teacher's guidance or expression of concern can make a difference. Research also shows that once the alcoholic goes into recovery, and children get the help they need, family functioning improves and children are happier and better adjusted.

- Help the child recognize and express feelings, resolve conflict, and master his or her realm through creative activities, children's literature, and play (see Chapter 7). Creative expression, in particular, helps children with locus of control, self-esteem, and overall psychological functioning. For instance, Rick wrote a poem that gave him a constructive outlet for expressing his anger and frustration of living with an alcoholic grandmother.

- Allow children solitude and privacy when they need it. If they spend an inordinate amount of time alone, however, this may be cause for concern. Balance is what you should look for, balance of alone time and social time.

- Help the child develop feelings of trust. The alcoholic home is often one in which promises are broken. COAs believe that they cannot trust their parents or any adult. Establishment of trust between you and the child can be the greatest gift you can give. Be consistent. Do not say one thing and do another. When you make a commitment, no matter how small it may seem to you, stick to it. Never make promises unless you plan to follow through.

- Make the classroom a sanctuary in which children feel secure, psychologically safe, and relaxed, and enjoy learning. Have predictable routines and rules. If you are going to change this predictable world (because of an emergency or a special event), be sure to tell children before and explain to them why the change is necessary.

- Let the children play, play, play. As a rule, COAs do not have the opportunity to play, and the time they spend with you may be their only leisure time. They may have more trouble than most children in playing with peers, and just plain having fun. Your role may be to literally help them learn to play and to have fun doing it. Integrate fun activities, jokes, and funny stories. Laughing is therapeutic, and a sense of humor is a powerful antidote against stress.

- Self-esteem building activities are important for the fragile self-concepts that so many COAs have.
- Explore psychoeducational and emotionally supportive ways to help nonalcoholic parents enhance sources of social support and perceived efficacy or to reduce stress or depression. These efforts may help strengthen family relationships sufficiently to temper the impact of the alcoholic parent on children's psychosocial functioning (Tubman, 1993).

5 RISKS AND HAZARDS IN BEHAVIOR AND DEVELOPMENT

CASE 5.1

Ted, a student in my first-grade classroom, had all the symptoms of a child living in active alcoholism. He showed signs of flagrant parental neglect. He bragged that he didn't have to do anything he didn't want to do at home or school. And he didn't. He was allowed to roam the neighborhood at will unsupervised, to stay up as late as he wanted to, and he boasted that his mom even gave him a cigarette to smoke. He came to school in tattered and torn clothes. His unlaced and untied shoestrings usually dragged the floor. His shirts had holes in them, and his pants were missing pockets or belt loops. His face was often crusty, and he had body odor from not bathing and from wearing the same clothes day after day. One morning, he showed me a severe burn across his chest that he said came from a kerosene heater. The burn may leave permanent scars.

Ted was quarrelsome and uncooperative with classmates and teachers. Late-night television watching of adult themes on cable channels caused him to repeat sexually explicit language to other children and to touch little girls in sexually aggressive ways. Ted had poor relationships with his classmates. His foul language, combined with his offensive smell and roughhousing, caused the other children to dislike and reject him.

Behaviorally, Ted commanded my constant attention by stealing and lying. Although he had free lunch at school, he repeatedly stole snacks and lunch from the other children. One day, I watched Ted, after he had eaten a full lunch, go into the book bags and coat pockets of several children. He stole and ate three apples, a sandwich, and three bags of carrots on top of his lunch. Show-and-tell toys and valuables (such as a digital watch) began to disappear from the classroom. I had given Ted some used clothing—sweatshirts and pants. It finally came to my attention that Ted was taking home other children's possessions and telling his mother that I had given him the toys just as I had given him the clothes. On different occasions, he took credit for other children's work and told classroom visitors that he painted a picture or wrote a story that had been done by another child. Ted's conduct was out of control not only in school but also in his neighborhood. Once while playing with matches he set fire in the woods, and the fire department had to be summoned to fight the blaze.

Academically, Ted had difficulty concentrating and made failing grades. He had a short attention span and always seemed to be on the move when he wasn't sleeping. He often slept during lessons or just simply refused to do his work. At the end of the year, he started to show some improvement in reading, but he was behind the other children in most areas. He still, for example, couldn't associate number values with manipulative objects. He was retained in first grade.

— Judy Watson, first-grade teacher

A. Health and Safety Hazards

Some children from alcoholic homes have serious health and safety problems in addition to psychological difficulties. Basically, alcoholic homes are psychologically unsafe and highly stressful. Stress has many physical side effects that impair children's health. These problems are best observed and addressed in schools, where kids spend most of their weekday time. Chronic stress and poor health interfere with academic performance and functional social relationships. Occasionally, poor health has a biological basis that will remain a permanent part of the child's makeup, as in the following case of Sheila. But more commonly, problems manifested in school are an outgrowth of unstable family conditions stemming from alcoholism.

Clinical reports and research studies agree that children of alcoholic parents have a greater number and variety of health problems, including psychosomatic illnesses and compulsive disorders, than children from nondrinking families. One of the reasons children miss so much school is that the quarreling, violence, and disruption caused by alcoholism is so upsetting that they actually become physically sick. Children of alcoholic mothers who drink during pregnancy also run the risk of being born with fetal alcohol syndrome.

Fetal Alcohol Syndrome

CASE 5.2

The first time I met five-year-old Sheila was at the beginning of the school year, and I noticed how small she was compared to the other children in my kindergarten class. She weighed about twenty pounds, whereas most kindergarten children weigh forty-five pounds. Her clothes fell off of her because she was so tiny. I thought perhaps she had anemia, and I referred her to the school nurse.

Not only were Sheila's clothes too big for her, but she couldn't concentrate or retain skills for very long. She could remember for a few seconds, but if you asked her the same thing again, she would draw a total blank. Her downfall was her nervousness, which at times got worse. She shook all the time, bit her fingernails, and her eyes darted from one place to another. She had a short attention span and couldn't sit or stand still for very long because of her nervous condition. She'd rather stand up to do seat work, and she preferred to do something that would allow her to move around the room such as looking at pictures in the book center or playing in the housekeeping area. She couldn't hold a pencil or crayon deftly and could barely write her name. She could put down the letter s for the first letter of her name. But the rest of the letters were out of sequence and ill-formed. From her brain to hand, she just couldn't make the correct formation of her letters. She could hold a crayon, but she couldn't stay inside the lines.

While the nurse was checking into the problem, I figured out on my own that she was probably a fetal alcohol syndrome baby because of her extremely small size, her nervousness, her emaciated appearance, and her inability to concentrate. The nurse found out that she was indeed a child of an alcoholic mother and that while the mother was pregnant with Sheila, an older sister was taken out of the home and put into a foster home.

It turned out that both parents were alcoholic. Sheila and her older sister took care of themselves. If they made it to school, it was because they dressed and fed themselves each morning. At a parent conference, her mother showed up greatly intoxicated. Her mother acted as if she felt very guilty. She told me she knew Sheila was nervous and small for her size, but she didn't know if the child's condition had anything to do with the fact that she drank when she was pregnant.

I know that a lot of Sheila's nervousness is biological and comes from her mother's drinking while she was in the womb. But a lot of it comes from the kind of home she still lives in, too. I'm afraid she's going to have big problems because of this in first grade.

— *Patti Young, kindergarten teacher*

Fetal alcohol syndrome (FAS) is a condition that results from maternal consumption of alcohol during pregnancy. FAS was discovered in 1973, but it is not known how alcohol causes this syndrome or how much alcohol must be consumed before FAS will occur. Despite our knowledge about the risks of alcohol consumption during pregnancy, the National Centers for Disease Control report that the rate of FAS increased almost sevenfold from 1979 to 1993 ("Use of Alcohol," 1995). Babies with FAS are usually quite small at birth, and they are slow to develop physically. Central nervous system damage causes irritability, hyperactivity, and retardation in intellectual development (Steinhausen, Willms, & Spohr, 1993). FAS children may have heart defects, disturbed sleep patterns, unusually small heads, and facial abnormalities. These abnormal facial features include abundant hair, short distance between the inner and outer portion of the eye, an extra portion of skin over the thinner portion of the eye, a flat crease that extends between the bottom of the nose and the upper lips, narrow eye openings, flat nasal bridge, thin upper lip, short upturned nose, and small chin (Holzman, 1983).

Research has shown that long-term behavioral effects are still present during the preschool and elementary school years (Steinhausen et al., 1993). Although FAS children never fully recover from their disorder, they can improve in motor functioning, attention, relations with siblings and peers, temper, phobias, intellectual performance, and psycholinguistic abilities (Steinhausen et al., 1984). No change, however, has been observed in their level of hyperactivity. It is clear from these findings and the case of Sheila that this birth defect continues to handicap children's academic performance throughout their school years.

Psychosomatic Complaints

Because they encounter an inordinate amount of stress and strain at home, COAs often store their feelings and anxieties in the confines of their bodies and, as a consequence, experience more health problems. They complain more often of headaches, difficulty sleeping, fatigue, nausea, stomachaches, and eating problems (Steinhausen, Nestler, & Huth, 1982). Although they are more likely to seek treatment for these ailments, there is generally no physical origin for their psychosomatic maladies. Wives and daughters of alcoholics are more prone to complain of psychosomatic problems, to seek treatment for them, and to receive specific diagnoses than sons and husbands of alcoholics and females in nondrinking homes (Biek, 1981; Roberts & Brent, 1982).

COAs often develop nervous conditions in reaction to an alcoholic environment that can be psychologically and physically unsafe. Kids who fear for their own safety or for that of another parent or sibling have shot nerves. Fingernail biting is the most noticeable sign of anxiety. Trembling, headaches, nervous tics, insomnia, and upset stomachs are also symptomatic. Gail said she got especially nervous at night. That was when her father drank the most and when he and her mother argued and brutally fought. Gail had a nervous stomach and shook so uncontrollably at times that she could barely hold a pencil in school. When she did complete assignments, Gail trembled so much that her teachers could not read the scribbling. But she loved school and saw it as a sanctuary from her unhappy home life. "My counselor helped me a lot with my nerves," Gail explained. "She gave me stuff to read about alcoholism and we talked a lot." Gail's counselor also referred the child to a COA group. Many of her nervous habits began to disappear as she took an active part in her own recovery.

Children whose parents are in recovery do not show the same pattern of psychosomatic problems. Studies in which parents were being treated for alcoholism found no significant differences in health problems, personality disturbances, or school problems between their offspring and those from nonalcoholic homes (McLachlan et al., 1973; Rimmer, 1982). Children of recovered alcoholics have no greater incidences of allergies, anemia, asthma, frequent colds or coughs, and overweight and underweight problems than children from nonalcoholic homes (Moos & Billings, 1982). In contrast, children of relapsed alcoholics have more psychosomatic problems than children from nonalcoholic homes.

Compulsive Disorders

Other health hazards taking their toll among COAs are addictions that do great harm physically as well as psychologically. As they progress through childhood, COAs have difficulty discarding their needs for perfection, compulsion, and control, which they used in an effort to manage all that is controllable in a chaotic home (O'Gorman & Oliver-Diaz, 1987). Having provided many years of comfort, these needs become an integral part of their adult personalities. Untreated in childhood, these compulsive dependency needs can be serious sources of stress in adolescence and adulthood when they are converted into addictions. COAs often attempt to assuage the anxiety through alcohol or other drugs, work, food, sex, and other compulsive behaviors. They are at high risk for becoming alcoholics, workaholics, compulsive gamblers, compulsive spenders, or sex and drug addicts. Eating disorders are also common.

BOX 5.1
Compulsive Eating

My brother and I are both compulsive eaters. I went through a year of treatment at the Center for Behavioral Medicine in a group for compulsive eaters. In my private sessions with a therapist, we talked about my father's alcoholism. I had never realized until recently that I suffered from low self-esteem and that the eating is tied into that as well.

It's one of those things where if you eat the first peanut M & M, you're sure that the nineteenth will taste even better. When I eat, I feel comforted. It's calming to some degree. And then I feel guilty and I eat some more. Compulsive eating is just like drugs or drinking or anything else. The therapist told me that I didn't express as much anger about my father as people generally do. I guess the pushing down of feelings is one reason I stuff food into my mouth. And I think I'm constantly trying to fill up that emptiness with food. I used to go on diets and starve and lose twenty-five pounds, and that's how I'd keep my weight down.

My therapist hypnotized me and did a regression to the point where I started overeating. And it was the strangest occurrence because all of a sudden I remembered being in the fifth grade. Mrs. Autry's 5C was our room. I remember we were the last class to eat, and they'd bring these huge trays of homemade yeast rolls, and they'd put the butter on with paintbrushes. If they had three pans left, the cafeteria workers would put them on the table and tell us to go to it. The boys were always the ones to gobble down the rolls, except I would enter the contest and remember winning one day with a total of fourteen rolls on top of all the lunch I had already eaten. I had been a good basketball player in the fifth grade. Al-

---

Eating Disorders

Overeating is the major eating disorder, followed by bulimia (bingeing and purging) and anorexia (starvation, laxative usage, and stringent exercise). Like all compulsive behaviors, overeating begins in early childhood and becomes full-blown in adulthood. Box 5.1 presents an interview with Emma, forty-two, who talks of her compulsive eating problem and how, through hypnosis, she traced it to the fifth grade.

Type A Children and Work Addiction

Many COAs are hurried children—youngsters forced to grow up too fast. They acquire adult responsibilities as well as the stressful and

though I was very small, I was fast and very wily. All of a sudden, I was as round as the basketball. I can remember my elementary school princi-pal—who was also the basketball coach—saying, "Emma, if you eat one more roll, I'm gonna use you for the ball." I traced my overeating back to that point. That's when I remember starting to overeat.

But in the last three years since I started back to work and my last child started kindergarten, the thoughts of denying myself and dieting just make me sick! So I've tried every magic potion. I've been to every weight loss program there is in town. When I was going through therapy, I thought, "Damn, I'm not an alcoholic. I'm compulsive when I drink just like I am compulsive when I eat or talk or used to be when I smoked. I've got a compulsive personality."

I have read that children of alcoholics are compulsive in some area. I bite my nails. I remember first biting my nails when (again in the fifth grade) my mother had been diagnosed with a fatal blood disease. I was in my grandmother's kitchen when my mother had gone to the hospital, and I knew she was very ill, and it seemed like the compulsive behavior had started around that point. Biting the fingernails came first, then the eating came along. In the process of therapy for my eating, my finger-nails grew. Just like a lot of people cope with stress by drinking or smok-ing, I cope by eating.

If anybody had asked me growing up if I'd ever drink, I'd have said, "Absolutely, positively not!" [because of my father's alcoholism]. But I do. Although I wish I were just like my mother, I have a whole lot of my father in me, which I don't like.

—Emma, age forty-two

tense side effects that accompany grown-up problems (Elkind, 1981; Robinson, 1996). Many of the pressures from taking on the hardships of alcoholic parents—such as calling in sick to a drunken father's em-ployer or making sure monthly bills get paid so utilities are not discon-nected—can produce severe childhood stress and burnout. COAs who assume the role of family hero and parent to a younger sibling (cooking, dressing, washing clothes, and overseeing household chores) or to a parent (becoming Mom's confidant and helping her solve her problems of the bottle or becoming her protector by keeping a violent father from assaulting her night after night) must become little grown-ups with adulthood's worries and burdens. Ultimately, they miss childhood al-together.

Hurried children often have what medical scientists call Type A personalities; being overly stressed and burdened leads to physical health problems. Type A behavior pattern is characterized by intense time urgency, impatience, a competitive achievement orientation, and aggressiveness-hostility (Raikkonen & Keltikangas-Jarvinen, 1992; Yamasaki, 1990). This compulsive need to achieve in children is linked to such cardiovascular risk factors as fluctuations in blood pressure and heart rate. The Type A behavior pattern is the most documented psychological risk factor for coronary heart disease, the origins of which have been traced to childhood (Raikkonen & Keltikangas-Jarvinen, 1992; Visintainer & Matthews, 1987). Type A characteristics have been observed among schoolchildren as young as five years of age, and these traits endured over a five-year period (Visintainer & Matthews, 1987).

Current research is exploring the ways in which children are put at increased risk for becoming Type A children. Although it has been suggested that Type A characteristics may be determined by both hereditary and environmental factors, there is as yet no clear evidence that Type A behavior is hereditary. Among environmental factors, however, family environments, parental psychological characteristics, and child-rearing practices have been found to be associated with the development of Type A behaviors in children.

Research suggests that children of alcoholic families develop Type A characteristics in response to parental behaviors for one or more of three reasons: as an effort to maintain family equilibrium by distracting attention from the alcoholic parent, as an effort to gain parental attention and approval, and/or as an effort to cope with the uncontrollable events of living in an alcoholic family.

First, children of alcoholic families may assume Type A behavior patterns in the context of the role of family hero. The family hero is the overachieving child who excels at every task in order to draw attention away from the painful dynamics of his or her alcoholic family system. Type A children are descriptive of those COAs who, through the family hero role, become compulsive overachievers and eventually workaholics (Robinson, 1998) (see Box 5.2). They attempt to control, suppress fatigue, are impatient, strive for competition and achievement, and have a sense of time urgency and perfectionism.

Alternatively, children may develop Type A characteristics in direct response to the child-rearing patterns of their alcoholic parent. For

---

BOX 5.2
Work Addiction

Weekends were difficult for me as a young adult because, as a child, that's when the crises with my father would erupt. Anytime there was quiet, it was the calm before the storm, and the rapid-fire jolt of my father's inebriated outbursts would hit me like a jackhammer. Waking up on Saturday mornings or holidays with nothing to do made me panic stricken. I felt out of control and that something terrible could happen during those idle hours. It was difficult for me to be flexible and live moment to moment. I learned to cope by packing my weekends full so that I knew exactly what would happen next and how to prepare for it. Although staying busy seemed to alleviate a lot of stress, it left no time for spontaneous, relaxing moments, no time for play, and no time for smelling the roses and living in the now.

Schoolwork helped me feel good about myself, and later the work world gave me the same sense of what I thought was fulfillment. It provided an escape so that I didn't have to deal with many feelings buried since childhood. It kept me disconnected from people and intimate relationships and gave me something with which to connect and with which to be intimate. Work also gave me a sense of total control of my life. I had found my drug of choice. I transformed my long hours of college study into long hours of work: weeknights, weekends, and holidays. I was hooked.

Like an alcoholic, I felt restless and became irritable when I went more than a few days away from my desk. Even when lounging on a tropical beach, all my thoughts revolved around my next project. Hardly a vacation passed that a stuffed briefcase of work didn't accompany me as part of my luggage. When family and friends complained about my overworking, I hid my work by sneaking it into my suitcase. While others swam and played in the surf, I toiled over a makeshift desk back in the cottage. I hid my work as my father had hidden his bottle. As a recovering adult child of an alcoholic, I came to realize that, like most adult COAs, I was repeating my father's compulsive dependency. Unrecognized in a different form, I had merely switched addictions.

—Bryan Robinson

Adapted from *Chained to the Desk: A Guidebook for Workaholics, Their Partners and Children, and the Clinicians Who Treat Them*, by Bryan Robinson, New York University Press, 1998. Used with permission.

example, Raikkonen and Keltikangas-Jarvinen (1992) found that hostile maternal child-rearing characteristics are associated with the development of the impatience and aggression aspects of Type A behavior in their adolescent children. These mothers used a strict, punitive disciplinary style, perceived their children as burdensome, and tended to ignore and avoid emotional contact with their children. These characteristics are consistent with Type A traits of competitiveness and time urgency, however, they are also consistent with parenting patterns common to alcoholic families: the inability to tolerate children's activity, a lack of comfort in the company of children, the need for overcontrolled behavior, and a belief that punishment is regularly needed to control children's behaviors and ensure obedience (Raikkonen & Keltikangas-Jarvinen, 1992). Type A adults are also very involved in their own lives and less interested in others. For nonalcoholic Type A parents, this preoccupation outside the family is focused on career development. For alcoholic parents, the preoccupation centers around drinking and activities associated with drinking. Children in alcoholic families are often ignored or left to their own devices; they may even experience themselves as invisible. Thus, although children of alcoholic families may not be exposed to classic Type A parents (i.e., parents may not have a strong achievement orientation); they may be parented in a less supportive and less positively involved family climate by adults with Type A characteristics (Raikkonen & Keltikangas-Jarvinen, 1992; Yamasaki, 1990). In response to these ineffectual parenting behaviors, COAs may themselves develop Type A behavior patterns. In an attempt to elicit more attention and expression of concern and affection from their parents, these children strive to prove themselves and develop more self-confidence by striving to excel (Yamasaki, 1990).

Finally, children in alcoholic families may develop Type A behavior patterns as an attempt to cope with the dysfunctional nature of their family environment (Compas, 1987). A central feature of development for all children involves coping with psychosocial stress, and the ways children learn to cope with stressful events or circumstances moderate the effects of those stressors. Children identify coping resources within themselves (such as problem-solving skills) and in their social environments (as in a relationship with another caring adult). They then use these resources to strengthen their ability to adapt to life stresses.

For children of alcoholism, Type A behavior patterns may reflect a distinctive style of coping with the chaotic, uncontrollable events of

TABLE 5.1. The Matthews Youth Test for Health

1. When this child plays games, he/she is competitive.
2. This child works quickly and energetically rather than slowly and deliberately.
3. When this child has to wait for others, he/she becomes impatient.
4. This child does things in a hurry.
*5. It takes a lot to get the child angry at his/her peers.
6. This child interrupts others.
7. This child is a leader in various activities.
8. This child gets irritated easily.
9. He/she seems to perform better than usual when competing against others.
10. This child likes to argue or debate.
*11. This child is patient when working with children slower than he/she is.
12. When working or playing, he/she tries to do better than other children.
*13. This child can sit still long.
14. It is important to this child to win, rather than to have fun in games or schoolwork.
15. Other children look to this child for leadership.
16. This child is competitive.
17. This child tends to get into fights.

SOURCE: Reprinted from K. A. Matthews and J. Angulo, Measurement of the Type A behavior pattern in children: Assessment of children's competitiveness, impatience-anger, and aggression, *Child Development*, 51, 466-475. © 1980, The Society for Research in Child Development, Inc. Used with permission.
*The scale is reversed for these items.

their family environments. Rigid time management, achievement, and aggression (classic Type A characteristics) can all be understood as a child's attempt to gain some degree of control over his or her life in the midst of the chaos of an alcoholic family environment. On some level, this child is reasoning, "I cannot stop my mother from drinking, I cannot change the craziness in this house, but I can achieve some sense of ownership of my own life by proving that I am in control of my time and my accomplishments, and that I am strong enough to not let others get in my way." The threat of total loss of control is thus diminished, even though all hell may be breaking loose around him.

The number of Type A children who come from chemically dependent families is unknown. The similarities, however, between behavior patterns of Type A kids and the compulsive overachievement behaviors of many COAs are striking. The Matthews Youth Test for Health (MYTH) was developed with the help of classroom teachers for research purposes (Matthews & Angulo, 1980) (see Table 5.1). Teachers and other interested practitioners can use the MYTH to distinguish Type A from Type B school-age children (youngsters who do not exhibit

Type A traits). The child is rated on how characteristic each of the seventeen items is on a scale from 1 = *extremely uncharacteristic* to 5 = *extremely characteristic*. Possible MYTH scores range from 17 (extreme Type B) to 85 (extreme Type A).

Childhood is threatened with extinction as youngsters are pressured to achieve, succeed, and please (Elkind, 1981). Although many Type A children are high achievers, they also have low self-esteem and insecurity about their ability to achieve their goals (Robinson, 1996). The period of childhood, compared to adulthood, is the shortest time in the life span, and some COAs burn out before they live through this brief period.

Physical and Sexual Abuse

Concern for the safety of children in alcoholic households is an important consideration in and out of school. Violence in an alcoholic home can become so heightened that it is unleashed on the child, causing physical injury and school absenteeism. Children often stay home to conceal welts, bruises, or other signs of abuse. One twelve-year-old girl told me she "couldn't go to school for three days" because of the huge welts caused by her drunk mother's abuse. Risks of sexual abuse also run high in alcoholic families. After school, large numbers of COAs are safety risks because they are home alone or left unsupervised with an inebriated parent.

Ginger tried to resist the sexual advances of her drunken father. Finally, he threatened to leave his wife and family unless the mother instructed their thirteen-year-old daughter to accept sexual relationships with him. Fearful of being abandoned, the mother and child succumbed to his sexual demands. During the next four years, Ginger replaced her mother as her father's sexual outlet.

Authorities estimate that two or three million children are victims of physical and sexual abuse each year. These estimates are low because many professionals never report cases or abused children are often afraid or ashamed to talk. Child abuse ranges from physical and sexual assault to neglect and failure to provide protection. About two thousand children die annually as a result of their circumstances.

Alcohol abuse is generally found among 50 percent to 80 percent of homes reporting physical and sexual abuse or neglect (Black, 1987;

Famularo, Stone, Barnum, & Wharton, 1986). COAs report greater frequencies of family violence than children from abstaining families. Physical violence includes abusive behaviors by and between parents and toward the children. Many children witness one parent abusing another.

A study of 409 ACOAs revealed that 95 percent described greater frequency of both parents being violent in general, and 56 percent said their parents were violent while drinking (Black et al., 1986). Fathers were ten times more likely to be abusive. COAs also described themselves and their siblings as performing violent acts more often than comparison groups. A total of 18.5 percent said they had been sexually abused as children either by fondling or oral sex. Daughters of alcoholics were two times more likely to be incest victims.

Eight-year-old Marla's dress and behaviors were sexually seductive and provocative. Dressed like an eighteen-year-old, Marla boasted, "All the boys at school [Marla is in the third grade] want to go with me. My daddy says the reason I dress nice is because I want to attract the boys and make them want me." Although her father said Marla dresses in high style to attract the boys, Marla argued that she just likes to dress nice. When her father gets drunk and throws things and yells, Marla lays in bed and hugs her oversized teddy bear. She said he gets crazy when he drinks and hits her mom and slams the phone down on her mother's fingers when she tries to call the police.

Marla has been told to call the police when her father gets violent, but she said she could never do that because she loves him too much. According to Marla, a next-door neighbor shared my concerns:

> This lady next door says that if my daddy ever touches me in places that I should tell her. Or that if he wants me to touch him somewhere I should tell her too. Yuk, I wouldn't want to do that. But he'd probably whip me if I didn't do what he said.

Documented physical abuse, sexual overtones in Marla's dress and behaviors, and sexual themes in her discussions about her father raise suspicions. These signs are among twenty indicators of child sexual abuse (Sgroi, 1982, pp. 40-41):

1. Overly compliant behavior
2. Acting-out, aggressive behavior
3. Pseudomature behavior

4. Hints about sexual activity
5. Persistent and inappropriate sexual play with peers or toys or with themselves, or sexually aggressive behavior with peers
6. Detailed and age-inappropriate understanding of sexual behavior (especially by young children)
7. Arriving early at school and leaving late with few, if any, absences
8. Poor peer relationships or inability to make friends
9. Lack of trust, particularly with significant others
10. Nonparticipation in school and social activities
11. Inability to concentrate in school
12. Sudden drop in school performance
13. Extraordinary fears of males (in cases of male perpetrator and female victim)
14. Seductive behavior with males (in cases of male perpetrator and female victim)
15. Running away from home
16. Sleep disturbances
17. Regressive behavior
18. Withdrawal
19. Clinical depression
20. Suicidal feelings

COAs become alcoholics or marry alcoholics or both; sexually abused children have kids whom they sexually assault, or they marry abusers; and physically abused children become adult child abusers or marry batterers (Weatherford, 1988). Youngsters who grow up under all three conditions are prone to repeat the cycle by living out a combination of sequences, unless practitioners intervene (Black, 1986).

All fifty states have mandatory reporting laws of suspected or known physical and sexual abuse cases (Slavenas, 1988). If you observe patterns of abuse, neglect, or harm, you can review the reporting policies and procedures in your respective school and state and file reports in accordance with them. You can obtain the specific laws that apply to you from your state's Child Protective Agency. Although you should ensure confidentiality in conversations with children from alcoholic families, the one exception would be in cases of physical or sexual abuse. Children should be encouraged to tell you in such instances, and you *must* always report it.

Latchkey Children of Alcoholic Parents

In addition to the hardships of everyday living in chemically dependent homes, many COAs are neglected by their parents. They have the added burden of before- and after-school responsibilities of caring for themselves, a younger sibling, and sometimes a drinking parent. All these factors combined can jeopardize safety, increase stress levels, and interfere with school performance.

Latchkey kids are underage children who care for themselves on a regular basis before and after school, on weekends, and during summer vacations and holidays while their parents work (see Lamorey, Robinson, Rowland, & Coleman, in press). There are roughly the same number of latchkey kids as there are COAs under age eighteen: seven million. Latchkey youngsters have received far greater attention and help in coping with their self-care arrangements than the millions of children like Nina, who are latchkey kids by default. Public school extended-day programs, neighborhood "block mothers," after-school hotlines, and "survival skills" training are just a few examples. Being a latchkey child is not necessarily detrimental when proper preparations have been made.

But because they are not officially classified as latchkey children, many kids who go home each day to an alcoholic parent do not get the adequate preparation they need for self-care. Those who have worked with COAs for any length of time know countless children who are technically latchkey kids, even though a drinking parent is home. The parent may be so physically and psychologically unavailable that the child is literally unsupervised. Such is the case of fourteen-year-old Fran and her eight-year-old sister, who are frequently left alone by addicted parents at all hours of the night. Fran, who had become the parent of the whole family, had the look of a child who carried the world on her shoulders. She spoke openly about her parents' use of cocaine and alcohol:

> It makes me sick to my stomach when they get high. They smile and ask me if I want some too. I feel like they don't really love me because they'll let me do anything I want. I can go anywhere and do anything and stay as long as I want to. But I don't because there wouldn't be anybody to take care of my sister.

Above and beyond the many problems encountered through alcoholism, COAs may be at high risk for added psychological or physical hurt that plagues some latchkey kids: accidents, fears of intruders, stress from emergencies that cannot be handled, sexual abuse, feelings of confinement, and isolation. Research indicates that COAs have more accidents and serious illnesses and report more emotional problems than children from nondrinking homes, presumably because of parental absence and neglect (Woodside, 1986).

Some children are alone at home, and some are supervised by an older brother or sister while the alcoholic parent is passed out in another room. Others are on their own but stop by a friend's house where no adults are present or "hang out" at a local mall or video arcade. Some children are supervised in absentia by a sober, working parent through telephone calls, while others have no communication with nondrinking adults at all. These diverse arrangements make a difference in children's adjustment. Children who hang out at a friend's house (where no adults are home) or on the street are at higher risk of getting into trouble than kids who promptly report home and remain there alone. Kids who are supervised in absentia by sober parents adjust in similar ways to other children who are supervised by nonalcoholic parents at home during after-school hours (Steinberg, 1986).

In addition to providing children of chemically dependent parents the necessary skills for surviving alcoholism, we can also give them the self-care skills they need to function more effectively on their own when proper supervision is not available. Of course, children need to know the basic skills and strategies necessary for maintaining their safety and well-being when they are home alone (see "Implement Self-Care Curricula" on p. 96). It is just as important, however, for us to provide these children with as much emotional support as possible. Whenever possible, children should be given a break from self-care in the alcoholic home while simultaneously doing positive things for themselves by participating in after-school activities that they can enjoy such as Scouts, sports, YMCA programs, and so forth. Children at home alone or with an alcoholic parent who are supervised in absentia by a nondrinking parent at work should have frequent opportunities to communicate with that parent through check-in phone calls. This connection to a caring, responsible parent can lessen a child's sense of isolation and provide a greater sense of security. Children should also be encouraged to talk about how they feel about being alone or with the drinking parent. Perhaps most important, children do better when they are praised and trusted for undertaking self-care responsibilities. They need to hear it, and they need special quality times with the nondrinking parent in which they are the sole focus of attention (Lamorey et al., in press).

Tips for Practitioners

There are several points you can keep in mind in regard to the health and safety of COAs. You need to know when to consult with another resource person and when to recommend referral to another community agency, how to build on the child's strengths, important points to emphasize for children at risk in self-care situations, and how to help relieve childhood stress.

Know When to Consult and Refer

You can consult with the school nurse when physical, psychosomatic, or medical symptoms appear. It is important to know when the symptoms are constitutional, as they were with Sheila, or environmental, as they are with most COAs. Medical staff can be helpful resources in determining the appropriate approach. FAS children who are obviously developmentally delayed can be referred to the school psychologist or social worker for testing. Special curricula can be developed out of their assessments. It may be more appropriate to refer other children to a counselor for a special COA group or for individual counseling. You also must be prepared to intervene in cases where children show symptoms of physical or sexual abuse. The appropriate steps in reporting should be followed according to the respective laws in your state.

Emphasize Strengths

Capitalize on the children's strengths. Although Sheila had attention and concentration problems, her teacher stressed the child's excellent social skills and put her into situations where she was able to interact and to give moral support to other children.

Implement Self-Care Curricula

Determine those children who are in situations where they must ultimately care for themselves. This might include latchkey arrangements or situations in which children are left alone for fifteen minutes while a parent runs errands. You can help children who are vulnerable to crisis acquire self-reliance skills, ensuring that they can cope safely on their own. Traffic safety, precautions with strangers, handling emergencies, accident prevention, and entering a safe house are topics that can be included as part of a health unit on safety. Although all children benefit from such instruction, COAs will automatically learn (even though alcohol is never mentioned) whom to call in case of an emergency or accident, or if they get abandoned at the mall or movie by a drinking parent or need a safe place to get away from a violent, abusive, intoxicated parent.

Community helpers can be brought in, and many of the points discussed earlier in this chapter can be included for children who are unprepared for self-care (see Lamorey et al., in press). Children who have self-confidence in their ability to care for themselves when alone are more likely to concentrate and perform better in school rather than dwell on their apprehensions. School counselors can help teachers plan special lessons on self-care and encourage children to talk about being alone. This way children learn that other children share many of their same feelings of fear or loneliness.

Help Relieve Stress

You can play a major role in children's lives by helping them keep the *child* in their childhood. Practicing stress-relief exercises will help all youngsters. Take a breather from learning each day, and teach children how to relieve tension by practicing relaxation exercises. With soft music playing, lead children through guided imagery and meditation. Emphasize the importance of physical exercise and good nutrition for stress reduction. Encourage children to practice these suggestions at home.

Many books on the market for ACOAs recommend healing the child within or getting in touch with the inner child (for example, Whitfield, 1980). Practitioners can help kids by ensuring that they have this opportunity while they are still young, unlike many grown COAs, who were deprived of their childhoods and must mourn that loss during recovery. Try practicing the following guidelines daily and sharing them with parents of all children.

- Avoid hurrying children. Let them grow and develop at their own unique pace, according to their unique developmental timetables.
- Encourage children to play and do things children do. Some of our fondest memories are of our childhood experiences.
- Do not force-feed learning. Have reasonable expectations based on what children are capable of performing at their respective ages.
- Let children have some daily and flexible schedule in school and at home, with free time built in for choosing from activities that match their interests.
- Protect children from the harsh pressures of the adult world, without overprotecting them, and give them time to play, learn, and fantasize.
- Try not to pass needless stress and worry on to children. Give them opportunities to talk about their own worries and stresses. Adults can save theirs for the therapist's couch.
- Guide children toward wise decision making by introducing limited choices that match their emotional maturity.
- Reward children for their triumphs and successes, no matter how small. Let them know you love them and are proud of them for who they are, not what you want them to be.
- Start the day on a positive note with pleasant words and calm routines.
- Plan special times together each week as a family (without television), and listen to what your children have to say.
- Do not burden kids with the adult responsibilities of raising a sibling, keeping house, and the emotional worry of being a parent at age ten or twelve.

B. Academic and Behavioral Concerns

Research indicates that boys and girls from alcoholic homes have poorer school performance and lower academic achievement than children from nonalcoholic homes (Chandy, Harris, Blum, & Resnick, 1993; Sher, Walitzer, Wood, & Brent, 1991). Problems with COAs naturally emerge in the classroom, where they spend a large portion of their time. Ted's teacher was smart enough to put two and two together and realize that lying, stealing, and poor study habits were not his real problems. Instead, they were symptoms of a deeper-rooted, more pervasive

problem of family alcoholism. Ted had many of the academic and behavioral signs that concern and puzzle classroom teachers. Fortunately
for Ted, he had a sensitive and caring teacher who communicated
closely with his parents and provided him with every opportunity to
learn. She was successful in getting the mother to work with Ted on his
reading, and, although he lacked in mathematical ability, the child became a proficient reader.

Academic problems occur with older children for many of the same
reasons but with the added pressure of the peer group, which has a
bigger influence. Aaron, for instance, had trouble with skipping school,
sleeping through classes, and "cutting up." Slightly rebellious but ar-
ticulate and charismatic, with coal-black hair and dark eyes, the fifteen-
year-old was already two grades behind.

> What do you do when you know you need help with algebra but you
> don't want to ask for it because the other guys will think you're not cool?
> I mean, if I don't understand a problem, the teacher will come over and
> spend all this time hovering over my desk, and everybody else laughs at
> me. So I just don't even ask anymore.

The peer group is essential for all teenagers, but for Aaron, whose
father was an active alcoholic, being accepted and fitting in was even
more important—even if it meant flunking his grade. He'd rather fail
than look "dumb" in front of his classmates.

A host of problems related to academic performance are associated
with drinking parents (see Box 5.3). The upheaval that typifies the alcoholic household interferes with concentration in and out of school. Psychosomatic disorders are often accompanied by behavioral disturbances. Sleepless nights, stress, and depression lead to daydreaming
and sleeping during class. Children have trouble keeping up. School
absenteeism, frequent changes of schools, and preoccupation with
problems at home lead to low scores on standardized tests, bad grades,
and, ultimately, grade failure.

Alcoholic Fathers and Academic Achievement

Two studies compared sixteen sons of alcoholic fathers with twenty-
five sons whose fathers were not alcoholic (Hegedus, Alterman, &

BOX 5.3
Academic Problems
of Children of Alcoholics

- Lower mental abilities for boys
- Lower verbal proficiency and lower reading comprehension
- Lower academic achievement for children of alcoholic fathers and children of alcoholic mothers
- Lower scores on IQ tests
- Deficits in perceptual-motor ability, memory, and language processing
- Attend more schools than children from nondrinking homes
- Repeat more grades than children from sober homes
- Higher school absenteeism than children of nonalcoholics
- Inability to concentrate and short attention span
- Restlessness and impulsivity
- More likely to be referred to school counselor or psychologist
- More likely to be expelled and less likely to graduate from high school among low-income children of alcoholic parents

---

Tarter, 1984; Tarter, Hegedus, Goldstein, Shelly, & Alterman, 1984). In the first study, sixteen-year-old boys were given a battery of intelligence tests. Results showed teenage sons of alcoholics performed more poorly on tests measuring attention, memory, perceptual motor coordination, motor speed, spatial sequencing, and language capacity. They also performed less well on reading comprehension. In the second study, the adolescent boys were given achievement tests. Although both groups were of average intelligence and in the same grade, sons of alcoholics scored two years below the sons of nonalcoholics on learning achievement. The researchers also discovered that the lower scores of COAs were linked not only to family instability and disruption but also to neuropsychological capacity—a hereditary function of the brain that could suggest a possible neurobiological basis for the vulnerability to alcoholism (Hegedus et al., 1984). The high risk of COAs for developing alcoholism will be discussed in a later chapter.

Two research investigations followed 134 sons of alcoholic fathers for twenty years and compared them with seventy sons of nonalcoholic fathers in Denmark (Knop, Teasdale, Schulsinger, & Goodwin, 1985;

Schulsinger et al., 1986). Schoolteachers rated sons of alcoholics as more restless and impulsive and poorer in verbal proficiency than sons of nonalcoholics. Performance on neuropsychological tests also indicated that sons of alcoholics had poorer impulse control. Sons of alcoholics had reading difficulties and, as a result, were referred to school psychologists more often than the comparison group. Based on the social history of sons of alcoholics, the investigators found that they attended more schools, repeated more grades, and had less happy childhoods in unstable homes.

Alcoholic Mothers and Academic Achievement

Adrienne Marcus (1986) conducted a major study showing that children of alcoholic mothers also have problems in academic achievement. She compared forty elementary school children of alcoholic mothers with forty children of nonalcoholic mothers. Children of alcoholic mothers were more often placed in some type of special education class and scored lower on mathematics, reading recognition, and reading comprehension subtests of academic achievement. These lower scores in some cases may be caused by broken homes (65 percent of the COAs were from single-mother households) and turmoil in the home environment that interferes with learning or contributes to a negative home learning environment. But significantly more alcoholic mothers drank during the term of pregnancy, so that the presence of FAS among some COAs could be a contributing factor, as it can be in all studies with alcoholic mothers. Early academic failure and special education placement by third grade were also noted in another investigation of heavy-drinking mothers (Shaywitz, Cohen, & Shaywitz, 1980). Other studies also show that children of alcoholic mothers have lower IQ scores than children of nonalcoholics (Aronson, Kyllerman, Sable, Sandin, & Olegard, 1985; Steinhausen et al., 1982).

Sex of Child and Academic Achievement

There is evidence that the academic achievement of boys, compared to girls, is more severely affected by parental alcoholism, both in terms of their lack of resiliance (Werner, 1986) and poor academic performance (Kern et al., 1981; Schulsinger et al., 1986). Sons of alcoholics, compared to sons of nonalcoholics, are at higher risk for repeated school grades and are more likely to be referred to a school psychologist for academic difficulties (Schulsinger et al., 1986). Kern and his associates (1981) compared the mental ability test scores of twenty COAs (ages eight to thirteen) with twenty children of nonalcoholics. Although girls from alcoholic homes were not affected, boys from drinking homes scored lower on mental ability than boys from nonalcoholic homes. The researchers speculated that depressed mental ability in male children may be an outcome of their perceived inability to control their destiny in the area of intellectual performance.

Research in the area of separation and divorce shows that young boys have a harder adjustment time than girls, and this is pronounced in schoolwork and cognitive tests (Flake-Hobson et al., 1983; Skeen & McKenry, 1980). Interference with school performance, thus, may be a factor not only of alcoholic parents but also of family turmoil or even family splits.

Poverty and Academic Achievement

A twenty-year long-term study of 147 low-income COAs revealed that, compared to 112 control children of abstainers, the outlook for academic achievement was not optimistic (Miller & Jang, 1977). Children of alcoholic parents were less likely to graduate from high school. More children of alcoholic parents dropped out because of early marriage or pregnancy, because they joined the military or became institutionalized, or because they were expelled. It is important to note, however, that all 147 children in the sample were from low-income families that were already beset by serious social problems.

Other studies of children from low-income families also conclude that poverty conditions, combined with parental alcoholism, place elementary school children at higher risk for being expelled, failing their grades, being truant, and dropping out of school before graduating from high school (Robins, West, Ratcliff, & Herjanic, 1977). Researchers in another study examined the records of one hundred children from alcoholic households (average ages ten and eleven) and compared them to those of one hundred children from sober homes (Chafetz, Blane, & Hill, 1971). All children were enrolled in a child guidance clinic, were mostly from low-income families, and had emotional problems. Alcoholic families consisted mostly of single mothers and had much less income than the nonalcoholic, mostly two-parent families. Findings revealed that during adolescence, children of alcoholic parents had greater school difficulties and police or court problems than children from nondrinking homes.

It would be incorrect to assume that mere exposure to alcoholic parents will lead to horrendous school failure. A lot has to do with how early kids are exposed to alcoholism, the presence of divorce or separation, other debilitating conditions (such as poverty and emotional stability), and how resilient kids are. Resilient children score higher on aptitude and achievement tests and are more achievement oriented than children who develop behavioral problems before eighteen years of age (Werner, 1986). School performance, as you saw with psychological adjustment, also depends upon the family environment, social support system, and coping behaviors (Clair & Genest, 1987). Some COAs appear relatively invulnerable to the stressors and ill effects of having an alcoholic parent, whereas others are clearly more dysfunctional.

Reasons for Poor Achievement

For some children, school is a hiding place, a place of safety and comfort. They like school because it is the one place where they can retreat from their unstable home life. As a result, these kids thrive in the classroom. Smart teachers and other school personnel will capitalize on these children's motivation and build self-confidence that will equip them with other coping skills. In contrast, there are those children who perceive school as another stress factor in their tormented lives. Fear of teachers, fear of failure, and fear that other students will not like them increase the anxiety and stress and lower children's performance abilities.

Actress Suzanne Somers (1988), who confessed that her thoughts were never far away from the problems of home, describes the school fears and bad grades that accompanied her father's alcoholism:

> Instead of school being a place to escape the trauma of my home life, it became another kind of prison. I was dumb and stupid in school. I hid from my dad at home, and I hid from my teacher at school. I always tried to sit at the back of the room out of Sister Cecile's eyesight. I would panic

when she called my name. I was never paying attention. The kids in my class made fun of me. I wasn't smart and I was skinny. (p. 32)

COAs do poorly in school for many reasons. Typically, parents are so consumed with their own problems that those of their kids take a backseat. Even if a child does well in school, it is often without the support and praise of a parent. When children do poorly in school, they are castigated or belittled by their parents, and when they do well, they receive little recognition at home. It is difficult for children to study or keep their mind on homework in a home where chaos is the norm. The unpredictability and inconsistency of alcoholic households, described in Chapter 4, has a direct bearing on children's school performance. Accomplishing homework assignments or concentrating on studying for a test can be a monumental task in the midst of constant upheaval. Many times, COAs are chastised for not having their homework by teachers who, although unaware of their home situations, have their best interests at heart.

Although alcoholic parents typically do little to provide a supportive environment at home, they may be sticklers about good grades and homework. Despite the constant noise and dissension, children may still be expected to do well in school. How they achieve that is their problem. Interestingly, Chandy and colleagues (1993) found that teenage COAs who managed to do well at school perceived that their parents had high expectations of them.

Often alcoholism zaps 90 percent of children's energies, and they may have only 10 percent to give in the classroom. Children become so preoccupied with maintaining calm and sanity at home that they may never think of school, much less homework, after the bell rings. All their energies revolve around the alcoholic parent and trying to control and stabilize their roller coaster existence.

Research indicates that difficulty concentrating on schoolwork is a common complaint of children with alcoholic parents (Fine, Yudin, Holmes, & Heinemann, 1976; Tarter et al., 1984; Wilson & Orford, 1978). Poor concentration and low attention span, when not linked with FAS, stem from lack of sleep or stress and worry about what happened the night before or what is happening at home in their absence. It is difficult for the attention of these children not to wander in the middle of a lesson, as they wonder if everything will still be in one piece when they get off the school bus in the afternoon. Alternatively, fantasizing and daydreaming about a better way of life, a different kind of home, can be a way for COAs to psychologically relieve themselves of the horrible reality of the night before and the terrible dread of what they will face in the night to come. Meanwhile, their grades suffer, and no one, least of all their teachers, knows why.

As a consequence of their disrupted family conditions, children of alcoholism usually attend more schools than children from sober homes (Knop et al., 1985; Schulsinger et al., 1986). Their families may be transients because of evictions, job changes, and other family disruptions that are used to keep the drinking problem a secret (Priest, 1985). Because of sleepless nights and bouts of parental alcoholism, higher rates of school absenteeism are found among children from drinking homes (Haberman, 1966; Kammeier, 1971). Children also stay home from school to protect the nonalcoholic parent, usually the mother, from the alcoholic parent (Wilson & Orford, 1978). School absenteeism makes it difficult for children to keep up with their assignments and often leads to poor grades. Many of these children come to school despite sleepless nights and end up sleeping or daydreaming through class.

Suzanne Somers (1988) described her bewildering school experience of trying to stay awake in class:

> I woke up with a start. I didn't know where I was. Then I realized that everyone in class was laughing at me. Sister Cecile was standing over my desk. "Miss Mahoney, what *is* the capital of Montana?" I couldn't think. How long had I been sleeping? "Maybe we should talk to the principal about why you can't stay awake in class. Don't your parents make sure you go to bed on time?" she questioned. . . . How could I tell her that we were up all night with screaming and yelling and hitting? How could I tell her I finally cried myself to sleep at 5 a.m.? How could I tell her how nervous I was? How could I tell her this was a normal part of my life; that most nights were like this? (p. 31)

Conduct and Developmental Disturbances

A strong body of research suggests that COAs who fit the scapegoat role develop a variety of delinquent and behavioral disturbances. As we have emphasized before, only a small portion of the seven million kids of alcoholics are so severely disturbed that their behaviors warrant attention from the justice or mental health systems. Still, COAs are overrepresented in these institutions. About 20 percent of the caseloads of juvenile courts and child guidance clinics are children from alcoholic homes (Ackerman, 1983).

Cases in which the behavior patterns become so disruptive that they require professional intervention are ordinarily based on information from therapists, mothers, and classroom teachers. COAs between ages eight and eighteen, admitted to a mental health clinic, were more disturbed in their behavior patterns than children from abstaining homes also attending the mental health center (Fine et al., 1976). Compared with children from nondrinking families, COAs were less able to pay attention, less responsive to environmental stimulation, and more prone to emotional upset. As a rule, they were more anxious and fearful children, they had trouble managing their excitement or mood, and they tended to be more dependent. They were more socially aggressive and domineering toward other children and often annoyed and provoked their peers into hitting or in other ways attacking them. They were also more socially and emotionally detached from the happenings around them and preoccupied with inner thoughts. As with autistic children, the COAs showed extreme sensitivity to noises, bright lights, heat, or cold and shut out visual and auditory stimuli by covering their eyes and ears.

Research also suggests that violence in alcoholic fathers is linked to developmental disorders in boys and girls (Wilson & Orford, 1978). Boys—but not girls—with alcoholic fathers showed a greater number of developmental disorders than a control group of children. More symptoms of developmental disorders existed among COAs with violent fathers.

Mothers' reports of their offspring unearthed eight behavioral symptoms that distinguished COAs from other children. COAs were more likely to stutter, wet the bed after age six, fight with peers, get in trouble in the neighborhood, isolate themselves from peers, have temper tantrums, have unreasonable fears, and have trouble in school (Haberman, 1966). Direct observations of 229 COAs, along with mothers' reports and teacher judgments, indicated a greater prevalence of emotional disturbances among the COAs than a comparison group of 163 non-COAs. Bed-wetting, hysterical symptoms, and speech disorders were more typical of the COAs than non-COAs. Classroom teach-

BOX 5.4
Common Conduct Disturbances Reported
Among a Small Portion of Children of Alcoholics

Socially aggressive behaviors
Isolation from peers
Fighting with peers
Quarrelsomeness and uncooperativeness
Delinquency
Disruptive, disobedient, and oppositional behaviors
Stealing
Lying
Truancy
Substance abuse
Temper tantrums
Hyperactivity

ers' comparisons of boys with alcoholic fathers and nonalcoholic fathers revealed that sons of male alcoholics tended to have the same
passive-aggressive personality traits as their fathers (Aronson & Gilbert, 1963).

Other studies confirm that COAs, compared to children of nondrinking parents, have an assortment of conduct disorders (Merikangas,
Weissman, Prusoff, Pauls, & Leckman, 1985; Steinhausen et al., 1984)
(see Box 5.4). They are more hyperactive (Aronson et al., 1985; Bell &
Cohen, 1981); have more temper tantrums as well as problems paying
attention (Steinhausen et al., 1982); engage in more avoidant coping behaviors such as smoking, drinking, and eating (Clair & Genest, 1987);
and are more often involved in fights and impulsive behaviors at
school (Schulsinger et al., 1986).

In one study (Rimmer, 1982), children from active alcoholic homes
had twice as many behavior problems as those from nondrinking families. The greatest problem was disobedience, followed by stealing at
home and discipline problems at school. Truancy and fighting were
also common problems. Other problems, although less common, were
playing with matches, stealing, cheating at school, being expelled or
suspended from school, and lying.

Sometimes COAs tell lies because they are embarrassed by the fact that their parents drink or because they are just trying to make things look the way they wish they could be. Ted, in the earlier case, often took credit for other children's work because he felt that his was inferior. Sheila's kindergarten teacher said the child constantly lied about her alcoholic parents by constructing a fantasy world at school:

> She lived in a fantasy world. I noticed this especially when we started having show and tell at the first of the year. She came up with some strange concoctions of where her mother was going to take her and it was always Disneyland or Disney World. Then I noticed a pattern. If the child ahead of Sheila happened to say something about their parents taking them to Disney World, then Sheila would get up in front of the group and say that her mom was also taking her to Disney World. She would describe in great detail how they were going to get there and when they were going to go. One time during show and tell Sheila picked up something that belonged to another child and told the class about it. Then the child that the object belonged to said, "But that's mine!" Sheila suddenly snapped out of her dream world and seemed very embarrassed.

It is difficult to know how much of delinquent and behavioral problems are due to divorce, and not alcoholism. But analysis of this body of work revealed that, once the influence of one-parent families is considered, parental alcoholism does not increase the risk for delinquency beyond that attributable to divorce (West & Prinz, 1987).

Children with behavioral disturbances are signaling to those around them that something is wrong. Behind the angry, hostile, and aggressive mask lies a frightened little child. At sixteen, Rick had become the family scapegoat. He had pulled away from his one-parent family by running away, fighting at school, and using alcohol and other drugs. The first night he came to the COA group, he wanted everyone to know he was a cool dude and tough enough to make it on his own. Through hostility and arrogance, he made it clear that he didn't want to be in the COA program and would rather be with his friends getting high and listening to music. On that first night in group, we unrolled a huge parachute and played with it in a large circle. Rick became absorbed in the activity, squealing with laughter and delight each time we made it ascend and descend and offering various suggestions on ways we could make the parachute "behave." His inner child emerged in all its glory. Much to our surprise, Rick thrived in the program, taking advantage of all its offerings. He actively pursued the creative writing and art each week. Gradually, he began to lose most of his tough exterior. He clung to parts of the role, though, because he still needed them to survive.

Suicide

All COAs need educational intervention. The few that need intensive therapy or confinement to correctional facilities are the ones who act out, rather than conceal, their pain and frustration. They direct it either against society, in the form of delinquent acts or conduct and developmental disorders, or against themselves in the form of suicide.

Almost one fifth of the adolescents who attempt suicide come from homes where one or both parents have drinking problems (Hafen & Frandsen, 1986). Patrick McKenry and his colleagues at Ohio State University conducted a series of studies suggesting that COAs are at high risk for suicide attempts (McKenry & Tischler, 1987; McKenry, Tischler, & Kelley, 1983; Tischler & McKenry, 1982). The researchers studied ninety-two adolescents between the ages of twelve and eighteen who entered the Children's Hospital Emergency Room in Columbus, Ohio. Half of the adolescent patients had attempted suicide, and the other half were admitted to the hospital for minor nonsuicidal injuries.

Parents of suicidal adolescents used more alcohol and drugs and used them more often than parents of nonsuicidal adolescents. Suicidal adolescents routinely used more alcohol, depressants, marijuana, and stimulants than the nonsuicidal group. Drugs, in fact, were used in the suicide attempt by thirty-nine of the forty-six adolescents. During clinical evaluations, 24 percent of the suicidal adolescents reported that at least one parent had a serious drug or alcohol problem, and one third of them actually used drugs belonging to their mothers or fathers in their suicide attempts. Parents of the suicide attempters, compared to parents of nonattempters, were coping more poorly, were more depressed and more anxious, and had more suicidal thoughts and lower self-esteem—many of the same symptoms shared by active alcoholics.

This research confirms earlier reports that some teenagers react to parental alcoholism with suicide attempts, acting out, psychiatric problems, and difficulty with the legal system (Kearney & Taylor, 1969). Other evidence suggests that adult men (average age fifty-six) who grew up in alcoholic homes where they had been abused as children had a higher incidence of serious suicide attempts, suicidal drinking, an increased level of anxiety, more legal difficulties, domestic violence, and violence against authority figures than a group of men without a history of child abuse (Kroll, Stock, & James, 1985). More recently, out of a sample of fifty thirty-year-old ACOAs, 44 percent had deliberately tried to hurt or kill themselves in adulthood (Weatherford, 1988).

Tips for Practitioners

Teachers, counselors, and school administrators are in a better position than most practitioners to help kids whose parents drink because of their greater daily contact. Although they cannot and should not be therapists, school personnel can follow many helpful practices that ultimately can make a difference in youngsters' lives. A speaker at the 1988 National Association for Children of Alcoholics Conference shared through tears that he had been a lost and shy twelve-year-old troublemaker when an angel turned his life around. That angel was his classroom teacher, who introduced him to Alateen. Today, that man is a recovering child of an alcoholic and a leader in the field of chemical dependency. Many behavior problem children, like this man, await the concerned practitioner's touch.

Look Beneath the Symptoms

Some COAs may need greater opportunities for success in school so that their performance will be commensurate with their potential. Look beneath the daydreaming, inability to concentrate, or sleeping during class and sympathetically address the reasons behind these and other symptoms. Once you have gained the ability to look past the symptoms and identify family alcoholism as the problem, you will begin to see significant changes in the attitudes and behaviors of both you and the child.

Give Extra Attention

You can help highly stressed kids by setting aside a special block of time toward the end of each day for homework completion so that they do not fall behind in their assignments (Brenner, 1984). Some COAs may need extra attention in order to complete in-class assignments. One way of providing this attention is to set aside a few minutes each day for the teacher, a counselor, a parent volunteer, or another child to work closely with children who have difficulty completing in-class and homework assignments. This can also be a time for the child to build rapport with this special person who functions as a supportive listener. Extra attention makes children feel someone cares, and it gives them a chance to talk about disturbing thoughts or feelings that could be interfering with school performance. Boys from alcoholic homes, in particular, may need individualized attention, because they appear to be more vulnerable to the negative effects of parental alcoholism. Depressed mental ability in boys may be an outcome of their perceived inability to master their destiny in the area of intellectual performance (Kern et al., 1981). By keeping a pulse on family transitions such as divorce or new stepfamilies, you will be more successful in helping children through these added conflicts.

Catch Children Being Good

Make a point to praise children for classroom successes and goals that are achieved—good work, good grades, good behaviors. They need the strokes that they may not be getting at home. Exercises that allow children to learn that they can gain a sense of mastery over their environment can instill feelings of competence and self-esteem.

Be Supportive of Parents

Make a concerted effort to remain objective and supportive of parents and to provide an informal atmosphere in which parents can share their problems and solutions about children. It is important that parents always feel that they can discuss their problems about their children with school personnel. You can often help parents share information about alcoholism without prying by saying, "Molly's mind hasn't been on her schoolwork lately. She seems to be daydreaming a lot. Is there anything that I should know about?" That way you have opened the door for parents to bring up any personal problems without making accusations or putting anyone on the defensive. It is important to remember that alcoholic parents are in a crisis situation and may not be able to parent as well as they would like. Contrary to their outward behavior, all chemically dependent parents love their children, but the disease of alcoholism gets in the way of expressions of love. Be sure to treat both the dependent and codependent parents with equal respect and concern. Never side with the codependent parent against the alcoholic parent or the child against alcoholic parents. Blaming and taking sides are counterproductive and contrary to the concept of alcoholism as a disease. Such strategies actually reinforce the battle lines to which children are accustomed in dysfunctional families and further divide the family. Although it may be difficult, you must remember that parents suffering from alcoholism need empathy and understanding too, as they are often in the midst of a bitter struggle to overcome their illness.

6 IDENTIFYING CHILDREN OF ALCOHOLICS

CASE 6.1

Everything I remember about my childhood is bad. My parents were really heavy into drugs, like LSD during the 1960s and later alcohol. They were so chemically dependent that they spent all their money on dope and alcohol and ended up broke. My mother beat on me from the time I was four years old. I remember my mother laying in her bedroom and staring up at the ceiling, and that's all she'd do all day long.

When I was four years old in nursery school, I wanted to make the babies cry for some unknown reason. I would go into the infant room and pull the babies' hair. I didn't know why I wanted to hear them cry. I remember my mother used to pull my hair when she'd get high. She'd yank it for no reason. Now that I'm grown, I know I was angry with her for doing that to me. It was the only way I knew how to cry out for help. I was trying to show in an outside way the pain I was having on the inside. But nobody listened. I can still see the preschool teacher right in my face, nose to nose, and all the little kids surrounding her, and she was yelling at me. And I can still see her face. I was getting real upset because I had to go to the bathroom, but the teacher wouldn't let me. She spanked me with a paddle as hard as she could, and the whole time I was using the bathroom while she was doing that. I'll never

forget that as long as I live. And I'll never forget that preschool. I
still remember the nightmares I had about that awful place!

Identifying Preschool Children of Alcoholics

Deidre is one of the millions of invisible, forgotten, and ignored
(Bosma, 1972; Black, 1982) COAs who live a life of silent suffering (Mac-
Donald & Blume, 1986). Most of these kids, who pass before our eyes
every day, remain unseen unless they make waves or cause problems.
Even when they cause problems, practitioners often focus on the symptoms rather than underlying causes, as illustrated by Deidre's preschool teacher, who punished and humiliated the child for pulling hair.
The last few chapters dealt with psychological, health, academic, and
behavioral problems that, although they appear at elementary age, are
already brewing long before in the preschool years.

The Need for Early Identification

The neglect of COAs is more pronounced among preschool children
than any other age. Identification, treatment, and research with this age
group are practically nonexistent. Instead, professionals tend to post-
pone identification and treatment until about age eight or nine when
kids are old enough to take a test or tell us that something is wrong.
That is too late. The implication of the blatant neglect of preschoolers is
that they cannot be seriously affected if they are preliterate. Child development research, however, shows that this is a fallacy: The preschool years are the most important ones in the life span for establishing the bedrock for adulthood.

Most authorities concede that schools are the best places to identify
and treat COAs because school systems have direct access to all children over the span of their youth (Ackerman, 1983; Deutsch, 1982;
DiCicco, Davis, & Orenstein, 1984; McElligatt, 1986; Morehouse &
Scola, 1986). Although schools should continue to play a primary role

in this process, identification efforts must start earlier, in the preschool years. Postponement of identification and treatment until the first or second grade is ill-advised, given the clinical observations that denial systems and family roles are already firmly entrenched by age nine (Black, 1987). Preschool intervention can interrupt the disease cycle of alcoholism before dysfunctional patterns are firmly in place.

Barriers to Early Identification

Many of the same good reasons that more COAs are not identified in elementary schools also explain the lack of detection in the early years. Most practitioners have not been trained in alcohol education and do not know enough about alcoholism to spot its effects. They may not know how to ask about substance abuse or feel uncomfortable about intruding into the family's personal business. They may be immobilized by their own fears of traumatizing the child, angering the parent, or stirring up trouble (McElligatt, 1986).

Despite these barriers, early intervention is possible today more than ever before with most preschoolers in some type of group care and with increasing public school support for three- and four-year-old classrooms. Although children are accessible, however, it is much more difficult to identify children under age six than it is elementary school youngsters. COAs are not easy to spot because they have no common distinguishing markings. Children with Down's syndrome or autism, or even those who have been physically abused, can be easily identified almost immediately because of certain common physical attributes.

Standardized procedures for identifying COAs have been developed for school-age children (see the discussion later in this chapter). The Children of Alcoholics Screening Test (CAST) (Jones, 1983), for example, and other standardized measures are designed for children age nine and older. But these tests are inappropriate for preschool youngsters because children must be old enough to read and write in order to complete the forms. Because preschool children and preliterate kids are automatically excluded from the standardized approach, identifying them is much more difficult.

One of the most effective techniques for identifying older elementary children, self-referral, is also developmentally inappropriate for preschoolers, because they cannot verbalize how they feel or what they think about alcoholism as older kids can. Because they are preliterate, they cannot write their feelings, respond to a survey, or take a test. Moreover, their art ability, which produces fewer elements of detail than the skills of school-age kids, has not developed enough to be used as a confident diagnostic medium.

Still, identification is possible in the preschool years, although it is totally contingent upon the subjective impressions of the caregiver. There are four areas of the preschool child's life that practitioners can examine to determine if stress and possibly chemical abuse are present in the home: (1) daily routines, (2) play observations, (3) emotional adjustment, and (4) parental relationships. Examining these four areas unearths the alert signs outlined in Box 6.1.

Monitoring Daily Routines

Developing habits for sleeping, toileting, eating, and adjusting to routines are important milestones in the lives of preschoolers. Persistent trouble in these areas is symptomatic of deeper problems, which could be alcohol-related. Preschoolers who are off developmental schedule in physical-motor, cognitive, language, or social-emotional areas also may have alcohol-related difficulties.

Sleeping Difficulties

By their first birthday, healthy infants have spent over half their lives asleep. During the first two months, they sleep about seventeen hours a day, but by three months, this time has dropped to fourteen hours. By six months, most babies sleep through the night. A lot of sleep is normal during the first twelve months. But as children approach one year of age, they require less and less sleep. After one year of age, persistent fatigue or lethargy and the desire to oversleep are signs of a physical problem or emotional depression that could be related to family alcoholism.

By age two, toddlers are expected to adjust their sleeping habits to those of the family, and most children do so with little difficulty. Sleep patterns are an excellent indicator of how well preschool youngsters are adjusting and how well other things are going in their lives. Just as adults have difficulty sleeping when something is bothersome, erratic

---

BOX 6.1
Twenty Signs for Identifying
Preschool Children of Alcoholics

1. Sleeping difficulties
2. Persistent fatigue or lethargy
3. Relapses in toileting habits
4. Extreme eating behaviors
5. Problems in adjusting to transitions and changes in routines
6. Developmental delays
7. Recurring alcoholic themes in dramatic play
8. Isolated play
9. Lack of sustained attention
10. Hyperactivity
11. Abrupt and uncharacteristic behavior changes
12. Frequent fussiness and fretfulness
13. Frequent temper tantrums or attacks on other children
14. Regressive behaviors such as thumbsucking or "baby talk"
15. Excessive fear of unfamiliar people or new situations
16. Persistent clinging and exaggerated fear of separation
17. Insecure attachment behaviors
18. Parental authoritarianism and unrealistic expectations
19. Parental indifference and frequent preschool absences
20. Signs of neglect or physical and sexual abuse

---

sleep patterns indicate problems among preschoolers. The first signs of nightmares normally appear in toddlerhood, and some bad dreams typically accompany the child's newfound ability of symbolic representation. Still, recurrence of bad dreams, disrupted or erratic sleep patterns, or refusal or fear of sleeping at nap time all are indicative of potential alcohol-related problems.

Toileting Habits

Although toilet training is developmental and unique for each child, most children are both bowel- and bladder-trained by twenty-seven months on the average. Most children sleep through the night without bed-wetting by thirty-three months. Soiling and wetting accidents are common occurrences, even after children are well in control of their toileting needs. Accidents also occur, however, when children become unusually upset or experience trauma. Regressive toileting habits are natural responses when preschool children get overly excited, become ill, experience a break in daily routines, or become fearful or worried about something. Family alcohol problems can lead to repetitive lapses in toileting habits—either frequent bed-wetting or soiling pants after toilet training has been achieved.

Eating Practices

By twelve months of age, most babies are eating three meals a day. Loss of appetite and refusal to eat new foods are normal behaviors in toddlerhood, as children grow taller and leaner. But starvation, compulsive eating, eating rituals, or preoccupation with food are not normal throughout the preschool years. We know that a compulsive eating disorder is a major symptom of adult COAs. Such a disorder can originate in the eating habits that are established in the first year of life. Overprotective or overanxious mothers, for example, often feed their babies every time they cry, and they sometimes overfeed infants as a substitute for love they are unable to give. Food for some children becomes a substitute for the love they never received from alcoholic parents. Overfed children can develop compulsive food habits and become obese children. Some overweight children develop adult-sized fat cells by two years of age. These excessive fat cells are difficult to remove by weight loss in adulthood, so obese babies tend to be obese adults (Flake-Hobson et al., 1983).

At the other extreme, continued loss of appetite, finicky eating, and malnourishment are signs of problems. Children of alcoholic families may reflect their worry and depression through loss of appetite, much as adults do. Children who are being neglected and are not getting proper meals at home may show it through their gauntness. Thin children who eat as if their stomachs are bottomless pits or who constantly take food from other children may suffer from alcoholic neglect.

Handling Transitions

All preschool children need the consistency and predictability of everyday routines whether at home or in the preschool classroom. Secure children from stable homes can handle occasional changes in daily routines. Children from insecure alcoholic homes, however, may show signs of upset when the order of the day is altered. In particular, caregivers will notice that insecure children have difficulty adjusting to transition times in the day care preschool curriculum. As one activity terminates and flows into another, COAs may have difficulty following the flow and may perseverate in the terminated activity or become anxious or aggressive as the change takes place. An unexpected event in the day that causes a change in normal routines also can be emotionally upsetting to these children.

Developmental Delays

Developmental norms can be useful yardsticks for practitioners to detect problems in development. Serious developmental delays, noted by the use of norms, could signal alcohol-related difficulties. When children are far behind the norm on language or motor skills, alert caregivers will perceive a possible developmental problem. Children who have fetal alcohol syndrome suffer from developmental lags in several areas, including physical and intellectual delays and perceptual-motor disturbances.

It is important for practitioners to remember that because norms are only averages, the ages at which individual children acquire skills will vary. Generally, it is only the sequence of skills that remains the same. Individual children, for example, do not begin crawling, sitting alone, or walking right on schedule according to the norms because they all have unique biological clocks that regulate the same skills at different rates. Still, norms are useful tools that skilled caregivers and medical practitioners can use to spot developmental delays that could possibly be associated with parental alcoholism. Preschool teachers, in cooperation with parents, can refer children with severe developmental delays for appropriate treatment.

Play Observations

Play serves not only as a workshop for the development of social skills but also as an important aid to emotional development. Through play, children often deal with reality in a nonthreatening way. Play helps children deal with fears aroused by trauma such as alcoholism.

The play of young children is a revealing mirror into the inner workings of their thoughts and feelings. Through play observation, practitioners learn many of the secrets of child development.

Dramatic Play

Preschoolers enjoy a type of play called dramatic play, in which they act out scenes they observe from everyday life. Preschool classrooms generally have an area especially designated as the housekeeping corner or dramatic play area. Props such as dress-up clothes, empty soup cans and cereal boxes, and dolls are usually on hand to help stimulate dramatic play. Children act out their joys and frustrations and, as they pretend, they will even repeat scenarios they have observed at home. Adults can gain a sense of trouble when children use props as bottles or beer cans and imitate drinking parents or when they perform acts of spousal hostility in the housekeeping area.

Some alcohol treatment programs place beer cans, wine bottles, beer glasses, liquor bottles, shot glasses, and an Alcoholics Anonymous Big Book in the play area for children from chemically dependent families to play out their feelings. Recurring themes in the play of preschool COAs are violence, anger, guilt, and fear (Hammond, 1985). Fears of being left and parents' fighting are commonly played out in the preschool classroom. Four-year-old Brad's fear for his emotional and physical safety was apparent when he picked up an empty beer can off the drama shelf, made pouring motions into the glass, and asked the therapist to drink it:

Brad:	It's poison.
Therapist:	Oh, no! I'm getting sick.
Brad:	I'll call the doctor.
Therapist:	Thanks.
Brad:	The doctor says you're better.
Therapist:	Oh, good.

(Hammond, 1985, p. 12)

The ability to create and resolve the consequences in such scenarios gives preschool children of alcoholic parents an enormous sense of control over their fears and worries.

Stages of Play

Between the ages of two and five, preschool children typically play alone less and become more socialized in their play (Parten, 1932). Children from alcoholic homes will have more difficulty progressing through these stages and can be observed playing in more isolated types of play (unoccupied, onlooker, solitary, and parallel) than social types (associative and cooperative).

In *unoccupied play,* children are not playing but are occupied with anything that happens to be of fleeting interest to them. During *onlooker play,* children spend time watching others play, often asking questions and giving suggestions to other children but rarely entering into play. The child plays alone and independently with toys in *solitary play,* sometimes within speaking distance of others. Between eighteen and twenty-four months, children begin *parallel play,* in which they play independently but alongside one another, frequently engaging in disputes over the same toy. Children play with peers who are engaged in similar activities in *associative play,* which ordinarily appears between three and four years of age. Sharing, borrowing, and lending play materials are typical. The most socialized play is *cooperative play,* in which children play in groups organized for the purpose of making some material product or attaining some common goal. Typical of five- and six-year-olds, children play cooperatively, assigning each other roles and acting in accordance with those designated roles. Five-year-olds who still spend most of their playtime as onlookers or in solitary or parallel play should be cause for concern.

Sustained Attention and Hyperactivity

Children who are unable to sustain attention when playing with toys and who flit from one activity to another are cause for concern. Hyperactivity among preschoolers is a chief symptom of parental alcoholism and a frequent side effect of fetal alcohol syndrome. It is characterized by difficulty paying attention and concentrating, high levels of motor activity, poor impulse control, and attention-seeking behavior. Ordinarily, preschool children have short attention spans, a need to be active, and difficulty sitting for long periods of time. The amount of time preschoolers spend paying attention to an activity increases gradually. Signs of potential family alcoholism are reflected in preschool youngsters who cannot sit through short group story or music times; children who cannot plan and complete activities they begin; and children who do not have the patience or enthusiasm to work on a classroom project that requires them to carry attention over several days.

Abrupt Changes in Play

Sudden changes in behavior can be indicative of alcoholism in the lives of school-age children. Similar abrupt changes can be observed in preschool youngsters where alcohol is a problem. An outgoing child, for example, who withdraws into a shell or a shy child who suddenly starts to act out could be troubled. The dramatic switch in Jacob, who overnight became apprehensive about exploring the playroom, and the abrupt appearance of Deidre's hair-pulling episodes are two extreme changes in behavior that indicate fear and frustration with alcoholic parents.

Of equal concern is the child who suddenly begins to attack other children or classroom pets during playtime. Caregivers should be alert to children, like five-year-old Lenney, who demonstrate an inordinate amount of dramatized violence in their play or who do not exhibit a broad range of play behaviors. Lenney had an array of activities to choose from in his preschool: transportation toys, blocks, art activities, dress up and housekeeping, and so forth. But in lieu of these activities he perseverated in walking about the classroom with a stick that one minute became his machine gun and the next a machete to cut and slaughter. One day, with the preschool teachers out of sight, Lenney took the class hamster from the cage and squeezed it to death.

A limited range of play need not be violently obtrusive, however, to warrant the practitioner's attention. Children who become suddenly preoccupied with one particular toy or activity and who play with that toy in the same ritualistic way day in and day out are cause for concern. Marcy, for example, got in the habit of holding and rocking her doll and repeating, "Mommy loves you."

Assessing Emotional Adjustment

The reactions of preschool children to a variety of situations can be an emotional barometer of the stability and security of their family lives. Observations of children's moods, their emotional control, their regressive behaviors, and the degree to which they handle separation anxiety can give practitioners possible clues to family alcoholism.

Moody Children

All children have unique temperaments. Even as infants, some children are labeled as "easy," whereas others are called "difficult." Difficult babies are described as irregular in biological functions, negative and withdrawn toward new people and situations, unable to adapt to change easily, and intense, mostly negative in mood. Easy babies are characterized by regularity of such biological functions as hunger, sleep, and eliminating; a positive approach to new people and situations; easy adaptation to new situations or changes in routines; and mild, mostly positive moods (Thomas & Chess, 1980).

Some children are temperamentally more difficult than others. Still, contrasting temperaments can be used to spot preschool children from alcoholic homes. In one study, infant temperament was a major distinguishing factor between babies (of alcoholic parents) who did and those who did not develop serious coping problems by age eighteen (Werner, 1986). Babies with easy temperaments, who were rated as "cuddly and affectionate" by their caregivers during the first year of life, were twice as likely to be resilient children than those who were viewed as difficult.

Temperamental children, who are fussy, cross, or fretful much of the time, are exhibiting their inner feelings that something is wrong. Irritability, nervousness, and erratic behaviors can be signs of fetal alcohol syndrome. Regardless of biological predisposition, children who remain stuck in depressed, mostly negative moods are evidencing emotional distress, as are children who have flat affect and whose emotions never change. Frequent mood swings from happiness to anger or vice versa also indicate problems that could originate from the stress of alcoholism in the home.

Temper Tantrums

Healthy preschoolers, like healthy adults, have a range of emotions toward others—from love to rage. Temper tantrums are normal emotional outlets for toddlers, who are still learning to balance adult boundaries with autonomy and inner control of their feelings. Brief aggressive conflicts over toys are also common in toddlers' play. Ordinarily, temper outbursts decline after two years of age and disappear by age four (Flake-Hobson et al., 1983). Preschool youngsters who persist with frequent temper tantrums after this age or who have difficulty controlling their emotions need special attention. Aggressive acts directed at other youngsters are also signs indicating children of alcoholic parents.

Regressive Behaviors

Caregivers should be alert to children who show regressive behaviors, such as bed-wetting, baby talk, or thumb-sucking. Although some relapses typically occur as children acquire new developmental abilities in other areas, prolonged and exaggerated regression is a sign of emotional maladjustment. Thumb-sucking, for example, is normal to some degree, and for some children, it replaces the familiar security blanket by providing comfort during moments of hurt and fear. Obsessive thumb-sucking among young children, however, and continued thumb-sucking past age five are signs of emotional insecurity that could stem from alcohol abuse in the home.

Separation Anxiety

Toddlers often display anxiety in the absence of those closest to them. Separation anxiety reaches a peak at eighteen months, diminishes gradually, and levels off by age three, usually disappearing in the preschool years (Weinraub & Lewis, 1977). It is normal for preschoolers to cling, follow, and remain near their parents and familiar caregivers as they adjust to such new situations as the preschool classroom.

Children who have established secure anchors with their parents experience less anxiety when separated from their parents or caregivers. In contrast, preschoolers who fret for long periods of time in the parent's absence, follow and cling to the caregiver for an inordinate amount of time, and become visibly upset when the caregiver leaves the room are displaying unhealthy adjustment problems. The same is true for preschoolers who are constantly afraid of strangers and new situations. Generally, their maladjusted behaviors stem from an insecure upbringing, one that could be linked to alcoholism.

Insecure Attachments

Child development research shows that the type of attachment patterns established in the first twelve months of a child's life remain stable over childhood (Flake-Hobson et al., 1983). COAs who received a great deal of attention from their primary caregivers during the first year of life were less likely than those who received little attention to develop serious coping problems by eighteen years of age (Werner, 1986). Preschoolers with an active alcoholic parent who is inconsistent, often inaccessible, and generally unresponsive to the child's needs early in life will develop insecure attachments. By one year of age, COAs who have developed insecure attachments become uncertain that their caregivers will be there when they need them. Signs of insecure children are visible by eighteen months of age, when toddlers are anxious and emotionally distressed even on the mother's knee. Unlike secure children, insecure preschoolers are upset when their mothers leave and remain fretful for longer periods of time, having difficulty getting involved in play.

Attachment patterns at twelve months are associated with personality traits two, three, and six years later (Ainsworth, Blehar, Waters, & Wall, 1978). Insecurely attached children of alcoholic parents, compared to securely attached youngsters, are more uncooperative, negative, quarrelsome, easily frustrated, and aggressive toward adults and peers in preschool and elementary schools. Insecure children tend to have difficulty forming close relationships with others and to be disliked by classmates and teachers.

Observation of Parents

Practitioners can gain information by observing the interactions of parents with their children and noting their attitudes and parenting practices and how interested and involved they are in their child's development. Parents' interactions with the preschool and cooperation with the administrator and caregivers also can provide clues to family alcoholism.

Child-Rearing Practices

Children may be at risk when their parents are unusually harsh, impatient, or highly critical. Practitioners can pay particular attention to authoritarian parents, who displace their anger and frustration onto their preschoolers. Authoritarian parents were first described by Diana Baumrind (1967) from her observations of parenting practices and their relationship to the personalities of three- and four-year-old nursery school children. Authoritarian parents, Baumrind noticed, use power and firm disciplinary controls without reason or explanation. Disapproval, physical punishment, and fear techniques are routinely administered. Authoritarian parents are generally more detached, less approving, and less affectionate in relationships with children. Their harsh and controlled practices lead children to develop behaviors governed by external controls of guilt or fear of being punished.

Clearly, scientists in the chemical addiction field have shown that alcoholic mothers (Krauthamer, 1979) and alcoholic fathers (Udayakumar et al., 1984) tend to use authoritarian parenting styles. Research in the field of child development indicates that children of authoritarian parents have many of the same characteristics as children of alcoholic parents. They are usually more withdrawn and hostile, easily upset, moody, unhappy, mistrustful, apprehensive in times of stress, and less competent in peer relationships than other children (Baumrind, 1967).

Child Development Knowledge and Attitudes

Children are also at risk when their parents have unrealistic child-rearing attitudes or expectations for them. Alcoholic parents with little understanding of normal child development might, for instance, view naughty behavior as the child's deliberate attempt to "get them." Or they might take it personally when a child spills food or breaks a prized vase. They may expect their child to respond in far more mature ways than is developmentally possible.

Misunderstanding children's developmental milestones, such as when they should begin walking, talking, or become toilet trained, and an attempt by parents to rush these developmental steps also put preschoolers at risk. Practitioners should be alerted when parents place unreasonable demands on children or depend on them to meet certain emotional needs beyond their capability. Either the alcoholic parent or the codependent parent may expect the preschool child to act as a source of reassurance, comfort, and love, a huge responsibility for such a small child.

Parental Indifference

A drinking problem also may exist when parents refuse to show an interest or become involved in the child's development. Parents who cannot be reached by telephone, refuse to respond to notes, or do not show up for conferences also have high-risk children. Parents who repeatedly fail to pick up their children after preschool or who are persistently late may have a drinking problem (Morehouse & Scola, 1986). Children who are frequently absent from preschool, especially on Monday mornings or after holidays, may be home with a parent nursing a hangover.

Parental Abuse and Neglect

Signs of parental abuse and neglect are the best indicators for identifying children of alcoholic parents, since 90 percent of the time, alcohol is involved in incidents of abuse. Practitioners should look for unusual cuts, welts, bruises, or burns on the child's body. Bruises or wounds that are in various stages of healing indicate that the injuries occurred at different times and may have been inflicted on a regular basis. Injuries that occur on multiple planes of the body or that leave a mark that looks like a hand or tool should also be considered nonaccidental. Physical abuse can be suspected if injuries show up a day or so after a holiday or long weekend, because bruises take a day or so to appear (Meddin & Rosen, 1986). A child who cowers when the preschool teacher raises a hand to catch the attention of the class may be a child who expects to be abused.

Neglect is apparent when children have poor hygiene, wear soiled or tattered clothing, wear winter clothes in warm weather and summer clothes in subfreezing temperatures, and are always famished. Neglect, in which preschool children are routinely left home alone for long periods of time without adult supervision, puts them in situations that they are developmentally unprepared to handle. Some preschoolers are latchkey children, in effect, even though a drinking parent is at home with them. The parent may be so wed to booze that the child is literally unsupervised. Such was the case of five-year-old Mark, who got off his school bus and stayed at home for two hours, unsupervised by an alcoholic father, until his mother got home from work. There is no such thing as a preschool latchkey child; there is only a preschool neglected child (Lamorey et al., in press).

Tips for Practitioners

None of the alert signs discussed in this chapter should be used alone to identify preschool children from alcoholic homes. When used in concert, however, these symptoms could form patterns indicative of alcohol-related problems in young children. Early identification can lead to primary intervention that can interrupt the disease cycle before it is implanted and before it takes its toll on the child physically, cognitively, emotionally, and socially.

Dealing With Denial

Once identified, you will find that preschool-age COAs are easier to reach in some ways than older kids (Black, 1987). A four-year-old will accept the family disease idea more easily than an older child, because the denial and the barriers have not had as much time to form. Younger school-age children (ages six to nine) also are much more willing to express their feelings honestly and talk about alcohol than older kids. Claudia Black (1982) found in her clinical work that children age nine and older were much harder to reach. As parents and older children dismiss what young siblings say as unimportant or as inaccurate, children begin to learn in the preschool years that they cannot trust their own realities: "The way I see it is not how it is" (Black, 1987).

Validating Preschoolers' Perceptions

One of the most significant contributions you can make when family alcoholism has been confirmed is to accept preschoolers' perceptions of what they see as accurate. Without doing anything with the information, you can simply validate what children say they see. This validation helps youngsters define the situation and learn to trust, rather than to deny, their own instincts and realities, thus betraying the disease of alcoholism.

Although they are a challenge in treatment, older COAs are much easier to identify because they have acquired more of the dysfunctional behaviors, as well as the prerequisite developmental skills—reading, writing, test taking, art ability, and verbal articulation—that aid in identification.

Identifying School-Age and Adolescent Children of Alcoholics

CASE 6.2

One day my mother was drinking and forgot to pick me up from elementary school. I knew she didn't really forget. She was just too messed up. The teacher took me home. I remember being really angry because the teacher believed my mother, who said, "Well, I didn't forget. I was going to be there." I was so mad because nobody believed me. I don't know whether children tell those things. I didn't, and I never told about my mother beating on me like that. But when my grandmother came to visit one time, she said, "Sara, you asked me when I spent the night, 'Grandmommie, are you not scared in this house?' I am." That was the only thing that I ever said that made my grandmother wonder what was happening.

When I was six, my mother beat me over the head with a frying pan. That was the day they took her off to the institution, and I lived with my grandmother ever since. Having grown up with my grandmother, now that I'm twenty-one, I don't even know my mother today. My father would visit occasionally, but he finally died of drugs and alcohol at the age of forty-one. The worse thing for me was that he led such a tortured, empty life and how sad he was. I feel relieved in a sense that I never have to worry about him again.

I'm majoring in child and family development because I want to make some kind of different impression about teachers than I had because it was such a nightmare. I had to take care of my little brother and nurture him. I even had to cook his meals. To this day I feel like I want to take care of everybody. I never thought I'd want to be anything else but a preschool teacher. I want to be somebody that makes a difference. I see some of the parents come into the day care center and ignore their kids and say, "Come on, let's go to the car." Then they walk ten feet in front of the child without even giving them time. I grew up with something like that, and I understand those kids who are going through those things.

Sara is among an estimated 95 percent of COAs who pass through elementary schools and are never identified or treated. Sara's grandmother was the only adult around her who was astute enough to pick up clues that she was being abused by her alcoholic mother. Estimates are that only 5 percent of the seven million school-age COAs are identified and treated (National Institute of Alcoholism and Alcohol Abuse, 1981). Classroom teachers are astounded to learn that one in five of the kids in their classrooms are COAs. That means in a classroom with twenty-five students, five are COAs. "No, that's impossible," is the general retort from teachers when hearing this news for the first time. But armed with new facts about COAs and upon closer scrutiny, most teachers come back and confess, "I would never have believed it, but it's true."

Research indicates that COAs are generally undetected by many practitioners, not just classroom teachers. One study found that none of the kids who were identified as COAs by a formal screening test (a total of one fourth) had ever been diagnosed as COAs by counselors or social workers, and none of them had been referred by teachers or had been self-referrals (Pilat & Jones, 1985).

Roadblocks to Identification of Older Children

Some of the same problems in identifying preschool youngsters also hinder the identification process with school-age children and adolescents. Lack of alcohol education and the practitioner's own attitude toward alcohol can make a big difference. Many practitioners have denial systems of their own that prevent them from dealing with alcoholism among children with whom they work (Whitfield, 1980). Some practitioners feel incompetent to deal with alcoholism, whereas others are afraid of causing trouble. They may be apprehensive and unknowledgeable about what to do with the information once children are identified. Still others fear parental reprisals, lack of administrative support, and even loss of their jobs. Or they may have seen drinking problems so often that they have become desensitized to their effects:

> They [may] no longer identify it as a distinctive condition requiring specific intervention strategies. Many caregivers cling to the belief that only by "curing" the parent can we really help the child, rather than viewing the child as a primary client who requires help, whether or not his or her parent is willing to accept help. (DiCicco et al., 1984, p. 1)

One problem that is more likely to hamper practitioners' identification of older children, compared to preschoolers, is the denial system. As Sara's case illustrates, school-age children have already developed enough denial not to bring up the topic, even if it is troubling them. Entertainer Suzanne Somers (1988) described how her problems in fourth grade were misunderstood by teachers:

> No teacher ever asked me if there was something wrong. They just assumed I was one of those lazy students. I'm not even sure if they *had* asked what I would have said. I was already, at nine years old, used to covering up; pretending that life inside our house was as pretty as the outside. (p. 31)

According to Claudia Black (1987), 80 percent of COAs look good, which is a chief reason they have gone unnoticed. Their survivor roles help them cope through the tough times until they are grown-ups. Then, just as they start to sigh with the relief of being out of the alcoholic home, their symptoms ambush them, jolting them back into turmoil. At twenty-one years of age, Sara had to seek counseling to cope with emotional barriers and difficulties with intimacy that she had devised as a child to "make me independent and determined to stand on my own two feet, to be absolutely different from my parents."

Another problem is that there are few reliable methods for identifying COAs. The lack of precise tools leaves a great deal to the subjective interpretation of practitioners, who may be ambivalent about their roles. Once teachers, counselors, and social workers feel comfortable enough to openly discuss alcohol and its accompanying problems, a climate of acceptance can be created and many roadblocks to identification removed. As practitioners reveal that it is normal for COAs to feel troubled and confused, more youngsters will come forward, identify themselves, and expose the family secret (McElligatt, 1986).

Importance of Identification

Because practitioners encounter COAs routinely but often may not be aware of the child's COA status, the identification of COAs takes on monumental importance. Intervening with a nine-year-old child can be a step toward primary prevention of another adult alcoholic. Identification breaks the denial system frequently operating in schools and opens the door for a multitude of services to children. It allows classroom teachers to match their expectations, goals, and interpersonal behaviors with knowledge of the alcoholic environment in which certain kids live. It also enables practitioners to establish support systems for COAs outside the classroom. Practitioners can refer COAs for such services as individual counseling, and they can create special COA groups that convene regularly in the schools.

Some children are easily identifiable because their parents are patients in alcoholic treatment centers or attend Alcoholics Anonymous. Because of their parents' recovery, these children may already be involved in some type of recovery program of their own—a COA group in treatment centers, for example, or Ala-Teen. But these children are more the exception than the rule. Most COAs are not that easily identified and are not getting the help they need.

To close this gap, numerous ways have been devised to spot school-age kids and adolescents from alcoholic homes. As with preschoolers, the practitioner's informal observational assessment is an important method. But two additional procedures can be used with older children that make identification more objective and precise: formal standardized procedures and the child's self-identification.

Identification Through Practitioner Observations

Although older COAs are not easily identified, practitioners actually have a better chance of spotting them than younger children because

BOX 6.2
Twenty Behavioral and Psychological Signs
of Children of Alcoholics in School Settings

Behavioral Signs

1. Difficulty concentrating
2. Persistent absenteeism
3. Poor grades and/or failure to turn in homework
4. Low scores on standardized IQ and achievement tests
5. Sudden behavior changes (quiet and moody or acting out)
6. Signs of physical abuse or neglect
7. Compulsive behaviors (e.g., overeating, overachieving, smoking, chemical abuse)
8. Shy and withdrawn from other children
9. Quarrelsome and uncooperative with teachers and classmates
10. Constant health problems (e.g., headaches, stomachaches)

Psychological Signs

1. Low self-esteem
2. Presence of anxiety
3. Easily embarrassed
4. Suppressed anger
5. Perceive problems as beyond their control
6. Poor coping skills
7. Prone to depression
8. Unreasonably fearful
9. Sad and unhappy
10. Difficulty adjusting to changes in routines

more concrete signs have had time to develop. Observing parents and looking for extreme behaviors also provide telltale signs. There are at least twenty behavioral and psychological signs that practitioners can look for that are best observed in school classrooms (see Box 6.2). Many of these signs were discussed in earlier chapters.

Behaviorally Versus
Psychologically Oriented

Some children's symptoms may appear behaviorally and thus are easily detected, whereas other children may manifest more psychological and thus more subtle symptoms of family alcoholism. Some children may manifest both. Behaviorally oriented children are more easily detected because they manifest their feelings outwardly where practitioners can observe the signs. They are often the classroom behavior problems and have difficulty getting along with their peers. Or on the other extreme, they may isolate themselves in the background from teachers and classmates.

Sometimes COAs are victims of physical abuse or neglect, which has a whole set of its own symptoms. The child who arrives at school early and leaves late, for example, may dread being at home. By the same token, children always in a rush to get home at the end of a school day may be concerned about how an alcoholic parent is getting along in their absence. Health care and school performance may be sporadic. School grades and concentration may nosedive, tardiness may increase, and homework may be incomplete. Tidy children may suddenly attend school unclean or unkempt, wear dirty clothing, or dress inappropriately for the weather. Children who never have lunch or lunch money, or who take food from other children, may be showing signs of alcoholic neglect. Children who refrain from activities where they must undress (such as costume plays or physical education) are often fearful of revealing bruises or other identifying marks of abuse. Cowering in the presence of adults is sometimes another sign of physical abuse.

COAs are frequently the kids who miss a lot of school, usually Mondays because of parental weekend drinking. They may use drugs themselves, overeat, overachieve, or frequently complain of headaches and stomachaches, or say they just do not feel well. They may have difficulty concentrating, staying on task, and sitting still. Some may be overactive, always fidgeting or on the move. Others may daydream or sleep through classroom lessons. They score poorly on standardized tests and may have poor grades for no apparent reason. They may show abrupt behavior changes, from shy to outgoing or vice versa. Or, like preschoolers, school-age children may suddenly regress into thumbsucking, bed-wetting, or "baby talk." Sudden changes in behaviors during alcohol education activities—the ears of a typically distracted child may suddenly perk up during a discussion—or absences from school during these activities are associated with COAs (Deutsch, 1982).

The more psychologically oriented COAs are those who may not manifest any outward signs that something is wrong. Their misery is internalized. They may be tops in the class—"a natural-born leader," the best and most popular student. They make the best grades and are sticklers for getting their work in on time—sometimes even before it is due. Because the signs are more subtle for psychologically oriented kids, practitioners must look more closely at these children to see their problems. Underneath their quiet success and achievement may be an obsessive drive to excel at everything and a compulsive need for approval, deep-seated unhappiness, and a sense of poor self-worth—children who browbeat themselves into perfectionism and refuse to allow themselves to make mistakes. They are overly serious, have trouble having fun, and judge themselves unmercifully. A closer look might show that these children have great difficulty when they are not in control of their lives, and their greatest fear is loss of control. Unusual changes in daily routines may make them anxious or upset or aggravate them or throw them into a panic. This is not to say that all successful children are COAs, but many are family heroes who have successfully disguised their misery to fool even the most astute professional.

Parental behaviors such as repeatedly missing appointments, calling the school at odd hours for irrelevant reasons, or consistently failing to pick children up on time are dependable signs of alcoholic neglect. Children's failure to return permission slips, absence slips, and other parental communications is also a clue. Ackerman (1983) suggests that parental report card signatures may develop a certain pattern that can cue practitioners to alcohol problems:

> A familiar pattern for COAs may be that one parent signs the report card on the occasions it is returned on time, and that the other parent signs the card when it is returned late. Although this may be a minor point, it can serve as a clue when other patterns are present that might suggest alcoholism. The nonalcoholic parent may sign the report card whether both parents have seen it or not. However, if the alcoholic parent was too inebriated to look at or understand the report card, the nonalcoholic may decide to wait for him or her to see it. (p. 101)

Looking for Extremes

It may sound contradictory to you that COAs can be both with-drawn and aggressive and both superachieving and incompetent, or that they either seem reluctant to leave the classroom at the end of the day or rush home immediately when school is dismissed. That pretty much covers the range of behavior. But it is the extreme behaviors that you must look for. It doesn't sound contradictory to be concerned over someone who is too fat or too thin. It is generally accepted that either extreme in body weight is indicative of an eating disorder that can be dangerous (obesity and anorexia, respectively). Analogously, COAs can be total failures or superachievers. But either avenue brings heart-break, unhappiness, and lack of self-esteem.

One way for you to look for extremes is to conduct a *sociogram*—a map of the relationships within a classroom or other specific group (see Figure 6.1). Simply ask the children to write down the names of two other children in the group with whom they would like to work·on a group project. Once you have assured the children of the confidential-ity of their selections, take this information and plot it into graph form.

Symbols are used to designate sex of child, and lines and arrows show direction of choices. Children like Caroline and Brad who receive a large number of choices are called *stars*. Class stars are the class mem-bers all the other children want to be with. Stars could resemble either mascots or heroes—chosen because they are fun to be around or be-cause they are considered group leaders and are efficient at their jobs. Those children like Velma and Nicky who receive no choices are called *isolates*. They are the children often on the outside of the social group. Isolates could resemble either scapegoats or lost children—unchosen because the children do not like them or are afraid of them or because the children simply do not pay much attention to them.

This technique was not developed to identify COAs. Still, it provides valuable information on who the children consider the class isolates and the class stars. The sociogram is more meaningful for pinpointing COAs when you use it in tandem with other data, for example, practi-tioner observation, anecdotal recordings, and examination of perma-nent folders. The information in the box on behavioral and psychologi-cal signs of COAs and the descriptions of the survival roles in Chapter 3 can also be used with these data. Once you have identified the isolates

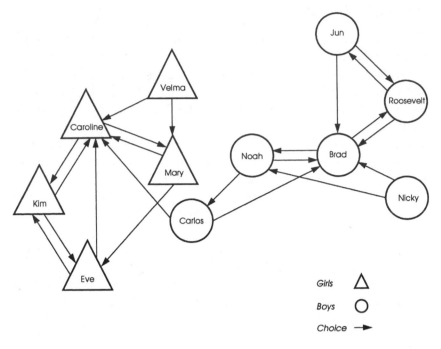

Figure 6.1: Sociogram

and stars by the sociogram, you can look more closely at these children to see if the characteristics of the isolate matches any of the characteristics of the lost child or scapegoat, or if those of the hero or mascot fit the class star. You can use this information to group children who are suspected or known to be COAs in various ways and to build social skills and self-esteem as suggested in Chapter 3.

Seeking Balance

Once extreme behaviors are identified—whether they be aggression, compulsive behaviors, persistent absenteeism, or withdrawal—the key to recovery is balance. The goal is not to rid heroes totally of their drive to accomplish. Instead, you can help them become more well-rounded through balanced play and leisure. Similarly, the lost child needs some time alone, but this alone time can be balanced with some social companionship. You do not want the mascots to lose their sense of humor, but just to know that life has its serious moments as well. And you would not want the scapegoats to become nonassertive and wimpish. Their balance comes from standing up for their rights without depriving others of theirs.

Caution in Practitioner Observations

Identifying COAs can be tricky business. The risk in identifying and describing a special group of children is labeling and stereotyping them through generalizations. Labeling COAs can have harmful effects on their self-image and cause school personnel to develop unfavorable attitudes, expectations, and responses toward them. It would be misleading for you to think that all COAs turn out the same way. There are many interacting factors that lead to diverse possible outcomes. COAs grow and pass through the same developmental stages as all kids. Aside from certain common developmental principles that govern everyone, and aside from having an alcoholic parent, COAs are a heterogeneous population.

Although COAs need special attention, you must avoid labeling them in a way that would cause others to behave differently toward them. COAs are not emotionally disturbed or mentally disabled as a population. One message COAs need is that although they are special, as are all children, they are not all that different from other kids. As children, COAs can believe that their situation is so unique that their thinking segregates them from other children and makes them feel so different that they start to act that way. COAs come into treatment believing they are different or something is wrong with them. They are always relieved to know they are not alone and that many children share their pain and suffering.

Ironically, special programs for COAs that help them feel "not so different" single them out as a group and set them apart, leaving them open for negative stereotypes. A worker mused on his first night in an outpatient group of COAs, "Funny, these kids don't look like children of alcoholics!" With a wave of books flooding the market drawing generalizations about adult COAs and COAs, it is easy to make sweeping conclusions.

The popular and scientific press have been criticized for making generalizations about COAs from anecdotal data on children whose parents are in treatment or who are otherwise atypical (DiCicco et al., 1984; El-Guebaly & Offord, 1977; Goodman, 1987). Most research investigations that show COAs have difficulty functioning were undertaken by clinicians who studied COAs with problems. These studies were usually conducted with children involved in treatment centers or support groups. Other sampling biases make it difficult to generalize all research findings to the whole population of COAs (see, for example, West & Prinz, 1987). Factors such as family size, psychopathology of parents, severity of alcoholism, divorce, and socioeconomic status can make a difference in how children turn out. Researchers still do not understand how these many factors, individually or combined with parental alcoholism, can influence children's development.

Recent evidence suggests that COAs from the general population who are not involved in treatment do not have the same coping problems as COAs undergoing therapy. Whereas COAs from the general population were as well adjusted as children from nondrinking homes, COAs in treatment had more coping problems in self-regard, intimacy, self-acceptance, feeling reactivity, and inner-directedness (Barnard & Spoentgen, 1987). Additional research indicates that COAs recruited for study from the general university student population also scored like non-COAs on self-concept, anxiety, and knowledge about the effects of alcoholism on children (Robinson, 1988). These studies further indicate that COAs are not a homogeneous group characterized by a host of psychological problems. Although some have interpersonal and intrapersonal problems, others appear to recoil from the effects of living in alcoholism.

As you begin to identify COAs from a set of published characteristics, you can avoid labeling and stereotyping these children by using this knowledge in conjunction with other information. The key is to remember that generalizations are guidelines and only guidelines and that, as an individual, each child is a creative wonder of the universe.

Identification Through
Standardized Procedures

Regardless of the procedure used, COAs should never be publicly identified. The best starting point in the identification process is with alcohol awareness programs that are provided to all children. During these sessions, children with alcohol-related problems can be identified anonymously, through teacher observations, tests, or self-referral, for further specialized help. Once identified, these youngsters can receive safe and confidential help individually and in groups.

The most confident way to confirm the identity of COAs is through a standardized test that has been subjected to rigorous scientific scrutiny. Data from these measures yield the most objective and self-assured results. A major drawback of standardized procedures, however, is that children must be old enough to read and write in order to complete the forms. As we discussed, preschool children and preliterate kids are automatically excluded from this approach. Still, standardized procedures for kids ages nine and older have been developed and have demonstrated beneficial results.

The Children of Alcoholics Screening Test

One of the most popular measures for identifying COAs is the Children of Alcoholics Screening Test (CAST) (Jones, 1983). It is an objective instrument that does not depend upon the practitioner's judgment, which could cloud the conclusions. The CAST makes it possible to identify at-risk children who are living with or who have lived with alcoholic parents. The instrument can be used by practitioners who need to identify at-risk children for inclusion in intervention programs. The CAST can also be used by the courts to determine if alcohol is involved in child abuse and custody cases. As Table 6.1 shows, the CAST is a thirty-item inventory that measures children's attitudes, feelings, perceptions, and experiences related to their parents' drinking.

The CAST can be administered to children nine years of age and older individually or in group settings. The yes answers are added to yield the total score, which can range from 0 to 30. A score from 0 to 1 indicates children of nonalcoholics; 2 to 5 indicates children of problem drinkers. These children have experienced problems due to at least one parent's drinking behavior. These are children of either problem drinkers or possible alcoholics. A score of 6 or more is indicative of COAs. These parents can be in the early, middle, or late stages of alcoholism.

Research has shown that the CAST has withstood scientific scrutiny and has yielded impressive reliability and validity (Pilat & Jones, 1985). In one study, for instance, the cutoff score of 6 or more accurately iden-

TABLE 6.1. Children of Alcoholics Screening Test (CAST)

Please check (✓) the answer below that best describes your feelings, behavior, and experiences related to a parent's alcohol use. Take your time and be as accurate as possible. Answer all thirty questions by checking either Yes or No.

Sex: Male_____ Female_____ Age:_____

Yes	No	Questions
___	___	1. Have you ever thought that one of your parents had a drinking problem?
___	___	2. Have you ever lost sleep because of a parent's drinking?
___	___	3. Did you ever encourage one of your parents to quit drinking?
___	___	4. Did you ever feel alone, scared, nervous, angry, or frustrated because a parent was not able to stop drinking?
___	___	5. Did you ever argue or fight with a parent when he or she was drinking?
___	___	6. Did you ever threaten to run away from home because of a parent's drinking?
___	___	7. Has a parent ever yelled at or hit you or other family members when drinking?
___	___	8. Have you ever heard your parents fight when one of them was drunk?
___	___	9. Did you ever protect another family member from a parent who was drinking?
___	___	10. Did you ever feel like hiding or emptying a parent's bottle of liquor?
___	___	11. Do many of your thoughts revolve around a problem-drinking parent or difficulties that arise because of his or her drinking?
___	___	12. Did you ever wish that a parent would stop drinking?
___	___	13. Did you ever feel responsible for and guilty about a parent's drinking?
___	___	14. Did you ever fear that your parents would get divorced due to alcohol misuse?
___	___	15. Have you ever withdrawn from and avoided outside activities and friends because of embarrassment and shame over a parent's drinking problem?
___	___	16. Did you ever feel caught in the middle of an argument or fight between a problem-drinking parent and your other parent?
___	___	17. Did you ever feel that you made a parent drink alcohol?
___	___	18. Have you ever felt that a problem-drinking parent did not really love you?
___	___	19. Did you ever resent a parent's drinking?
___	___	20. Have you ever worried about a parent's health because of his or her alcohol use?
___	___	21. Have you ever been blamed for a parent's drinking?
___	___	22. Did you ever think your father was an alcoholic?
___	___	23. Did you ever wish your home could be more like the homes of your friends who did not have a parent with a drinking problem?
___	___	24. Did a parent ever make promises to you that he or she did not keep because of drinking?
___	___	25. Did you ever think your mother was an alcoholic?

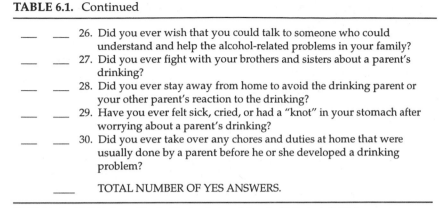

TABLE 6.1. Continued

___	___	26. Did you ever wish that you could talk to someone who could understand and help the alcohol-related problems in your family?
___	___	27. Did you ever fight with your brothers and sisters about a parent's drinking?
___	___	28. Did you ever stay away from home to avoid the drinking parent or your other parent's reaction to the drinking?
___	___	29. Have you ever felt sick, cried, or had a "knot" in your stomach after worrying about a parent's drinking?
___	___	30. Did you ever take over any chores and duties at home that were usually done by a parent before he or she developed a drinking problem?
	___	TOTAL NUMBER OF YES ANSWERS.

SOURCE: © 1983 John Jones. Used with permission of Camelot Unlimited, Publisher.

tified 100 percent of a group of COAs who had been clinically diagnosed by psychiatrists, counselors, and psychologists.

Survey and Interview Responses

Another objective means for identifying adolescent COAs is by their responses on surveys and interviews. DiCicco et al. (1984) say that it is impossible to identify COAs by having them describe their parent's drinking. Alcoholics cannot be diagnosed by how much they drink. It takes multiple criteria to diagnose alcoholism—a process that becomes too complicated for kids to accurately perform. Plus, the denial system would interfere with the child's objectivity about parental drinking.

It has been suggested that a more efficient approach aims questions to children on how they have been affected by or react to parental drinking (DiCicco et al., 1984). By focusing on the child's reaction, it is possible to raise the issue of alcoholism in an unobtrusive way that promotes more reliable disclosure. In a case in which a child is afraid, mad, confused, or embarrassed by his or her parent's drinking and wishes for the parent to stop, the parent should be considered alcoholic, simply because of the negative effects drinking has on the offspring. The child's perception in this case is the more critical variable in producing behavioral and self-image problems.

For eight years, the Cambridge and Somerville Program for Alcoholism Rehabilitation (CASPAR) has used a single question on a survey form to identify COAs. That item is known as the Children from Alcoholic Family (CAF) item:

> Have you ever wished that either one or both of your parents would drink less?
>   1. Parents don't drink at all
>   2. Yes
>   3. No

DiCicco and her associates (1984) found that the CAF is statistically reliable and valid as an identifier of COAs. There is considerable stability over time in the way teenagers answer the CAF item, which suggests that their "wish" is a relatively enduring characteristic. Other data confirm that the CAF item coincides with clinical judgments. Among seventy-one respondents who said yes to the CAF item, for example, 83 percent also were identified by the clinical staff as COAs. Correlations also have been drawn between the CAF item and COA reports of frequency of parental drinking. Among respondents who say yes on the CAF, 61.5 percent also report that their father drinks "fairly regularly" and that they are concerned about this drinking.

Another more detailed screening interview permits the identification of adolescents adversely affected by a problem-drinking parent (Biek, 1981). The brief interview questions, shown in Table 6.2, are appropriate for use with teenagers in a variety of settings but are especially recommended as a routine part of the evaluation process for all adolescents attending primary health care settings. This screening test fosters early identification, referral, and intervention to treat families in which there is alcohol abuse, thus promoting healthier psychosocial development. Teens with high scores on the screening interview had twice as many somatic complaints and health questions as those who gave no indication of having a problem-drinking parent. Teen COAs complained more of such problems as shortness of breath, stomach aches, headaches, sleep problems, and tiredness. Early identification of and intervention to treat alcohol-related problems help medical personnel to place vague, somatic complaints in a more meaningful perspective. This identification and intervention potentially could also lower the chances of teenagers with high scores becoming problem drinkers because, as offspring of alcoholics, they would be at higher than average risk.

TABLE 6.2. Screening Interview for Identifying Teenagers With Problem-Drinking Parents

---

1. Do you know any teenager who has ever had some difficulty because of either parent's drinking?

    YES   NO

2. Have you known either of your parents to ever take a drink? (This item to rule out possible abstainers' children, for whom the following questions would be irrelevant.)

    YES   NO

Following a "No" response to item 2, exit the interview.

3. Has the drinking of either parent ever created problems between him/her and the other parent or near relative? ("Yes," meaning recently or "Yes" meaning long ago?)

    YES   NO

4. Do friends or relatives think either of your parents has a drinking problem?

    YES   SOMETIMES   NO

5. Do you ever worry because of either parent's drinking?

    YES   SOMETIMES   NO

6. At any time in your life, have you ever felt hurt, scared, or angry because of either parent's drinking?

    YES   SOMETIMES   NO

7. Has your parent's drinking ever made things more difficult for you in any way?

    YES   SOMETIMES   NO

Following all "No" responses to items 3-7, exit the interview. Following any "Yes" or "Sometimes" responses, the interview is continued with the open-ended question.

8. How has the drinking of your parent affected you?
    a.
    b.
    c.
    d.

9. At any time in your life has your own drinking caused any trouble or concern for you?

SCORING: Questions 3 through 7 are scored as follows:

Yes = 3 points; Sometimes = 2 points; No = 1 point.

The possible range of scores is 5 to 15 points:

Low Score:	5 points, with no "Yes" or "Sometimes" responses
Medium Score:	6 points with 1 "Sometimes" and 4 "No" responses;
	7 points with 2 "Sometimes" and 3 "No" responses
High Score:	8-15 points with 1 "Sometimes" and 1 "Yes" response OR
	2 or more "Yes" responses

SOURCE: From Biek, 1981. Used with permission.

BOX 6.3
Steps in Self-Identification

1. Conduct alcohol education awareness classes.
2. Introduce the concept of an ongoing group for those who have drug or alcohol problems in their homes.
3. Disseminate self-referral forms.
4. Hold screening interviews with all children who indicate interest in the COA group.
5. Select the number of children based on prioritized criteria that best fit your unique situation.

Self-Identification

Perhaps the most successful method of identification is self-referral by the child. This approach puts the assurance of psychological safety and anonymity in children's hands. Those youngsters who come forth and join groups of their own free will are motivated to learn more about COA issues and to work on the problem. They also end up with close-knit relationships that support and carry them through their ordeal. Steps in the self-identification process are simple, easy to implement, nonthreatening, and highly effective (see Box 6.3).

The Self-Identification Process

Counselors Betty Newlon and William Furrow (1986) found that classroom guidance activities combined with small-group counseling offered a way to reach COAs. They began the steps in their identification process by giving two guidance lessons on alcoholism and the family in the classroom. Sessions comprised films, lectures, handouts, and group discussion to cover the differences between alcoholic and responsible drinking, alcoholism as a family illness, and the characteristics of COAs. At the conclusion of the two sessions, children were given a self-evaluation form on which they could indicate interest in attending a small group in which alcoholism was discussed on a more personal level. A brief screening interview was conducted with each

---

BOX 6.4
Sample Self-Referral Form

Sometimes we all need someone to talk with, especially if we don't understand what's going on. If you think that a parent, grandparent, sister, brother, or someone else that you care about has a drinking or drug problem, and you would like to join a group of kids just like you, fill out the form and return it to the office. Your guidance counselor [the name of the appropriate person could be substituted here] will get in touch with you about the group.

Name _____

Grade _____

Teacher _____

Yes, I'm interested in the group _____

No, I'm not interested, but thanks _____

SOURCE: Cleveland County Community Organization for Drug Abuse Prevention. Used with permission by Vicky V. White, Program Director.

child who expressed a desire to participate in a small group. Those who disclosed that they had an alcoholic parent were automatically eligible for the group. Selection of the remaining children was done by teachers, who were asked to choose from the list of volunteers the ones who might be having difficulty at home. Of the eighty children who participated in the classroom guidance lessons, eleven were successfully identified as COAs.

Similar self-referral steps used by the Cleveland County School System in North Carolina are expedient and highly successful. At the end of the alcohol education program for fifth and sixth graders, school personnel introduce the idea of an ongoing small group. Children are informed that a group will be started for those who think one or both parents might have a drinking problem. Counselors ask them to complete a simple form, such as the one in Box 6.4. Once forms are collected, counselors hold individual screening interviews with each child who indicates an interest in participating in the group. Children considered to be in the most trouble and those in the sixth grade (because this will be their last chance for help before going on to junior high school) are given priority slots in the group. The final group size is usually between twenty and twenty-five students.

Legal Considerations

Alcoholic parents love their children, and they do not want them to be stigmatized. An active alcoholic parent is not going to say, "Yes, teach my kids about the problems they are having because of my drinking." The denial is too strong. You should check the laws of your respective state, as some states require written parental consent in order for children to participate in groups. Programs in those states can send home permission slips requesting parental permission for children to participate in groups to improve self-esteem and to learn about drug and alcohol prevention. This approach gets around stigmatizing anyone concerned and has a high success rate of getting children into programs that meet their needs.

PROGRAMS AND TREATMENT STRATEGIES FOR CHILDREN OF ALCOHOLICS

7

CASE 7.1

Pauline was shrewd, and, at only twelve years of age, she had convinced herself that she could control the drinking of her parents—both of whom were alcoholic. When she came to the treatment center, she had already developed a sophisticated system of manipulating and controlling her mom and dad's drinking. When they went out to eat, she made sure the restaurants they frequented did not serve alcoholic beverages. That way she didn't have to worry about her parents getting out of hand and embarrassing her or getting too drunk to drive her and her younger sister home.

When shopping, she encouraged her parents to spend as much money as possible so there would be none left over to buy booze. When drinking friends called, Pauline deliberately "forgot" to give her parents telephone messages so they wouldn't get mixed up with company that would encourage their drinking. Pauline was constantly emptying liquor bottles and disposing of unopened beer, hoping her parents would not notice and punish her.

Constantly conniving and creating ways to prevent her parents from drinking, Pauline had become consumed with the alcoholism, and her life revolved around it. Her preoccupation with trying to control the disease was heartbreaking because inevitably, no matter what she did, Pauline admitted that her parents somehow got their beer and wine. The child started to blame and feel badly about herself because she could not accomplish her goal. All the while, she was missing out on the most important period of her life—childhood.

Untreated, Pauline's compulsive need to control would ultimately insinuate itself into school, work, and friendships. In adulthood, it would interfere with trust and intimate relationships with people for whom she cares. In the weekly program sessions she attended, we tried to help her see the consequences of her actions and to help her learn to refocus her energies on taking care of herself. The six-week curriculum was just the beginning of a path of recovery in which she learned to let her parents be responsible for their drinking while she gave up that burden in lieu of fun, play, and being good to herself, while still caring about and loving her parents.

Effective Programs
for Children of Alcoholics

Once on a radio show, a caller asked, "What's the point in trying to help kids whose parents are alcoholic if they have to go right back home and live in it?" This is an important question and one that lurks in the minds of many who are unfamiliar with the disease of alcoholism. The answer that we as professionals give is even more significant. Children must have a distinct and separate treatment program of their own, regardless of whether or not the parent is recovering from alcoholism. Children like Pauline, who live in active alcoholism, can learn that they cannot control or cure the disease and that ultimately their best recourse is to take care of themselves. They learn it is OK and even advisable not to get into a car with an intoxicated parent, for example. They also learn that it is good practice to carry correct change to call a relative or neighbor in case they get abandoned by a drinking parent.

Underlying the radio caller's question was the myth that the welfare of the child hinges on the parent's actions. It is assumed that when alcoholic parents get treatment, their kids will automatically recover or conversely, that if parents do not get help, then it is hopeless for their children. Today, we know that children can recover regardless of their parent's behaviors, and as a result, programs for COAs have begun to appear in school systems and in treatment centers that historically treated only the alcoholic and the codependent parents.

Psychoeducational Programs

Most COAs, like Pauline, do not need intensive therapy. They need education, the most powerful weapon against alcoholism. Educating children about the disease removes the mystique surrounding it and provides them with a language and context for understanding and expressing their personal experiences with it. Knowledge also equips them with an intellectual mastery that will help them solve problems and cope with parental alcoholism in their future lives (Bingham & Bargar, 1985). Professionals and potential caregivers can be educated about simple, easy, low-cost, and effective ways to help this huge and generally neglected population of kids. Considering their numbers, children from alcoholic families can be found in all kinds of programs and service organizations. Rather than creating new bureaucracies, the helping professions can implement psychoeducational programs through the systems already in place: public schools, colleges and universities, and treatment centers.

The School System

Classroom teachers and counselors are not in the business of alcohol rehabilitation, but it is incumbent upon the schools to ensure that all children's educational opportunities are met. The fact that parental alcoholism severely interferes with children's learning is rationale enough for schools to play a big role in helping COAs. Schools are the most logical resource to educate children about alcohol use and abuse. Teachers and other school personnel are already in key positions to identify and help COAs. Because of their contact with children on a regular basis, school personnel can establish an ongoing relationship of security and trust that is a prerequisite to working with COAs. Teachers can lighten the child's load and give kids one special person who understands and listens. In the rare instances when families ask schools for help, teachers, counselors, administrators, and others can refer them to appropriate treatment.

The Phoenix Union High School District in Arizona offers an exemplary program on chemical awareness and its positive outcomes (Watkins, 1988). The program provides comprehensive prevention intervention for students from K to 16 who are harmfully involved with their own chemical use, affected by a family member's use, or experiencing problems unrelated to chemical use but considered at risk. The Phoenix program is a systematic effort to identify, refer, and support students having problems that interfere with their education and life development. All staff are given in-service training on chemical dependency. Alcohol and substance abuse education for students is provided through assemblies, course curricula, and class presentations. COAs, students involved with chemicals, and other troubled students are identified through referrals from peers, teachers and staff, families, community agencies (such as social services or police), and themselves. Special group facilitators are trained to lead student support groups. In-house student support groups meet weekly and are scheduled throughout the school day. Four groups, designed with diverse needs of students in mind, meet separately: to maintain a chemically free lifestyle, to get help when having problems resulting from substance abuse, to get support when concerned about the chemical abuse of a family member or friend, and to receive support for other problems not related to chemical dependency. Groups meet once a week and are scheduled during a teacher's preparation period.

Results of the program have been dramatic. A survey of 335 students revealed that 73 percent were able to find new positive ways to deal with problems and to communicate and express feelings in a positive way. Fully 61 percent of the students using alcohol and other drugs decreased their intake or stopped as a result of the support group. Feelings of self-worth improved for 71 percent of the students. Improvements were also noted in general attitude toward school (50 percent), school attendance (35 percent), and overall schoolwork (31 percent).

Higher Education

College and university campuses are also prime settings for psychoeducational programs for future practitioners and adult COAs. Courses on substance abuse and family dynamics can be added to curricula. Special lectures on children and alcoholism can be added to such existing courses as child development, sociology, psychology, nursing, and family studies. Special psychoeducational groups for students with alcoholic parents, established by university staff through campus counseling centers, have achieved success. A five-week collegiate group at a major university helped sons and daughters of alcoholics understand the roles they had assumed in the family and other useful information in the event alcoholism becomes a possibility in their lives (Donovan, 1981). An eight-week educational support group on another university campus improved the psychological functioning of students with alcoholic parents (Barnard & Spoentgen, 1987).

Treatment Centers

Psychoeducational programs for children are also important components in treatment centers in which the primary aim is the dependent and codependent parent. Survey results from treatment agencies during the 1980s indicate that COAs still remain on the periphery of the treatment process. When they do receive services, it is generally in the form of individual counseling (Regan, Connors, O'Farrell, & Wyatt, 1983).

The number of treatment programs for COAs nationwide has grown. The impetus for this gain was the resolution passed by the National Association for Children of Alcoholics in 1987, requesting that all chemical dependency treatment programs establish a component especially for children of dependent parents. Each of these programs should have the common denominator of appropriate goals, plus a built-in system of evaluation.

Establishing Program Goals

Program planners must understand that children's programs should contain appropriate goals for treatment to be meaningful. Intervention

---

BOX 7.1
Key Points for Children of
Alcoholics Programs

1. Alcoholism is a disease.

2. Everybody gets hurt in the alcoholic family, including the children.

3. Children whose parents drink too much are not alone.

4. Children do not cause, cannot control, and cannot cure their parent's alcoholism.

5. There are many good ways that children can take care of themselves when parents drink so that they feel better about themselves.

6. It is healing for children to identify and express their feelings about parental drinking.

7. It is OK for kids to talk about parental drinking to a friend or within the safety of a group.

8. Kids of alcoholics are at high risk of substance abuse themselves.

9. It is important for children to identify and use trusted support systems outside the family.

10. There are many practical ways of problem solving and coping with parental alcoholism.

---

programs have a number of messages that are important to convey to children. Numerous curriculum packages have been marketed especially for COAs for implementation in schools or in treatment centers simultaneously as parents receive treatment. Most of these various curricula have several key points in common. The key points, shown in Box 7.1, are important goals that should be part of any psychoeducational program for COAs. Most programs incorporate these ten key points in a variety of ways around designated central themes—one for each week in the program cycle.

Alcoholism Is a Disease

Children need to understand that alcoholism is a disease that the drinking parent cannot control. Frequently, children equate their parent's drinking with not being loved. As Robert Bly (1987) said, "Every child of an alcoholic receives the knowledge that the bottle is more important to the parent than he or she is" (p. 96). Kids need to know their parents love them, even though the disease symptoms may make them think otherwise. As children begin to understand the disease concept, the stigma of alcoholism can be removed, and they feel safer talking about it. They also acquire a language and context in which to verbalize their thoughts and feelings, and they learn that parents can and do recover from the illness.

Everybody Gets Hurt

Kids must know that alcoholism affects all family members in negative ways. Individual family members devise roles (such as hero, lost child, scapegoat, mascot) to cope with and survive the disease. These roles cover up poor self-esteem, anxiety, depression, and a host of other feelings. They also prevent children from expressing their true emotions and getting close to others. Programs stressing that alcoholism influences everyone in the family help kids to realize, if they are not already aware, that indeed, they too have been hurt.

Children Are Not Alone

A major relief for children whose parents drink too much is to learn that they are not alone. They discover that there are many other children just like them—seven million to be exact, nationwide. The importance of group work is that children learn firsthand that they are not so different after all and that other kids who have had similar experiences living in alcoholism also think and feel the same way about a lot of things. Young children are usually surprised to hear that famous people —such as Chuck Norris, Brooke Shields, or Suzanne Somers—also grew up in alcoholic homes. Such discussions send children the message that they are not isolated, different, or crazy and that their reactions to parental alcoholism are normal ones.

Cause, Control, Cure

Quality COA intervention programs address the issues of cause, control, and cure. Children often feel that their parent's drinking is, directly or indirectly, their fault. They need to know they are not responsible for their parent's drinking, and no matter what they do and how hard they try, they cannot control or cure their parent's alcoholism. Because it is an illness, they cannot change it any more than they can change the course of heart disease or cancer. Unyielding attempts to control parental alcoholism only lead to self-defeat and poor self-worth. Children can learn, however, that there are other things in their own lives that they *can* successfully manage, mainly themselves, that will make them feel better and help them recover from the disease.

Taking Care of Self

Although powerless over their parents' drinking, children need to know that they deserve help for themselves and that preoccupation with trying to stop or alter the course of parental drinking leads to frustration, anger, and numerous emotional side effects. Children need help in letting go of serious adult problems and embracing the carefree world of childhood. They must learn how to take care of themselves when a parent is drinking and whom they can call or where they can go for help when they need it. Children need to recognize their own good points and develop their strengths by learning to feel good about themselves, thereby separating parental alcoholism from self-concept. Practitioners can implement many self-esteem exercises to help COAs in this area. Research substantiates that self-regard and capacity for intimacy with others improves after short-term educational intervention with COAs (Barnard & Spoentgen, 1987).

Identifying and Expressing Feelings

Children learn that many emotions are common reactions when parents drink too much. They find that identifying the ones they have and expressing them in appropriate ways make them feel better inside and about themselves in general. Using creative media for the expression of emotions—art, music, puppets, role play, clay, and so on—is a nonthreatening way for children to share their feelings. Once expressed, the creative medium serves as a springboard for a discussion on feelings. It is important to point out that feelings are neither good nor bad. All feelings are appropriate. Even hate (a common report from

COAs) can be a genuine feeling and a natural reaction to the disease. There are, however, appropriate and inappropriate ways of expressing these feelings. Anger expressed as violence against another person, for instance, is always forbidden, even though children may observe this at home. An appropriate release of anger would be talking about it, telling the person with whom you are angry, strenuous exercise, drawing a picture of the anger and talking about it, role-playing it, or hitting a pillow or a solid surface with a plastic bat.

Talking About Parental Drinking

Denial, especially among older kids and adolescent youth, can be a difficult barrier to break. Because children have an emotional need to disbelieve alcohol educators, it is common for them to deny that their parents have a drinking problem. Even when they know deep down, they sometimes try to hide the truth from others.

At age twelve, Seth's defenses were firmly in place. A soft-spoken, blond child, he denied his mother and father were alcoholic, that he had beaten his drug-addicted mother and put her in the hospital, or that anything was wrong at all. He remained closemouthed and body-tight in group and listened intently to the other children's stories as if their problems were totally alien to him. When his father relapsed and got drunk on his fortieth birthday, Seth, with a smile and shrug of his shoulders, said simply, "I don't care. It doesn't bother me. I just ignore it. I slept in the car on the way back from the bar." Seth's ambivalence toward his dad's drinking was reflected in a letter the child wrote during a group exercise:

Dear Dad: I don't like when you drink. It's OK on birthdays. I know you don't like to but you do sometimes. I don't really care too much. I just ignore you. I am glad you have stoped [sic].

From one sentence to the next, Seth vacillated from not liking his father's drinking to feeling OK about it, to not really caring at all, to feeling glad his dad had stopped. Outwardly, Seth was struggling with denial of his true feelings of being upset, scared, and disappointed when his dad drinks. Our goal in the program was to create a safe setting for Seth to exhume his real feelings and deal with them in a constructive way.

Children need to know that it is OK to talk about a parent's drinking to a trusted friend or in the confines of a safe group. Creating a safe setting for children to talk about alcoholism takes time. Children gradually begin to feel safe once they know practitioners are sincere and care and that conversations will remain confidential within the group and will not be repeated to parents. It is crucial that practitioners never minimize or deny the child's perceptions of his or her experience with alcoholism.

High Risk for Addiction

The nature of the disease of addiction is that it can carry over into many areas of one's life. COAs are at high risk for becoming alcoholics, workaholics, compulsive eaters, gamblers, spenders, and sex and drug addicts. COAs are four times more likely to become chemically dependent than children from nondrinking homes. Children often fool themselves into thinking they are in full control and may even frequently repeat the old adage, "It will never happen to me." They may even boast, "I don't drink like my old man. I might do crack or weed. But I'll never be an alcoholic." Switching addictions is the way COAs often cope with parental alcoholism, unaware that all addictions are part and parcel of the same disease package. Children need to understand that these switches are abuse, too. They need to learn to break the cycle for their own sakes.

Caution should be exercised in drawing the analogy of cancer to alcoholism when explaining the disease concept to younger children. Sometimes they express anxiety over "catching" the disease of alcoholism. These kids need reassurance and understanding that becoming addicted can be prevented by learning about alcoholism and making wise decisions regarding its use.

Support Systems

The group experience is only the beginning of a child's journey into recovery. Children need to know about resources they can depend upon for support, once they have completed a program. They need to know that supports exist all around them and that they can reach out to these support systems when they need help. Children need practical information about how to reach out, as well as to whom and where to reach out—a friend, counselor, teacher, relative, neighbor, Alateen, and so on.

Problem Solving and Coping

Children get help with problem solving and coping by devising advanced plans of action to fit a variety of situations. Dad stops off at a bar and, after three or four hours of drinking, staggers back to the car to drive home. What should the child do? Mom forgets to pick the child up after the movie. A violent father has beaten Mom and threatens the child. Or the child just needs a quiet place to study. These are examples of the kinds of situations with which children are generally unprepared to cope. Children will have their own agendas in regard to coping and problem solving. Practitioners must be prepared to listen and help derive options and solutions that will maximize the child's well-being. Through small-group exercises, children can brainstorm ways to deal with troublesome situations, try to anticipate the consequences, then share and evaluate their plans (Schall, 1986).

An excellent activity, called Wheel of Misfortune, involves cooperation and teamwork in solving the real-life problems found in alcoholic families (Moe & Pohlman, 1988). The activity helps children come to see that they have choices and options in handling tough situations. After the facilitator divides the children into groups of three, each group selects a team name. Each team spins the wheel and lands on a letter of the alphabet that corresponds to various scenarios, as illustrated by the following example:

> Bobby, Jeremy, and Lori, all nine, called their team The Cool Cats. With a spin of the wheel, they found Mom passed out on the living room rug. What to do? The suggestions flew back and forth—some silly, some outrageous, others ingenious. Bobby suggested that they go get a neighbor. Lori wanted to call 911. Jeremy said, "It's a good idea to try and wake Mom first." They finally agreed to do all three—try and revive Mom, call 911 for an ambulance, and then get a neighbor. They were met with cheers and clapping when they shared with the larger group. (Moe & Pohlman, 1988, p. 48)

Through such exercises, children learn that they can face and solve their problems relating to alcoholism and that they are capable of handling unexpected situations. Increased competence, in turn, will improve self-esteem and help children overcome feelings of helplessness.

Tips for Practitioners

Effective psychoeducational programs hinge on establishing a climate of trust and safety. Children who have been deeply traumatized bring with them a natural resistance to intervention. Practitioners should not expect them to talk about what is bothering them right away. Whether in a weekly intervention program or during daily classroom routines, trust and safety are created by patience. Assuring confidentiality, providing nurturance, listening to children, and showing them you care without lecturing, prying, or pushing will earn their trust. Given time, practitioners and children can form a natural, gradual relationship built on mutual trust and respect.

Advocate for Children

Another way of showing compassion for COAs is being their advocate. Because of the nature of the disease, COAs do not have parents who advocate for them, as parents of the children with disabilities or emotionally disturbed children. So their voices must come from practitioners who can speak for their rights and needs. Classroom teachers, counselors, and social workers working in schools or practitioners already employed in chemical dependency treatment facilities can start a children's program, using points discussed in this chapter. In most instances, it is possible to develop children's programs using the current level of facility resources.

Conduct Alcohol Education Programs

Counselors can work closely with other school personnel to help children adjust to parental alcoholism. School counselors can help teachers structure special lessons on family alcoholism, using the program goals presented in this chapter. Conducting in-service workshops for classroom teachers and administrators on the plight of children from alcoholic families can generate better understanding of the problems these kids face and thereby enable teachers to help children better adjust to their tough situations. Establishing alcohol awareness days throughout the school, where all children learn about drinking and its effects, will reach COAs in a nonthreatening way and serve as a springboard to establishing special groups for children of alcoholism.

Treatment Strategies
for Children of Alcoholics

CASE 7.2

It was Rodney's first night at the treatment center and not unusual for him to be quieter than the other kids. Still, I was baffled by him. Something about his moves and gestures puzzled me, but I couldn't put my finger on exactly what it was at first.

Rodney, a six-year-old handsome Italian child, was by no means mentally disabled or autistic, but he appeared to be suffering from shell shock. He was emotionally disconnected from everything and everyone around him. On the playground, he appeared to be carrying on conversations with himself or imaginary companions. As the game of kickball swirled around him, Rodney entertained himself in his own make-believe world with hand motions and inaudible verbalizations. No wonder. He already had been in three different first grades this school year. He didn't know the name of his current school. His family had been evicted six times because his alcoholic father hadn't paid the rent. He told me that when he lived in Seattle, he came home from school one day and all the family belongings were on the front lawn, packed in huge black plastic bags.

Knowing his past and his need for a self-created fantasy world, the staff's goal was not to jerk that away from him. Many children often withdraw into their imaginations. Their mental creations become their survival tools because imagination is the one thing that is theirs—the one thing they can latch on to when all else around them is falling apart. Our approach was to gently keep Rodney in present time during kickball. "OK, Rodney, this one's coming to you" or "Get ready, Rodney, watch third base." Each time he was pulled back to reality from a self-created fantasy world. Rodney didn't know how to play kickball. I explained the rules to him and compared it to softball. I was stunned that the child didn't understand the concept of "outs," changing sides, or running bases. A half hour into the game, he tugged at my shirt sleeve and asked, "When are we going to play?" Shocked beyond belief, I thought I had misunderstood. "Pardon?" I asked. "When are we going to play?" was his retort. I looked down at his innocent face waiting for an answer and said the only natural thing, "We *are* playing, Rodney."

Rodney had never played before, and he didn't even recognize play when he saw it or was involved in it. Gradually, I began to understand what it was about him that caught my eye from the beginning. Play deprivation, clearly reflected in his demeanor, had negatively affected Rodney physically, cognitively, socially, and emotionally. He was clumsy and uncoordinated when he walked and ran. He lacked the cognitive concepts of play, the notion of rules, and how to play with others. He had poor social skills and didn't know how to interact with children his own age. I asked him if he had any playmates or friends to play with. He reflected on the question, and after a long pause he excitedly proclaimed, "My next-door neighbor's dog is my friend!"

In some ways, Rodney is unusual, but in other ways, he is typical of COAs. In fact, we can add a fourth rule to Claudia Black's three rules of don't talk, don't feel, and don't trust. The fourth rule that all COAs learn either directly or indirectly is don't play or don't have fun. The case of Rodney is an extreme example of a child of alcoholism so deprived of play that he was affected physically, cognitively, socially, and emotionally. We had to literally teach him step by step what play is and how to do it. Other children learn the rule perhaps to a lesser degree, but they internalize it just the same. Alcoholism is serious business, and surviving it takes every ounce of energy for everyone in the family. None can be "wasted" or "frittered away" on something as trivial or frivolous as play. Play is only one of many strategies that practitioners can use in treating COAs.

Therapeutic Value of Play

Play is the work of young children. Although all children need play opportunities, play is doubly important for COAs. According to Lerner (1986), "Connecting the head and the heart through humor and play can be just as healing as the work we do with anger, misery, and anxiety" (p. 114). Through interactive play, COAs learn to work out mutual problems and to internalize rules and roles of society's norms. Through play, COAs learn spontaneity and flexibility and to negotiate and interact with peers on an equal basis. Kids do not learn these important skills in an alcoholic home, where it is "the parent up and the kids down." (Black, 1987). All COAs need to be taught to play and to have fun as part of their treatment program. It is through play that the free child emerges and kids learn to deal with their feelings. Children develop motor coordination and balance, as well as competence in social interactions, and they learn to negotiate problems and work them out on their own. Roles and rules in childhood games provide children with opportunities to learn about similar roles and rules in adult society. Feelings of cooperation and competition are developed through play, and concepts such as justice and injustice, prejudice and equality, leading and following, and loyalty and disloyalty begin to take on real and personal meaning. Play also provides kids with sheer fun and diversion in an otherwise serious and traumatic life. Many types of play strategies can be integrated into treatment interventions.

Dramatic Play

As we discussed in Chapter 6, dramatic play can be a vehicle for observing inner feelings and frustrations related to alcoholism, especially among preschool children who act out domestic scenes. An area in the room designated as the housekeeping corner or dramatic play area, complete with props, helps stimulate children to act out troublesome situations they have experienced at home. Many times, these scenarios involve a drinking parent ordering everyone else around or episodes of spankings or spousal arguments. Adult guidance during dramatic play can help children sharpen their questions, clarify issues, and explore alternatives of action. By joining a domestic quarrel, for example, a practitioner can model successful ways of handling interpersonal conflict or dealing with fears by acting out a situation.

Stages of Play

Some young children, like Rodney, who were deprived of play at earlier ages may need to be taken through the stages of play that they missed. The goal may be to move the child into parallel play and then gradually into associative and eventually into cooperative play with other children. Although these stages are ordinarily reached by five or six, older school-age children who are having difficulty may need opportunities to retrace their steps through these stages.

Imaginary Play

Play does not always involve "real people." Sometimes young children invent imaginary playmates—especially when they have few real friends, no siblings, or problems such as family alcoholism that they need to work out alone. They get emotional satisfaction from carrying on lengthy conversations and sharing toys with these unseen friends. Imaginary playmates help children reduce loneliness, cope with fears or unsatisfactory relationships such as violent, drinking parents, and find an outlet for anger and hostility. Most imaginary playmates appear between the ages of two and a half and ten but disappear as children enter school, meet other friends to play with, or receive treatment for severe problems (Flake-Hobson et al., 1983).

Noncompetitive Group Games

Group games such as hopscotch, blindman's bluff, chasing games, hide-and-seek, and Red Rover are popular games among school-age children. Adolescents from alcoholic homes generally like group games, too, because many of them missed these activities when they were younger. These games allow children to let off steam and pent-up energy as well as develop physical-motor capacities and build social skills.

Programs that stress competition and open comparison of children are setting kids up for failure and inadvertently sabotaging their recovery programs. An alternative approach is to emphasize noncompetitive games that kids enjoy playing where nobody wins and, more important, nobody loses. It is important to avoid any games in which the self-worth of the child is at stake, because one of the points of COA programs is to build self-worth that has already been shattered. Games in which some children are chosen and others left out should also be avoided. Being excluded can only add to some children's personal history of isolation and rejection from the group. Many of us can remember the fear and humiliation of being the last one chosen for a team sport. Practitioners can prearrange teams for balance of abilities or can organize them around a numbering system. Children can count off by ones, twos, or threes, or they can choose a number of which two group leaders are thinking. Those closest to the numbers are on the respective sides.

It is important that group games requiring teams, such as kickball or volleyball, deemphasize winning and stress team spirit and fun of the game. COAs need to learn that both losing and winning are a part of life. But most of them have already learned how to lose. The focus of COA programs is to convey to kids that they are all winners. Noncompetitive games help children develop their free spirit of childhood and to feel a part of the group, while teaching mutual cooperation and working together without taking anything away from anyone. Two excellent resources for noncompetitive games for all ages are *The New Games Book* and *More New Games* (New Games Foundation, 1976, 1981).

Psychodrama

One of the most effective techniques used with adolescents is letting them play out their feelings associated with alcoholism. Adolescents can be asked to think about a specific instance when their parent was drinking and how they felt during that situation. Having cards that name specific feelings helps them identify their own emotions. Once an emotion is identified, one of the group leaders or another group member can be enlisted to act out the scenario. Although this approach is extremely effective, practitioners must be prepared for the frequently powerful accompanying reactions of anger or tears. Group processing of the scenario follows. The role play often taps emotions of group members on the periphery who need a chance to share their reactions. It is advisable to have two group leaders with a small number of adolescents (a maximum of ten), so that one leader is always free to attend to emotional flare-ups.

Other types of psychodrama, such as the empty chair technique, are also effective. A group member sits in front of an empty chair surrounded by a circle of supportive group members. The member in the middle of the circle pretends the alcoholic parent is sitting in the empty chair and carries on a conversation with the parent. Practitioners encourage the participant to get out unexpressed feelings toward the parent through words and actions: "What would you like to say to your mom/dad that you've never been able to say before?" This can include things the child would never actually say or do to the parent, such as yelling or hitting the "parent" with a plastic bat. After the conversation, the whole group participates in processing the experience.

Creative Outlets

No treatment program for children of alcoholism is complete without regular use of creative activities. Most child-oriented programs use some type of creative outlet as an integral part of every session. Each week, for example, sessions might alternate between painting, clay, music, creative writing, movement, puppets, collage, woodworking, and so forth. These are just a few creative outlets that serve as vehicles for communicating any of the ten key points for COAs programs (discussed earlier in this chapter). The possibilities are endless. Presenting the points through creative activities makes the process fun, interesting, nonthreatening, and relevant at the child's level. Creative activities not only provide outlets for an array of pent-up emotions—anger, sadness, fear, embarrassment, rage, loneliness—but also give children some say-so and sense of control over their lives.

One of the most successful activities used with COAs is having them express the feelings they have when a parent drinks. With stations set up around the room (such as puppets, art materials, writing areas, dramatic play areas, and musical expression), children and adolescents can be given free time to move about the room expressing the feelings that come up. Younger children gravitate toward puppets and artwork, whereas older school-age children and adolescents will write letters, poems, songs, and plays or use psychodrama. The activity is always followed by a group discussion. Children share with the group their creative outcome (a song, a picture, a puppet vignette) to express how they feel when a parent drinks. For some children, this is a difficult activity because their feelings have been denied and suppressed for so long. The identification of even one feeling is an accomplishment. Most youngsters approach the activity with interest and enthusiasm and feel more comfortable with something concrete in hand that helps them put into words how they feel. COAs are often children of fear. They are afraid of what is happening at home and terrified that something awful is going to happen to them. Many of them cope by building walls around themselves. This activity helps them remove a few stones from the walls.

Bibliotherapy

Literature can have a dynamic effect on children and family members. Bibliotherapy—the use of books as a therapeutic tool for helping families adjust to difficult situations—is a valuable intervention strategy in alcohol education (Brisbane, 1985; Fassler, 1987; Manning, 1987). An advantage of bibliotherapy is that it presents problems and possible solutions in a nonthreatening way. Practitioners can use children's books that tell stories about a parent who drinks too much, how it makes the character feel, and how the characters deal with these feelings. Bibliotherapy helps COAs to identify, understand, and deal with their feelings about family alcoholism, and it helps them confront and overcome many of alcoholism's problems. Children's stories let kids know they are not alone in their heartache and pain. Storytelling offers typical lifelike situations and gives the reader the opportunity to experience a variety of possible actions vicariously without having to actually experience the consequences. Conversations between adults and children can be stimulated by books. When children see story characters experiencing their own problems and feelings, the fear of uniqueness diminishes.

Practitioners who implement bibliotherapy must be sensitive to the child's age and developmental level, the child's reading level, and any special reading problems (e.g., disabled children) (Pardeck & Pardeck, 1987). The stories should provide a fair and realistic picture of the problem with accurate information and not be moralistic, "preachy," condescending, or "pat" (Manning, 1987). Successful bibliotherapy leads kids through three stages: (1) identification with the character or situation, (2) vicarious sharing of the feelings and motivations of the book's character, and (3) achievement of insight as readers internalize some of the coping behaviors exhibited in the book and apply them to their personal problems with alcohol (Jalongo, 1983).

Filmed Vignettes

Another nonthreatening approach to treating COAs is through film and other audiovisuals. As in bibliotherapy, the viewer can identify with the character on-screen in a protective group situation that is enhanced by a darkened room. Filmed vignettes help children express and deal with situations that emerge on the screen. Audiovisuals can be effective because they trigger children's reactions to experiences that are similar to those in the film and promote discussion.

Practitioners should exercise caution in showing strong films that strike at the heart of children's problems. Movies about alcoholism sometimes arouse in children some of the frightening emotions that they have felt at home before. Once during group time, for instance, Rodney sat stone-faced as other children chatted about the problems they were having with parental alcoholism. Not until the showing of the film *Soft Is the Heart of the Child* did his feelings erupt into a flood of words. During one scene where the father was drunk and behaving violently, Rodney blurted, "I hate it when people drink! I hate my dad when he gets drunk! We're not going back home until he gets well, either!" This release marked the beginning of Rodney's recovery.

As practitioners show filmed vignettes, it is crucial that they keep a constant visual survey on the children for signs of disturbance or erupting emotions. Younger children especially must be monitored during dramatic films that realistically portray active alcoholism. They will often slide toward grown-ups or crawl up on their laps for comforting. After the films, children are almost always eager to discuss what happened and to tell about similar experiences they have had.

Group Work

Group work offers several advantages over individual counseling and is the preferred strategy for treating COAs. Children learn through group experiences that they are not alone, and they can say and hear things that are mutually beneficial and growth productive. Group more than individual experiences increase the likelihood of breaking the silence and denial associated with family alcoholism. The therapeutic group process can provide the safety and protection that children need as they become aware of their feelings and begin to risk sharing them with others whom they trust (Bingham & Bargar, 1985). Group work also gives kids the experience of healthy social interactions, as well as building trust in social situations, an experience that many COAs are severely lacking. Group process also gives children opportunities for group validation and the building of confidence and esteem.

Positive peer group support helps children try out new approaches to old problems. The encouragement and empathy provided by peers lessens the child's resistance to making healthy changes. Positive peer support often extends beyond the group, as when group members exchange phone numbers, become friends, and call each other when problems occur (Morehouse, 1986). Morehouse also cites empathetic confrontation as a special advantage of groups. For example, if one group member confronts another: "You can't keep blaming your poor grades on your mom's drinking. We discussed several weeks ago how you could stay after school to study," children may rethink how responsible they are being for their own behaviors.

The short-term nature of most group intervention programs limits observable outcomes. Visible results may be few and far between, but the seeds of recovery have been planted. Children will continue to recover long after they have left the group. One of the final goals of the group is to help them connect with supports in their everyday worlds so that continuing recovery is ensured. The group experience prepares older children for Alateen, a peer therapy group that helps children keep their own lives and personal development from being affected too deeply by the close association with an alcoholic parent or family member. Alateen attendance or encouragement to attend Alateen occurs in the final phase of most treatment programs. Some regions of the country also have Alatot, a special group for younger COAs. Research confirms that self-help groups such as Alateen, Adult Children of Alcoholics, and Al-Anon are effective in helping participants with self-esteem, relationships, and other problem areas related to parental alcoholism (Cutter & Cutter, 1987).

Tips for Practitioners

Aside from the basic treatment strategies discussed in this chapter, there are numerous points practitioners should keep in mind in working with children of alcoholic parents.

Disseminate Information

Provide families with books and pamphlets on alcoholism, especially those that discuss the effects on children. Where appropriate, sharing the results of research studies could be beneficial to parents. This might include the detrimental effects on children who have alcoholic parents and the positive effects of early treatment intervention on these children. Other media, such as filmed vignettes, pamphlets, or books, can be useful informational tools for other uninformed professionals in your workplace, parents, and children.

An easy and effective way of disseminating information to alcoholic families is to establish a lending library where newsletters, magazines, pamphlets, and books are catalogued and can be checked out on a regular basis. A corner of a classroom, a waiting area, health room, lounge, or other underused area can house the collection in a minimal amount of space. Reading of these materials promotes knowledge, changes attitudes, and reduces feelings of isolation.

Address Individual Differences

It is important to remember that COAs are not a homogeneous population and the depth and degree to which each child experiences difficulty is a function of individual differences. Although group context is the preferred treatment strategy for kids, do not lose sight of their individual uniqueness and that they will need some individual attention.

Help Children Center Themselves

Achieving and maintaining balance is the goal of all human beings. Most COAs are off balance by virtue of their unbalanced upbringing. Unbalance is perpetuated by the adoption of any addictions that can throw us off center. If we think of the child as a physical, mental, social, emotional, and spiritual system that functions as a harmonious whole, we must be balanced in all component parts in order for the whole to optimally sustain itself.

You can help children become balanced or well-rounded. Teachers, counselors, and other school personnel are in an especially advantageous position because of the lengthy daily contact they have with children. A child who studies too much may be encouraged to socially interact with other kids. A child who suffers from poor self-concept can be put in leadership roles that are likely to lead to successful experiences and to result in accolades from peers. A child who excels in athletics may do so at the expense of his or her studies and may need direction in the academic domain. These practices are not revolutionary. Accomplished helping professionals, in fact, abide by them already. But capable helpers easily get sidetracked with daily humdrum routines and often forget or lose good habits that are so basic yet so imperative.

Empower Children

Help children see themselves not as victims of alcoholism, but as survivors, which they truly are. This positive approach helps children understand that everything that has happened to them is part of a total picture of who they are. It also empowers them to continue to transform their personal lives forever—no matter how horrific an experience—into a positive end. Recovery is gradual. You can help kids be patient, while recognizing and affirming the baby steps they make in their growth.

8 INTERGENERATIONAL TRANSMISSION
▖▖ OF ALCOHOLISM

CASE 8.1

My name is Irene, and both of my grandfathers were alcoholic. There was lots of vicious conflict in my mother's home. As a very young girl, she made a suicide gesture, and she has spent much of her life borderline depressed. I think her way to survive the viciousness that went on between her parents—the name-calling and the brutal verbal stuff—was to be nice and try to keep an insulation around herself so that it affected her as little as possible. My mother became the peacemaker in the family. She was very pleasant and had the incredible ability to accept just about anything.

My dad became a high achiever who gets his thank-you notes out the day after Christmas. He just does it right. A perfectionist workaholic, he holds those same standards for everybody. If he could do it, then everybody else ought to be able to do it and should do it. There were lots and lots of "shoulds" in my family. He was a traveling salesman on the road constantly working much of the time as I was growing up. No wasting of time, both of my parents were always busy and doing.

My parents were determined that things would be different for my brother and me. Our family would not be like the horrible family life they experienced as children of alcoholic parents. Alcohol was never around as I was growing up, and my parents rarely drank. Instead, Mom became a placater and Dad, a family hero.

Both of them have always been primarily other-directed, and that was reinforced in them and in myself through my family's active church involvement. It was a regular part of our life, a social as well as a religious place. The message was always taking care of other people, pride in ego, being good, and putting other people first. The fact that I was female made the layering of that message very thick. My family was a good family; they are very good people. They worked hard to send us to summer camp. They wanted to be Ozzie and Harriet, and they tried real hard to be.

There was very little open conflict in my family. Everybody was always trying to do everything right—anticipating anything that could create trouble before it happened. We operated from the avoidance of conflict. My dad didn't get angry; he got sarcastic. I learned very early that the consequence of wrongdoing around my house was freeze time, a tangible chill. It was awful. I'd rather have been beaten. It was worse than a slap across the face. I always feared that if I didn't meet my parents' expectations, they would withhold their love and abandon me emotionally. That had a big effect on my self-esteem. The way to have self-esteem was to be good, to be right, to do well, to be perfect.

There was a sense of something missing. I always wished there was more closeness in the family. I never felt a sense that my parents were people to talk to or to turn to when I was in trouble. I didn't feel loved and accepted, even though I know my parents were very well-intentioned. They were always the last people in the world I wanted to know my real business because there was no real history of that kind of intimacy. Instead, there was more focus on "You are what you do." The adage, "What would people think?" became a real measure. When I was a child, my dad gave me a dollar every time I read *How to Win Friends and Influence People*, and I really internalized that book. It emphasizes the people-pleasing stuff—tuning in to others and making them feel important. What I understand now is that underneath all that kind of manipulation is the basic need to control how others feel about me. That's how I can feel about myself. Today, at forty-two, I still struggle with whether or not it's OK for me to be different from others. It's been OK for other people to be different from me, but the issue of my being different from them is based on a security within myself that I'm OK even if others don't like me.

I still don't know how to deal with sarcasm. My response to my father's cold sarcasm was to be crushed inside and not to react in a way that would let him know that I was hurt. In fact, my mother and I both ate a lot and became overweight to deal with our stuffed feelings. It was also a form of rebellion for me because my eating was an issue for my dad, who'd say, "Oh, you're having more potatoes?" For a long time as an adult, there was no recognized conflict in my life. I bypassed any awareness of conflict and went right to accommodation so as not to have conflict. Being accepting and understanding has been one of my own coping devices, being a good girl, a good daughter, doing all the things you're supposed to do. If I wanted Chinese and you wanted Mexican, I was willing to give up Chinese, no problem! I became exactly like my mother—a placater.

The major disadvantage of being the grandchild of alcoholics is that there is no obvious dysfunction in my immediate family to point to as the reason for my discontent, lack, and frustration. So the logical conclusion I arrived at was that there's something wrong with me. It's my fault. It cannot be them. Christ, my parents are fine, upstanding, righteous people. So there must be something wrong with me for wanting to have intimate, feeling conversations and relationships and for feeling like I wasn't loved or accepted.

My understanding of adult children issues has helped me to clarify my own confusion. Now I understand how my mom and dad became who they are and therefore why I have some of the feelings I have. With that awareness has come a sense of more choice that I don't have to always be a placater simply because that was what I learned. I can learn that it's OK to be tougher and can learn that it's OK for me to disagree, be angry, or for your behavior not to be acceptable to me. As an adult, I have learned that there is something to be said for clearing the air in relationships. Not only is conflict normal, but it is OK and sometimes even very productive. If I had children, the biggest thing I would hope to do would be to promote an atmosphere of intimacy, of being able to really talk. I would see myself as the kind of mother who would want to hear how your day went and would want to talk more about how I felt and how my children felt.

— Irene, age forty-two

The transmission of alcoholism from parent to child to grandchild is an intriguing and complex issue, as the case of Irene illustrates. Although it is clear that alcoholism is carried in families, the degree to which hereditary and environmental factors contribute to this transmission is unclear. Scientists are still trying to untangle the puzzle of how the disease is transmitted. Researchers have found that both genetic predisposition and family dynamics play major roles in perpetuating the disease. During the 1980s, for example, genetic research revealed overwhelming support in favor of biochemical differences in COAs, compared to children of nonalcoholics. But the evidence is equally convincing that alcoholism is perpetuated in a generational cycle from parent to child and from grandparent to grandchild, not just genetically but also environmentally, because of certain behavioral patterns that piggyback the disease and carry it forth.

In 1988, actress and recovering alcoholic Margaux Hemingway spoke of following in the alcoholic footsteps of her famous grandfather: "I think alcohol drove my grandfather to suicide, but I'm still alive because I did something about it" ("Not the vintage Margaux," p. 95). Unfortunately, Margaux Hemingway took her own life in 1996, an indicator of the powerful force that alcoholism exerts on family members across generations.

Family Dynamics

A principal school of thought on the transmission of addictions is that the disease alters the operation of the family system, rendering it dysfunctional. The dysfunctions are passed on to future generations, not necessarily through alcoholism, but through dysfunctional family dynamics. According to Smith (1988), author of *Grandchildren of Alcoholics,*

> Many of us have heard others ask the question, "Why do I identify with adult children of alcoholics when my parents didn't drink?" The answer lies not in the family's addiction or lack of it, but in the codependent family dynamics which are subtly passed on from one generation to the next. (p. 3)

Through the family operation—its rules, beliefs, and behavior patterns—codependency is passed on to further generations, even though chemical dependency is not. Irene is a case in point. Codependency was passed on to Irene's parents. Athough they never drank, they continued the dysfunctional cycle by passing it on to Irene through the daily operation of the family. Despite the fact that Irene's parents were not alcoholic, the rules of don't talk, don't trust, and don't feel applied throughout her childhood. Her well-intentioned parents grew up with these rules and inadvertently passed the disease to their daughter through the disguised roles of family hero and placater. Food and work addictions replaced the grandparents' alcoholism. Irene developed with the identical traits of a child reared in an active alcoholic home. The major difference is that COAs, once grown, have the experience of active drinking and active family dysfunction to point to as the source of their problems. But grandchildren of alcoholics do not have those markers and thus suffer greater confusion.

Irene was never told about the grandparental alcoholism and accidentally discovered it as an adult: "I had early memories of the awful smell of bourbon and cigars as a little girl sitting on my grandfather's lap. To this day, I hate that smell." Aside from these early memories, however, Irene had nothing overt to identify as the source of her discontent, emptiness, and frustration. Still, the symptoms were there.

> It kills me to be a disappointment. Oh! It just kills me if I let someone down. It's a carryover of what will people think and what will they do if I don't meet their standards. And I still have a terrible fear of abandonment.

Irene said that she overcompensated for the don't trust rule by becoming too trusting:

> I'm still not very good at figuring out who's trustworthy and who's not. I have to take a massive abuse of mistrust before I will learn to mistrust a person. I too often laid myself open too much and too soon and ended up hurt and resentful and a lot of self-doubt about not being smart enough on how to discriminate who to trust and how much.

Feelings of intimacy were always missing in Irene's family. After her first therapy group, it was she who introduced hugging into her family, followed by saying, "I love you," which she still has to say first, if it is said at all.

Family Types

Irene's account is substantiated by what clinicians call the adult children of alcoholics (ACOA) syndrome—common personality traits that originate from common dysfunctional family experiences (see Box 8.1). This syndrome is directly related to being raised in an unsafe, dysfunctional, alcoholic family system. Four types of alcoholic families that can transmit the disease to future generations have been identified (Kritsberg, 1985).

Family Type 1 contains an active alcoholic in all three generations of the family: grandparent, grandparent's child, and grandchild. In *Family Type 2*, the active alcoholic family member has stopped drinking. Although active alcoholism has been arrested, without treatment, the family dysfunction will continue to carry the disease. The grandparent, for instance, may be an alcoholic who stops drinking. But the family remains untreated, and the disease is transmitted to the second-generation children and third-generation grandchildren, who will re-create the dysfunctional dynamics of the alcoholic family when they have families of their own, even if they never drink.

Family Type 3 resembles Irene's family structure. This type occurs when active drinking has been removed from the family for one generation or more. Suppose, for example, that a grandfather was an alcoholic but his daughter and her spouse were teetotalers. Their children (the grandchildren) are still at high risk for addiction because of the continuation of dysfunctional family dynamics and adherence to the rules and behaviors of the actively drinking alcoholic household of the past.

Family Type 4 is one with no previous history of alcoholism. Grandparents from both sides of the family are abstainers, but one of their children becomes alcoholic even though the alcoholic's spouse does not drink and has no family history of alcoholism. The grandchildren will have adult children issues with which to deal and be at high risk for dysfunctional behaviors themselves.

Analysis of these four family types provides two convincing arguments regarding the family transmission of alcoholism: (1) Although active drinking is not present, the effects of alcoholism on the family

BOX 8.1
Common Characteristics of
Adult Children of Alcoholics

Children who grow up in severely dysfunctional families where parents are alcoholics usually have many adult personality traits in common. Adult children of alcoholics who identify with many or all of the following characteristics may find some comfort in knowing that they are not alone. This list of characteristics can be a guide for personal healing. Those who learned these behaviors in a dysfunctional, unhealthy family can learn how to change them through a personalized program of recovery.

Adult children of alcoholics

___ 1. guess at what is normal.
___ 2. have difficulty in following a project through from beginning to end.
___ 3. lie when it would be just as easy to tell the truth.
___ 4. judge themselves without mercy.
___ 5. have difficulty having fun.
___ 6. take themselves very seriously.
___ 7. have difficulty with intimate relationships.
___ 8. overreact to changes over which they have no control.
___ 9. constantly seek approval and affirmation.
___ 10. feel that they are different from other people.
___ 11. are either extremely responsible or irresponsible.
___ 12. show extreme loyalty, even in the face of evidence that the loyalty is undeserved.
___ 13. look for immediate as opposed to deferred gratification.
___ 14. lock themselves into a course of action without giving serious consideration to alternate behaviors or possible consequences.
___ 15. seek tension and crisis and then complain about the results.
___ 16. avoid conflict or aggravate it, rarely dealing with it.
___ 17. fear rejection and abandonment, yet reject others.
___ 18. fear failure, but sabotage their success.
___ 19. fear criticism and judgement, yet criticize and judge others.
___ 20. manage time poorly, and do not set priorities in a way that works well for them.

SOURCE: Adapted from Woititz, 1983.

can persist; (2) untreated, the alcoholic family system will re-create itself generation after generation (Kritsberg, 1985). Where alcoholism is in one's family history, ACOA issues will exist.

Family Rituals

Another body of research suggests that the existence of certain family customs are associated with the transmission of alcoholism. Transmitter and nontransmitter families were studied to determine why transmission of alcoholism occurred in some families and not in others (Wolin, Bennett, Noonan, & Teitelbaum, 1980). It was found that the disruption of family rituals in alcoholic families contributes to the transmission of the disease. Rituals such as family celebrations, family traditions, and patterned family interactions are the glue that holds the family fabric together and gives it meaning and an identity of its own. When one or both parents are alcoholic and family rituals—such as family meals, birthdays, holidays, vacations, or graduations—are abandoned or altered during periods of heavy drinking, alcoholism is likely to be transmitted to children. Failing to respond to intoxicated parents as they abandon participation in rituals, transmitter families accept the demise of family rituals. In contrast, nontransmitter families reject or confront the drinking parent and protect the rituals by refusing to allow alcoholism to interfere. Nontransmitter families where rituals remain intact are less likely to pass on the disease, even when drinking is heavy. Families that stick together and present a united front are less likely to transmit alcoholism to the next generation.

Developmental Passages
for Children of Alcoholics

Another popular view on alcohol transmission holds that family dysfunction caused by parental alcoholism interferes with the natural progression of personality development from birth. The nature of childhood experiences, strategies of coping, and ways of understanding and reacting to parental alcoholism depend upon children's ages at the onset of parental drinking problems (Wilson & Orford, 1978). The earlier in life a child is exposed to parental alcoholism, the more severe are the side effects. Parental drinking begins to affect chil-

TABLE 8.1. Erikson's Eight Stages of Personality Development

Developmental Period	Age	Personality Crisis Stage
Infancy	Birth to 1 year	Trust vs. mistrust
Toddlerhood	1 to 3 years	Autonomy vs. shame/doubt
Early childhood	4 to 5 years	Initiative vs. guilt
Middle childhood	6 to 11 years	Industry vs. inferiority
Adolescence	12 to 18 years	Identity vs. role confusion
Young adulthood	19 to 34 years	Intimacy vs. isolation
Middle adulthood	35 to 64 years	Generativity vs. self-absorption
Older adulthood	65 to death	Integrity vs. despair

dren in infancy. Research confirms that youngsters reared in alcoholism from infancy are likely to have more serious social and psychological adjustment problems than children who face parental alcoholism for the first time in adolescence (Morehouse & Scola, 1986; Werner, 1986).

Developmentally, there is a natural time when all humans struggle with the same emotions that COAs experience in greater intensity and depth. At certain sensitive times in childhood, youngsters are more susceptible to develop the dysfunctional traits associated with adult COAs. During each developmental period, personality crises naturally occur that must be resolved in a positive way for healthy development to continue (Erikson, 1963) (see Table 8.1). When people fail to resolve a crisis in a particular stage, they will still go on to the next stage, but they cannot completely resolve the crisis in this new stage until crises of earlier stages have been resolved. It is possible to "go back" at a later time and work through the conflict, but it is more difficult.

For COAs, the crisis at each stage is multiplied, and passing the test is much more difficult. Active parental alcoholism at any one of these sensitive times during the life span can impair the successful resolution of the crisis and passage to the next developmental stage.

Infancy

Children living in active parental alcoholism at birth will be negatively affected by the disease in many ways. Those whose mothers drank during prenatal development can be FAS babies and suffer permanent neurological and cognitive deficits. Aside from prenatal influences, successful resolution of the conflict of *trust versus mistrust* depends upon the quality of the parent-infant relationship.

Infants are dependent on their caregivers to *consistently* gratify their needs for food, security, love, and touching. If infants are fed when hungry, if their cries are answered within a reasonable time, if their discomforts are removed, and if they are loved, cuddled, played with, and talked to, they will begin to feel that the world is a safe place and that they can trust others to care for them. When their needs are not met in a loving adult-child relationship, or if needs are inconsistently met one day and not another, they will grow to mistrust their world and those in it. Because of consistent care, trustful children develop a general "feeling" that their caregivers are accessible and responsive, whereas those who receive inconsistent care are mistrustful and unsure that their caregivers will be there when they need them. In active alcoholic families, infant trust is challenged from the first day of life because parents are too consumed with alcoholism to provide adequate support and nurturance to children. The inconsistency, neglect, and abuse that characterize many alcoholic homes will leave children with an overriding sense of mistrust, insecurity, and separation anxiety. They learn very early that they cannot count on anything. These infantile feelings build across the life span and are transformed into problems that many COAs have with intimacy, insecure relationships, and fear of abandonment in adulthood. Unless treatment intervention occurs, difficulty trusting others and abandonment anxiety will become integral and lifelong parts of their personalities. The inability to trust also extends to one's self, opinions, and confidence.

Toddlerhood

Toddlerhood ushers in the struggle between *autonomy versus shame and doubt*. At this stage, children develop abilities to manage and control their bodies and their world. They learn such self-control as walking, dressing, feeding, and toileting. They no longer need to depend on adults to carry them or push them in a stroller. They can move about by themselves and climb, push, and pull to get things without asking. Along with this newfound ability to control themselves and their surroundings, children develop autonomy and a will of their own. They express a desire to make independent choices and decisions that often conflict with parental wishes. Sometimes, unwanted help or demands from adults are met with negativism and resistance from toddlers. Conflicts centering around the basic routines of eating, sleeping, and elimination are unavoidable at this age.

Children who develop a healthy sense of autonomy have parents who are patient and supportive, especially during conflict situations. Their parents praise them for using self-control and making good choices. A positive sense of self and a healthy outlook on control develop when adults encourage autonomy while lovingly and consistently setting firm, reasonable limits. Toddlers develop a sense of shame or doubt about their abilities when their newly discovered independence is restricted, discouraged, or poorly guided. Shame and doubt and problems with control arise from children in alcoholic homes when they witness parents who lack self-control, who scold and criticize them for making poor choices and mistakes, or who deny them opportunities to make choices and develop self-control. COAs develop self-doubt about their abilities to manage their lives and to stand on their own two feet. Rigid parental demands and oppressive rules without some room for choices lead to codependency. Toddlers who live in active alcoholism, where autonomy cannot be exercised, begin to show the marks of codependency during this stage. As adults, they have difficulty making decisions and often marry people who will make decisions for them. Without treatment, they will carry issues around control and negative attitudes toward authority into their adult personalities. They overreact—become angry or sad—to situations in which they have no control or in which the future is unknown, and they both fear and resent authority figures.

Early Childhood

It is during this stage that children struggle with the conflict between *initiative and guilt*. Children must internalize right from wrong and adhere to the rules of society. Parents generally require children to assume more responsibility for supervising themselves, their pets, and their toys at this age. Hitting others and stealing are prohibited. Such rules are internalized in the conscience. Trouble typically arises as free-spirited, initiating children must learn to control their own behavior and follow the rules of society. Reality testing, a critical lesson, is difficult at this stage because children view the world as magical and cannot think logically. Imagination, fantasy, and fairy tales are the child's reality at this stage, so it is typical for children to have difficulty separating reality from fantasy. This developmental characteristic makes reality testing in alcoholic homes doubly problematic, because children are often told that what they saw didn't really happen or was not as bad as they perceived it to be. The line between reality and imagination becomes blurred, and children become confused. They often decide that their fantasy world offers a gift of escape, which they overuse to cope with the harsh reality of alcoholic family conflict. Rules of right and wrong change daily in unpredictable alcoholic homes so that children never understand what the rule for today is. They also have trouble predicting what is appropriate from one situation to the next and may feel guilty for thoughts and behaviors that others consider perfectly proper.

This stage is also characterized by egocentrism when children believe that they cause everything that happens to them. They feel guilty because they believe their parent drinks because of something they did, perhaps not putting away all of their toys or not eating all of their mashed potatoes. In alcoholic homes, being responsible for toys is extended to taking on adult responsibilities such as getting your own meals and getting yourself to school on time. As adults, children who have trouble at this stage will not be able to distinguish what normal is and will feel they are to blame for their parent's drinking. They may become overly responsible for others and blame themselves for others' failures. They have guilt feelings when they stand up for themselves, and so they give in to others, putting others' needs before their own. Failure to successfully resolve this stage results in children and adults who overcontrol themselves by obeying all the rules of their restrictive consciences without meeting their own needs in order to avoid guilt. Such people are also often intolerant of others who do not rigidly adhere to their strict set of rules.

Middle Childhood

School-age children have moved to a stage of personality development that involves the struggle of *industry versus inferiority* in which success comes with the child feeling productive and competent. Failure comes with feelings of inadequacy. Whether a child develops industry or inferiority is strongly influenced by the support and feedback that come from important adults and peers. Feelings of worth and industry come when children's efforts and products are recognized and approved by others. Accomplishments come from doing well in school, learning new skills such as playing musical instruments, or achieving distinctions in Scouts or other civic organizations.

When frequent failure or disapproval is common, as in most alcoholic homes, children may come to believe that the results of their work are not worthwhile and that they themselves have low worth. Poor work habits and feelings of uselessness are sometimes the consequence. In adulthood, these people have difficulty following through on projects, or they are prone to procrastination. On the other extreme, some children in alcoholic homes get stuck in this stage and spend the rest of their lives trying to prove to themselves and to others that they are competent and worthwhile. They become overly serious and do not know how to have fun. Achievement becomes a compulsion, and external accomplishments become sources of self-esteem. They may become high achievers in school and prized workaholics in their careers, but inside they feel driven, unhappy, and worthless. Although their standards are unrealistic, they judge themselves and others harshly for not meeting them. Nothing they accomplish can ever be good enough to change these feelings of incompetence, except for the completion of a good recovery program.

Adolescence

Identity versus role confusion is the struggle during adolescence. It is a time to struggle for a sense of self as well as an outlook on life that is acceptable to the teenager and society. Resolving this conflict involves satisfactory answers to many questions: Who am I? Where am I going? What will I do with my life? Adolescents who have resolved the struggle develop a positive identity and move into adulthood knowing who they are and where they are going. They find a fit between who they are and what society wants them to be.

This fit is impossible for children of alcoholism who have been unsuccessful at the previous stages. Lacking the inward resources to affirm their own worth, they become approval seekers. They constantly change their values to gain the affirmation of others or lose their identity in another person altogether. A backlog of unresolved residue from previous stages interferes with the identity crisis and leads to role confusion, negative self-concept, and doubts about the future:

> As teenagers, they are unable to develop adequately the social skills and attitudes necessary for separating from the family and establishing their own identity. As they limp into adulthood, they often leave a trail of poor relationships and they have difficulties with intimacy. They often feel

unable to meet life's challenges adequately, even when they are. They feel different; they feel frightened; and they feel misunderstood. (Gravitz, 1985, pp. 15-16)

This confusion is sometimes exaggerated when COAs turn to substance abuse, delinquent or psychotic behavior, or suicide attempts in order to deal with their failure at resolving personal issues.

Adulthood

It is not until COAs reach adulthood that many of the dysfunctional characteristics from their upbringing start to demand resolution. A lifetime of unresolved issues makes healthy and happy relationships extremely difficult. *Intimacy versus isolation* becomes the struggle in young adulthood. Unmet needs are stockpiled. Difficulty being intimate is the hallmark at this stage because stuffed feelings from childhood impair the ability to feel or express emotions. Feelings of being different and isolated from other people are also commonly reported by young adult children. Seldom do they, however, trace this difficulty to parental alcoholism.

Adult COAs unconsciously are attracted to one another because they feel less isolated and more at home with those who were also raised in codependency and chemical dependency. They confuse love with pity and are prone to care for codependent people whom they can pity and rescue. They tend to help and seek out victims and are attracted by that weakness in love and friendships. Marriages and friendships typically occur with others who are COAs, substance abusers, or members of dysfunctional families.

Middle adulthood brings the conflict of *generativity versus self-absorption*. Untreated, the disease of alcoholism continues to eat away at the happiness and fulfillment of middle age. At a time in life when self-actualization comes from doing things for others, raising children, leading society, and making the world a better place, nonrecovering COAs are self-absorbed in their own misery. They remain codependent and continue to suffer from the disease of alcoholism, even though they may never drink. By midlife, many adult children are chemically dependent themselves. They unwittingly pass the disease on to their offspring and thus perpetuate the addiction cycle to another generation. More fortunate ones, like the adult child of an alcoholic whose words follow, are breaking the cycle of addiction through recovery:

Growing up was hard for me, and it wasn't until I entered a treatment program for alcoholism that I understood my dependency on alcohol. I grew up with an alcoholic father who beat my mother and tormented the kids. My mother escaped the craziness with her own dependency on such prescribed drugs as Librium and amphetamines. I knew I too had to escape it all to survive, so as a young child I entered my own fantasy world. But as an adult, I couldn't live in the world of make-believe, so I drank instead. I started using alcohol in my teens and marijuana in my twenties. At forty-three, I am just beginning to live. Undergoing treatment for alcoholism and learning about ACOA issues has opened up my eyes to a new world. For the first time I am facing my past sober. Childhood confusion has been replaced by awareness and direction in my life. Again I can view the real world with the eyes of a child—sober eyes full of wonderment and excitement—living and loving every minute of it. My family's cycle of addiction stops with me!

The end of the life cycle in older adulthood brings the struggle of *integrity versus despair*. Those still suffering from the disease are displeased with the way their lives have turned out and are destined for despair, bitterness, and fear of death. Those who have sought spiritual healing from the disease have an outlook of integrity, a sense of satisfaction with their lives, and envision death as a normal ending to a fulfilling existence.

Genetic Predisposition

Genetic research has shown great promise as a source of information on why alcohol runs in families (see Box 8.2 for a summary of evidence supporting a genetic link to alcoholism). Biologic determinants have been studied for many years, but only recently has increased attention been given to the association of genetics to alcohol addiction (Talashek, Gerace, & Starr, 1994). In fact, the genetic component of alcoholism was cited for the first time in 1990 (National Council on Alcoholism and the American Medical Society on Addiction Medicine, 1990). The initial goal of genetic research was to determine the presence and extent of hereditary influence on the development of alcoholism (i.e., can a predisposition to alcoholism be inherited?). Scientists have differentiated inherited factors from environmental factors by using classical techniques for human genetic analysis: studying differences among identical and fraternal twins and among adopted children.

BOX 8.2
Evidence Supporting a
Genetic Link to Alcoholism

- Incidence of alcoholism is greater among identical than fraternal twins.
- Alcoholism occurs more often among adopted children, separated from biological alcoholic parents at birth, than among adopted children without family histories of alcohol.
- Adopted daughters and sons of alcoholics are three to four times more likely to become alcoholics than adopted children of nonalcoholics.
- Children of alcoholics are metabolically more prone to alcoholism than children of nonalcoholics.
- Neurological differences among children of alcoholics, compared to nonalcoholics, predispose them to become alcoholics as adults.

Ultimately, the goal of this research is to identify the specific genetic factors predisposing certain individuals to alcoholism. Twin and adoption research is being extended by studies that attempt to pinpoint the specific genetic and/or biochemical transmitter of alcoholism among some children and not others. Premorbid identification of individuals predisposed to alcoholism would allow primary prevention efforts to be directed toward these high-risk individuals.

Twin Studies

Twin investigations have compared the incidence of alcoholism among monozygotic or identical twins with dizygotic or fraternal twins. Monozygotic twins can provide evidence for genetic involvement in the development of alcoholism because if these twins, who have the same genetic makeup, do not have identical outcomes with regard to alcohol use and abuse, it is implied that something in the environment affects the development of drinking behavior patterns. Twin studies do indicate that an increased risk for the development of alcoholism can be inherited. Identical twins have been found to be more similar for alcoholism than fraternal twins (see Crabbe, McSwigan, & Belknap, 1985). However, research indicates that alcoholism is not absolutely determined by genetic factors because monozygotic twins have not, in fact, been found to have developed identical patterns of alcohol abuse.

Adoption Studies

A related strategy for separating out the influences of genetic predisposition from those of the environment is to study children who have been adopted at a very early age. A series of adoption studies were launched in the early 1970s by an investigation that originally sought to determine if full siblings would more often be alcoholic than half siblings (Schuckit, Goodwin, & Winokur, 1972). Findings revealed no real differences in alcoholism between the two groups. But when researchers studied half siblings from broken homes separately, the significance of biological factors was striking. Even when raised apart from their parents, a larger portion of half siblings with alcoholic biological parents became alcoholics themselves, compared to half siblings without alcoholic parents.

With the groundwork laid, an entire body of adoption research confirmed the contributing influences of genetic factors to alcoholism. Adoption studies from three different nations—Denmark, Sweden, and the United States—reported the existence of similar inheritance themes (Bohman, 1978; Bohman, Sigvardsson, & Cloninger, 1981; Cadoret, Cain, & Grove, 1980; Cloninger, Bohman, Sigvardsson, & Knorring, 1981; Goodwin, 1985; Goodwin, Schulsinger, Hermansen, Guze, & Winokur, 1973). Sons of alcoholics were four times more likely to become alcoholic than sons of nonalcoholics, whether raised by their alcoholic biological parents or by nonalcoholic adoptive parents. Adopted sons reared by nondrinking parents were just as likely to become alcoholic as sons reared by alcoholic biological parents. By contrast, sons of nonalcoholic biological parents adopted by alcoholic parents did not become alcoholic at an unusually high rate. Adopted daughters with alcoholic biological mothers were three times more likely to become alcoholic than other women, even when reared from an early age by nondrinking parents.

Physiological Research

Twin and adoption studies give evidence for genetic involvement in the development of alcoholism. As yet, however, we have relatively little information about exactly *what* may be inherited that puts some individuals at higher risk for developing alcoholism. For example, it may be found that genetic factors that influence a person's response to alcohol predispose some individuals to alcoholism. Genetically predisposed individuals may be found to inherit a hypersensitivity to the pleasurable effects of alcohol. Alternatively, individuals may inherit a lack of sensitivity to the unpleasant effects that follow excessive drinking (Crabbe et al., 1985). Most physiological research has studied high-risk candidates for alcoholism, usually COAs, who are still too young to have developed the disease. These studies have examined differences in drug absorption, metabolism, brain activity, and other biochemical mechanisms as possible mediators of the disease (Bardo & Risner, 1985).

Metabolic research has revealed that COAs ranging in age from eight to thirteen had lower zinc levels than children of nonalcoholic parents. This finding suggests that before any alcohol ingestion, COAs have the same zinc deficiency that manifests itself in the chronic adult alcoholic population (Kern et al., 1981). Zinc deficiency has been associated with cerebellar dysfunction, learning disabilities, and schizophrenia. This deficiency suggests school-age children may already be physiologically prepared for alcoholism and supports other research that indicates abnormalities in alcohol metabolism in adult COAs (Schuckit & Rayses, 1979).

When intoxicated, sons of alcoholics also have lower levels of the hormone prolactin in their bloodstreams, compared to sons of nonalcoholics (Schuckit, Gold, & Risch, 1987). It takes more alcohol for sons of alcoholics to become inebriated, and they have less ability to detect the effects of alcohol than their peers (Schuckit, 1984a, 1984b, 1984c). It is believed that prolactin may ultimately provide clues about the development of alcoholism and act as an early warning signal for those at risk. The presence of blood chemicals also has been effective in distinguishing adult alcoholics from nonalcoholics and may someday serve as a basis for spotting children who are at high risk of becoming alcoholics when they grow up (Tabakoff et al., 1988).

Several studies suggest that neuropsychological deficits predispose children to alcoholism. Findings indicated, for example, that compared to sons of nonalcoholics, sons of alcoholics are deficient in emotional self-regulation, planning, memory, perceptual motor functioning, and language processing (Tarter et al., 1984). Researchers attributed these neurotransmitter disequilibrium at the biochemical level. Scientists observed brain abnormalities (for example, rapid EEG activity), resembling that of adult alcoholics, to be more common among sons of alcoholics than among sons of nonalcoholics (Begleiter, Porjesz, & Bihari, 1984; Gabrielli, Mednick, Volavkar, Pollock, Schulsinger, & Itil, 1982).

Hennecke (1984) found that *stimulus augmenting* (i.e., perception that something is of greater magnitude than it really is, including sensitivity to pain, sound, and light) is higher in children of alcoholic fathers than children of sober fathers. Augmenting is believed to reflect a biochemical deficiency in the brain and is prevalent among alcoholics. Augmenters drink to reduce the augmenting tendency that preexists the active phase of alcoholism. Other studies have also cited more neuropsychological disorders in adults with family histories of alcoholism than in the average person. One such study reported that adults with alcoholic family histories had more difficulty than adults without such histories in performing abstract problem solving and perceptual motor tasks (Schaeffer, Parsons, & Yohman, 1984). Contrasting these findings, other data report that poor neuropsychological performance among COAs was not upheld and that, in fact, they scored as well or better than non-COAs (Workman-Davis & Hesselbrock, 1987).

The evidence linking inheritance to alcoholism is strong. Findings on familial transmission indicate that parents and siblings of alcoholics are seven times more at risk to develop alcoholism (Talashek et al., 1994). That does not necessarily mean, however, that COAs are biologically doomed and that all COAs will become alcoholics. Genes do not act independently in determining whether or not a person will become an alcoholic. Many COAs, approximately two thirds in fact, never have problems with alcohol. Although all the pieces of the puzzle are not yet in place, scientists suggest that genes somehow combine with what happens throughout life to determine patterns of alcohol use and abuse. This is consistent with a biopsychosocial or a biobehavioral perspective of alcohol abuse, which emphasizes that multiple biological, psychological, and environmental factors interact to produce alcoholism (Barrett, 1985; Talashek et al., 1994). Researchers are beginning to uncover different types and degrees of alcoholism that originate from the interactions of genetic determinants with environmental factors, such as patterns of family functioning, cultural norms, socioeconomic conditions, alcohol availability, peer-group influence, and moral and legal considerations (Cloninger et al., 1981). Even children who carry a genetic predisposition can live a healthy lifestyle, free of chemical abuse, and never become addicted. But regardless of whether alcoholism resides in our genes, family patterns, or a combination of both, when parents drink, hope and help are available for children who can recover from the disease.

Genograms

Genograms can be helpful in working with older children and adolescent children of alcoholic parents. Genograms are graphic representations that can be used to trace family patterns by recording the family structure and family information (Anderson & Sabatelli, 1993; Davis, 1996; McGoldrick & Gerson, 1985; for an example, see Figure 8.1). The amount of information the practitioner is able to obtain for the genogram will depend upon resources available, including the knowledge held by children about their family and the willingness of other family members to contribute information. A genogram typically includes three generations of a family. When used in working with COAs, the child would be represented as the index person for whom the genogram is being developed. Information about the child and his or her siblings, the child's parents' generation, and the grandparents' generation would be included. The core of the genogram is constructed around the index person and includes a depiction of family members connected by lines that represent how different family members are related to each other biologically and legally. For example, two persons who are married would be connected by a straight, horizontal line and children of that marriage would be depicted by symbols dropping off the marriage line. In the example of a genogram in Figure 8.1, Phillip and Theresa are married and have one son, Daniel, and one daughter, Gwen. Gwen is the index person in this genogram—that is, the family member for whom the genogram is being developed. Also recorded is information about family members, including dates of births, deaths, marriages and divorces; causes of deaths; occurrence of serious health problems, mental illnesses, or addictions; and other significant family events and transitions. This representation of the family's structure will indicate the transgenerational prevalence of alcoholism and other relevant characteristics of the family across generations.

However, genogram information can be extended beyond family structure to delineate family relationships. Various kinds of lines can be used to depict different types of relationships among family members.

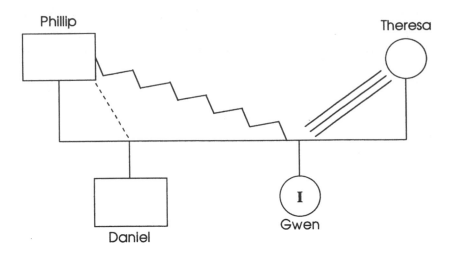

Figure 8.1: Genogram

For example, a close relationship between a child and sibling could be represented by two parallel lines. A distant relationship between a child and an alcoholic parent could be drawn as a dotted line, whereas a fused relationship could be indicated by three parallel lines drawn between that child and parent (McGoldrick & Gerson, 1985). In the family represented in Figure 8.1, the alcoholic parent is Phillip, the father. The relationship lines in this figure indicate that Daniel is emotionally cut off from his father (represented by the broken line between the two). Gwen maintains a relationship with her father; however, its conflictual nature is indicated by the jagged line connecting them on the genogram. The three parallel lines between Gwen and her mother, Theresa, tell us that the mother-daughter relationship is very close, perhaps even to the point of being fused. In addition to the use of relationship lines, important family subsystems can be indicated by surrounding those family members in the subsystem with a line representing an internal boundary. Examples of such subsystems could include a coalition of a child and sober parent against an alcoholic parent, or an alliance between siblings who share interests and activities that buffer them from the pain of their family dynamics. External boundaries can also be depicted to indicate other nonbiological kin who are considered to be "in" the family by the child, such as a trusted neighbor or a caring extended family member.

Genograms can be constructed in many different ways. The information presented here is offered to introduce the concept of the genogram as one means of working with children of alcoholic families. Although genograms may be used as a tool for gathering intergenerational family information, they can also serve as a way to build rapport between the practitioner and the child and to initiate discussion on issues of concern for the child. Finally, practitioners working with COAs can use the genogram as a way to gain a greater understanding of the dynamics of the current alcoholic family system and can use this information to support children in finding the best ways to take care of themselves within the family.

A New Beginning

As this book draws to an end, we would like to leave you with the message that it is really just the beginning. The grassroots COA movement will continue to grow nationwide as children, young and grown, become aware of issues that lend clarity to their past history with the disease of alcoholism and start on the road to a new life's beginning. This newly found knowledge is call for a celebration that, as one recovering child exclaimed, "makes me want to shout it from the mountaintops!"

COAs are survivors. They have many positive traits and remarkable skills that helped them triumph against incredible odds. That in itself is reason to celebrate. They grow up with many gifts that they bestow on others, among which are help and hope for a brighter future. Without adult COAs, the human services field would collapse. The discovery of being a child of an alcoholic is a joyous occasion that brings with it a wondrous sense of hope for growth and fulfillment. It is a second chance at self-discovery, an exciting life adventure. Every alcoholic childhood—no matter how devastating—is an opportunity for personal and spiritual transformation that can bring an exceptional tone to the quality of life. As more and more practitioners become aware of the complexity of alcoholism and its powerful effects upon kids, they will have a chance to contribute to the self-actualization of millions of children.

9 RESOURCES FOR WORKING WITH CHILDREN OF ALCOHOLICS

This chapter contains annotations of books for adults and children, unpublished research reports, organizations, periodicals, and videotapes pertaining to children from alcoholic families.

Books for Adults

Many books have been written about and for children of alcoholic families. Some books emphasize the childhood years, whereas others focus on adulthood, when the impact of an alcoholic upbringing continues to be felt. In the following list, I have organized readings by their emphasis into one of the following categories: Children of Alcoholics, Adult Children of Alcoholics, Alcoholic/Dysfunctional Families, Autobiographical, and Fiction.

Children of Alcoholics

Ackerman, Robert. (1987). *Children of alcoholics: Bibliography and resource guide* (3rd ed.). Pompano Beach, FL: Health Communications. A complete bibliography and resource on COAs, including youngsters and adult children.

Ackerman, Robert. (1983). *Children of alcoholics: A guidebook for educators, therapists, and parents* (2nd ed.). Holmes Beach, FL: Learning Publications. The author describes what it is like to be a child of an alcoholic and presents suggestions for educators, therapists, and parents. A comprehensive list of resources and materials is included in the appendixes.

Ackerman, Robert. (1986). *Growing in the shadow: Children of alcoholics.* Pompano Beach, FL: Health Communications. The book is divided into four parts and addresses COAs from childhood to adulthood. Written for anyone who has an interest in or who is currently working with COAs.

Black, Claudia. (1982). *It will never happen to me.* Denver, CO: MAC Publications. This book shares some of the experiences of COAs and explains the process of what happens, as well as what can be done to both prevent and handle these problems.

Chandler, Mitzi. (1987). *Whiskey's song: An explicit story of surviving in an alcoholic home.* Pompano Beach, FL: Health Communications. Told in verse, this is a story of chaos, pathos, and survival, relating how a child grows up in an alcoholic family where violence and neglect are everyday occurrences.

Cork, Margaret. (1969). *The forgotten children.* Ontario, Canada: General Publishing. Based on her interviews with 115 children, this pioneering work answers some of the unresolved questions pertaining to children in families where there is alcoholism.

Deutsch, Charles. (1982). *Broken bottles, broken dreams: Understanding and helping the children of alcoholics.* New York: Teachers College Press. This book explores the problems children experience in alcoholic homes and ways of helping them cope.

Gravitz, Herbert. (1985). *Children of alcoholics handbook: Who they are, what they experience, how they recover* (25-page pamphlet). South Laguna, CA: National Association for Children of Alcoholics. Provides for the layperson a clear understanding on the important issues relating to being raised in an alcoholic home.

Hammond, Mary. (1985). *Children of alcoholics in play therapy.* Pompano Beach, FL: Health Communications. An overview of how play can be an integral vehicle for working with COAs. Topics include the structure of the play environment, necessary equipment, and techniques to use in play intervention.

Lewis, David, & Williams, Carol. (1986). *Providing care for children of alcoholics: Clinical and research perspectives.* Pompano Beach, FL: Health Communications. Aimed at professionals who work with COAs, this book provides clinical insights and research findings.

Moe, Jerry, & Pohlmen, Don. (1988). *Kids power: Healing games for children of alcoholics*. Redwood City, CA: Sequoia Hospital District. An excellent resource of games and activities to help kids learn about parental alcoholism and how to cope with it on a daily basis. Includes music, art, puppets, and many innovative approaches, such as the Wheel of Misfortune.

Morehouse, Ellen, and Scola, Claire. (1986). *Children of alcoholics: Meeting the needs of the young COA in the school setting* (30-page pamphlet). South Laguna, CA: National Association for Children of Alcoholics. Written for professionals in the school system, this pamphlet describes the COA and offers advice on how to help these children.

Pickens, Roy. (1986). *Children of alcoholics*. Center City, MN: Hazelden. Reviews research on COAs and the emotional and medical problems that result. Implications for treatment and prevention are also presented.

Richards, Tarpley, Tuohey, Martha, & Petrash, Patricia. (1987). *Children of alcoholics: A guide for professionals*. South Laguna, CA: National Association for Children of Alcoholics. A pamphlet for practitioners involved in facilitating the recovery of COAs.

Seixas, Judith, & Youcha, Geraldine. (1985). *Children of alcoholism: A survivor's manual*. New York: Crown. Shows what happened in childhood to make adult children as they are. Also presents ideas on what to do about dysfunctional behaviors.

Veenstra, Susan. (1987). *Children of alcoholic parents: A handbook for counselors and teachers*. Cleveland, OH: Alcoholism Services of Cleveland. A guide for professionals in creating a system of identification, intervention, and treatment for children in the schools.

Adult Children of Alcoholics

Ackerman, Robert. (1987). *Let go and grow*. Pompano Beach, FL: Health Communications. An in-depth study of the different characteristics of adult COAs, followed up with guidelines for recovery.

Ackerman, Robert. (1987). *Same house, different homes: Why adult children of alcoholics are not all the same*. Pompano Beach, FL: Health Communications. A study of over one thousand adults who grew up in dysfunctional homes and how the findings can produce positive solutions for adult COAs.

Black, Claudia. (1985). *Repeat after me: A step-by-step workbook for adult children of alcoholics to set a new course in their personal lives*. Denver, CO: MAC (1850 High Street, Denver, CO 80218). Written to help adult COAs recognize how their present lives are influenced by the past, to help them release the parts of the past that they would like to put behind them, and to take responsibility for how they live their lives today.

Cermak, Tim. (1988). *Evaluating and treating adult children of alcoholics: A guide for professionals.* Minneapolis, MN: The Johnson Institute. Presents an integrated approach to evaluating and treating adult COAs. A theoretical framework for understanding adult children characteristics and problems and specific guidelines for initial interviews and clinical evaluations.

Cermak, Tim. (1985). *A primer on adult children of alcoholics.* Pompano Beach, FL: Health Communications. This booklet is written on adult COAs and identifies issues and steps to recovery.

Curtin, Paul. (1986). *Tumbleweeds: A therapist's guide to treatment of adult children of alcoholics.* Rutherford, NJ: Perrin & Treggett Booksellers. A brief guide with tips on therapeutic issues.

Dean, Amy. (1987). *Making changes: How adult children can have healthier, happier relationships.* Century City, MN: Hazelden. Brings the awareness and the tools necessary for changing unhealthy ways of interacting with others that were derived from living in an alcoholic home.

Friel, John, & Friel, Linda. (1988). *Adult children: The secret of dysfunctional families.* Pompano Beach, FL: Health Communications. Defines the problems of dysfunctional families, analyzes the characteristic symptoms, and offers guidelines to live healthy, happy lives now.

Gravitz, Herbert, & Bowden, Julie. (1986). *Guide to recovery: A book for adult children of alcoholics.* Pompano Beach, FL: Health Communications. Answers more than 75 questions typically asked by adult COAs and presents a description of the stages of recovery from the effects of parental alcoholism.

Health Communications. (1988). *Bread and roses: A poetry anthology for adult children.* Pompano Beach, FL: Author. A series of poems by adult children who have survived childhood in an alcoholic home. Their word-pictures in poems are sometimes graphically violent, at other times gentle, forgiving, and always touching.

Kritsberg, Wayne. (1985). *The ACOA syndrome, from discovery to recovery.* Pompano Beach, FL: Health Communications. The foundations for healing the wounds of an alcoholic-influenced childhood are laid in this book.

Lerner, Rokelle. (1985). *Daily affirmations for adult children of alcoholics.* Pompano Beach, FL: Health Communications. This book provides a daily source of inspiration to change the distorted and undermining messages of childhood in an alcoholic family.

Marlin, Emily. (1987). *HOPE: New choices and recovery strategies for adult children of alcoholics.* New York: Harper & Row. The author shows how all adult COAs have similar legacies, helps them reexamine the past to better understand themselves, and presents strategies for self-change.

McConnell, Patty. (1986). *A workbook for healing adult children of alcoholics*. New York: Harper & Row. The workbook is divided into two parts: "The Hurt," in which the reader is invited to explore childhood experiences with adult awareness, and "The Healing," which suggests that the reader can change behaviors by modifying feelings and defenses.

Middleton-Moz, Jane, & Dwinell, Lorie. (1986). *After the tears: Reclaiming the personal losses of childhood*. Pompano Beach, FL: Health Communications. A child raised in an alcoholic environment will perpetuate an alcoholic legacy even if they never drink. This book shows readers how to mourn the loss of childhood and recapture their self-worth.

Perrin, T. W. (1985). *This new day: Daily affirmations for adult children of alcoholics*. Rutherford, NJ: Thomas W. Perrin. An inspirational reading for each day of the year, these affirming messages are used by many adult children in their recovery process.

Robinson, Bryan. (1989). *Work addiction: Hidden legacy of adult children of alcoholics*. Pompano Beach, FL: Health Communications. Explores the disease of workaholism and how it destroys relationships and kills people. Provides help for adult COAs for whom work has become the drug of choice.

Rosellini, Gayle. (1982). *Taming your turbulent past: A self-help guide for adult children*. Pompano Beach, FL: Health Communications. This practical book is directed at troubled adult children, advising them that they are capable of happiness and how they can achieve it. It deals with anger and the power of forgiveness, fear and self-esteem, unhappiness, and the tyranny of always needing to please.

Smith, Ann. (1988). *Grandchildren of alcoholics: Another generation of codependency*. Pompano Beach, FL: Health Communications. Pinpoints the problems of those living in families where a grandparent is or was an alcoholic and where the parents are therefore COAs, with the resulting dysfunctional parenting skills.

Wegscheider-Cruse, Sharon. (1985). *Choicemaking*. Pompano Beach, FL: Health Communications. For those recovering from codependency, the author integrates her personal experiences as a child of alcoholic parents with professional knowledge to foster spiritual transformation.

Wegscheider-Cruse, Sharon. (1987). *Learning to love yourself: Finding your self-worth*. Pompano Beach, FL: Health Communications. The author points out that self-esteem is not inherited but learned. She presents, step-by-step, how self-worth can be developed.

Wegscheider-Cruse, Sharon. (1987). *Understanding me*. Pompano Beach, FL: Health Communications. Helps readers in their quest for self-understanding and self-respect.

Whitfield, Charles L. (1987). *Healing the child within: Discovery and recovery for adult children of dysfunctional families.* Pompano Beach, FL: Health Communications. Defines, describes, and discovers how we can find our child within and gently heal and nurture it until we can reach the role of spirituality within our child and live the free life we were meant to live.

Woititz, Janet. (1983). *Adult children of alcoholics.* Pompano Beach, FL: Health Communications. This best-selling book is an excellent overview to the insights of how upbringing in chemically dependent families can be carried into adulthood and what can be done to change these patterns.

Woititz, J. G. (1987). *Home away from home: The art of self sabotage.* Pompano Beach, FL: Health Communications. Raises and answers questions such as: What are the best jobs for ACOAs? Do all ACOAs end up as workaholics? How can they prevent burnout?

Woititz, Janet. (1985). *Struggle for intimacy.* Pompano Beach, FL: Health Communications. Reveals the barriers to trust and intimacy learned early in life by COAs. Tips for rebuilding intimacy in adult relationships are provided.

Wood, Barbara. (1987). *Children of alcoholism: The struggle for self and intimacy in adult life.* New York: New York University Press. A look at COA issues through traditional psychological theories. Also a reinterpretation of the survival roles.

Alcoholic/Dysfunctional Families

Bepko, Claudia, & Krestan, JoAnn. (1985). *The responsibility trap: A blueprint for treating the alcoholic family.* New York: Free Press. Presents a treatment plan that includes the alcoholic as well as all family members.

Bradshaw, John. (1988). *The family: A revolutionary way of self-discovery.* Pompano Beach, FL: Health Communications. The author guides the reader out of dysfunction and proposes how problems within the family can be remedied.

Brown, Stephanie. (1985). *Treating the alcoholic family: A developmental model of recovery.* New York: John Wiley. Focuses on how practitioners can best understand and meet the needs of the person who is addicted to alcohol. A major section is also included on treating the families of alcoholics.

Goodwin, Donald. (1976). *Is alcoholism inherited?* New York: Oxford University Press. Addresses the age-old nature/nurture question of genetic predisposition versus environmental influences. Surveys the research on both sides of the issue.

Meagher, David. (1987). *Beginning of a miracle: How to intervene with the addicted or alcoholic person.* Pompano Beach, FL: Health Communications. Step-by-step instructions on what can be done to stop alcoholic or addicted persons from their downward spiral.

O'Gorman, Patricia, & Oliver-Diaz, Philip. (1987). *Breaking the cycle of addiction: A parent's guide to raising healthy kids.* Pompano Beach, FL: Health Communications. Especially for parents or prospective parents who were raised in addicted or dysfunctional families, this book helps break the compulsion that is frequently passed on through family dynamics.

Orford, J., & Harwin, J. (1982). *Alcohol and the family.* New York: St. Martin's. Covers how alcohol affects the entire family and examines treatment needs for everyone concerned.

Perez, Joseph. (1986). *Coping within the alcoholic family.* Muncle, IN: Accelerated Development Publishers. Explores the emotional deprivations experienced by family members when one is an alcoholic. An important focus is on the COAs. This book is intended for family members as well as counselors and therapists who treat alcoholic families.

Porterfield, Kay. (1985). *Keeping promises: The challenge of a sober parent.* Center City, MN: Hazelden. A one-day-at-a-time approach to the parenting challenges faced by people recovering from chemical dependency.

Steinglass, Peter. (1988). *The alcoholic family.* New York: Basic Books. Over ten years of study on alcoholism in the family are presented. Covers understanding, treatment, and research into alcoholism.

Subby, Robert. (1987). *Lost in the shuffle: The codependent reality.* Pompano Beach, FL: Health Communications. Written for those who seek to understand the condition of codependency, the problems, the pitfalls, the unreal rules the codependent lives by, and the way out of the diseased condition to recovery.

Wegscheider, Sharon. (1980). *Another chance: Hope and health for the alcoholic family.* Palo Alto, CA: Science and Behavior Books. Integrates family therapy and alcoholism and explains and exposes the feelings and frustrations of family members living with an alcoholic.

Wegscheider, Sharon. (1976). *The family trap.* Palo Alto, CA: Science and Behavior Books. Identifies and describes the survival roles family members play when living with an alcoholic.

Autobiographical

Burnett, Carol. (1986). *One more time.* New York: Random House. A touching and candid account of the famous entertainer's alcoholic childhood and how it affected her life as a grown-up.

Crews, Harry. (1983). *A childhood: The biography of a place*. New York: Morrow. A biography of the novelist's tumultuous, alcoholic upbringing and the long-lasting effects it had on his life and career.

Dean, Amy. (1987). *Once upon a time: Stories from adult children*. Center City, MN: Hazelden. Twenty adult children share their stories, revealing the problems they had to overcome in their alcoholic upbringing to free themselves of their past.

LeBoutillier, Megan. (1990). *Little miss perfect*. New York: Ballantine. The author describes her efforts to survive her alcoholic home and suggests a way for others to move beyond their past into healthy adulthood.

Scales, Cynthia. (1986). *Potato chips for breakfast*. Rutherford, NJ: Perrin & Treg-gett Booksellers. An autobiography of a 16-year-old girl with two alcoholic parents. A story of tragedy and triumph.

Somers, Suzanne. (1988). *Keeping secrets*. New York: Warner. A retrospective and candid account of how alcoholism robbed this celebrity of her child-hood.

V., Rachel. (1987). *Family secrets*. New York: Harper & Row. Life stories of adult COAs are given to help millions of people recover from the ill effects of growing up in an alcoholic household.

Fiction

Anderson, Peggy. (1988). *Coming home: Mending memories for adult children of alcoholics*. Seattle, WA: Glen Abbey. This story concerns a healing experience between a recovering father and his daughter.

Heckler, Jonellen. (1986). *A fragile peace*. New York: G. P. Putnam. This novel tells of a family's journey through the agonizing torture of a father's alco-holism.

Nilsen, Mary. (1985). *When a bough breaks: Mending the family tree*. Center City, MN: Hazelden. This novel follows a family who enters a five-day treatment program and relates the dramatic and exciting changes they experience.

Books for Children and Adolescents

Al-Anon. (1977). *What's "drunk," mama?* New York: Al-Anon Family Group Headquarters. Deals with a little girl's feelings about her father's alcohol-ism. Presents the problems through the child's eyes and presents the con-cepts of Alateen and Al-Anon. The story ends with the father going to AA.

Anders, Rebecca. (1978). *A look at alcoholism*. Minneapolis, MN: Lerner. Provides factual information about alcohol and drinking.

Balcerzak, Lois. (1981). *Hope for young people with alcoholic parents*. Center City, MN: Hazelden. Helps kids deal with their feelings of hurt, fear, embarrassment, and confusion that stems from parental drinking.

Berger, Gilda. (1982). *Addiction: Its causes, problems, and treatments*. New York: Watts. This thorough overview of addiction covers abuse of and dependence on alcohol, caffeine, food, tobacco, and legal and illegal drugs. Discusses the psychological, genetic and physical causes, and effects of addiction.

Bissell, L., & Watherwax, R. (1982). *The cat who drank too much*. Bantam, CT: Bibulophile Press. An alcoholic cat named Willoughby is the main character of this story. Shows all the problems of alcoholism through the cat's behaviors.

Black, Claudia. (1979). *My dad loves me, my dad has a disease: A workbook for children of alcoholics*. Denver, CO: MAC Publishers, 1850 High Street, Denver, CO 80218. A workbook for COAs that is designed to help them work through and better understand alcoholism as well as their own feelings. The basic premise is that alcoholism is a disease. Illustrations were created by children up to age fourteen.

Brooks, Cathleen. (1981). *The secret everyone knows*. Center City, MN: Hazelden. This story for children and adolescents expresses feelings commonly experienced by COAs and offers suggestions for honestly coping with problems in the home. The author's true story lets kids know they are not alone.

Brooks, Jerome. (1973). *Uncle Mike's boy*. New York: Harper. A father's drinking causes many psychological problems for an eleven-year-old boy.

Brown, Michael (Ed.). (1986). *Letters from the children of alcoholic parents*. Charlotte, NC: Randolph Clinic, Inc., 100 Billingsley Road, Charlotte, NC 28211. A series of moving letters and illustrations written by children of alcoholic parents, revealing their pain, hurt, frustration, and anger.

Childhelp U.S.A. (1983). *How could momma say she loved us?* Woodland Hills, CA: Author. In this ten-page booklet, a fourteen-year-old boy describes his attempts to protect his younger siblings and himself from his alcoholic mother's neglect.

DiGiovanni, Kathe. (1986). *My house is different*. Center City, MN: Hazelden. This storybook for children ages six and up interprets the twelve steps of recovery. Joe and his dog Fuzzy travel down Rainbow Road and encounter a variety of creatures and adventures that help Joe learn how he can feel good about himself even if his dad continues to drink.

Duggan, Maureen. (1988). *Mommy doesn't live here anymore.* Weaverville, NC: Bonnie Brae. For children who suffer from parental alcoholism, this is a comforting true story written by a mother. Especially written for professional use with six- to twelve-year-olds who have one parent who is alcoholic.

Guy, Rosa. (1979). *The disappearance.* New York: Delacorte. A powerful story for teenagers about a black 16-year-old named Imamu and his wino mother who lives in poverty and alcoholism. Shows how the adolescent never stops loving his mother and returns to help her with her disease.

Hammond, Mary, and Chestnut, Lynnann. (1987). *My mom doesn't look like an alcoholic.* Pompano Beach, FL: Health Communications. A story written about living in an alcoholic family told through the eyes of a nine-year-old child. This well-illustrated book can be read by parents to their children or by children themselves.

Hastings, Jill, & Typpo, Marion. (1984). *An elephant in the livingroom.* Minneapolis, MN: Comp Care. When children live in a family where drinking is a problem, it's a lot like living with an elephant in the living room that no one talks about. The book's purpose is to help children realize they are not alone, understand that alcoholism is a disease, learn to express their feelings, improve self-esteem, make decisions, and seek support. Written for children ages seven to early adolescence.

Hip, Earl. (1988). *Fighting invisible tigers: A student guide to life in the jungle.* Minneapolis, MN: The Johnson Institute. Talking teens' language and using cartoon humor and quotes from famous people, the author explains what stress is and how to handle it. Intended as a preventive measure for alcohol and drug abuse, this book emphasizes being the best person you can be.

Hornik, Edith. (1974). *You and your alcoholic parent.* New York: Association Press. Uses questions and answers to address topics of interest to teens to prepare them for circumstances that might arise in an alcoholic family.

Hornik-Beer, Edith. (1985). *A teenager's guide to living with an alcoholic parent.* Center City, MN: Hazelden. Teenagers' questions and anxieties about parental alcoholism are answered in this book. Family arguments, unkept promises, and misdirected responsibilities are discussed.

Hyde, Margaret. (1978). *Know about alcohol.* New York: McGraw-Hill. Emphasizes the dangerous consequences of drinking. Also includes a question-and-answer section with vignettes that allow individual responses.

Jance, Judith. (1986). *Welcome home: A child's view of alcoholism.* Washington, DC: Franklin. Tad's father is a problem drinker. This book not only informs the child about alcoholism but emphasizes that he or she is not to blame. Ages five to eleven.

Johnson Institute. (1987). *A story about feelings coloring book.* Minneapolis, MN: Author. Using cartoon characters from the film *A Story About Feelings,* this coloring book helps children gain a clearer understanding of chemical dependence and the role that feelings play in their lives.

Jones, Penny. (1983). *The brown bottle.* Center City, MN: Hazelden. This brief little story is about a caterpillar named Charlie who discovers a bottle of alcohol and spends many hours inside because of the pleasant feelings he gets. Spending time there began to fill all his time, eventually it became his home, and ultimately it was his doom.

Kenny, K., & Krull, H. (1980). *Sometimes my mom drinks too much.* Milwaukee, WI: Raintree Children's Books. Details Maureen's account of her mother's drinking and the feelings the child has around the drinking and the disease of alcoholism. Several embarrassing situations are depicted in which the mother is drunk and the father tries in vain to shield the child. In this instance, a caring teacher comes to the support of the child.

Kranyik, M. (1985). *Coping with adult problems when you're still a kid.* Mount Dora, FL: KIDSRIGHTS. Addresses the special problems of kids who must assume adult responsibilities due to stress, both parents working, divorce, alcoholism, and other crises.

Lee, Essie, & Israel, Elaine. (1975). *Alcohol and you.* New York: Julian Messner. Gives vignettes about the tragedy of alcohol. Uses cartoons to illustrate points on the devastation of the disease.

Leiner, Katherine. (1987). *Something's wrong in my house.* New York: Watts. Stories about children growing up in alcoholic homes.

Leite, Evelyn, & Espeland, Pamela. (1988). *Different like me: A book for teens who worry about their parents' use of alcohol/drugs.* Minneapolis, MN: The Johnson Institute. Looks at the problem from the kids' point of view. Written especially for teens who are concerned, confused, scared, and angry because their parents abuse alcohol and drugs.

Mathis, Sharon. (1974). *Listen for the fig tree.* New York: Viking. A story for teens about a black sixteen-year-old blind girl named Marvina, who rises above her disability to help her alcoholic mother, who feels defeated by the disease.

Melquist, Elaine. (1974). *Pepper.* Frederick, MD: Frederick County Council on Alcoholism. A heartwarming story told through the eyes of a dog, Pepper, whose master is alcoholic. Pepper describes how he felt when his master neglected him and treated him badly when drunk.

Miner, Jane. (1982). *A day at a time.* Maleato, MN: Crestwood House. Anger, fear, and denial of a little girl whose father is alcoholic are described in this story. The little girl eventually attends Alateen and is able to understand and cope with her father's illness.

Nelville, Emily Cheney. (1975). *Garden of broken glass*. New York: Delacorte. A story of a thirteen-year-old boy and how he copes with his mother's alcoholism. Shows the roles that the boy and his siblings take on as a result of parental alcoholism.

Operation Cork. (1983). *Winthrop and Munchie talk about alcohol*. La Jolla, CA: Author. (Write: Operation Cork, 8939 Villa La Jolla Drive, Suite 203, La Jolla, CA 92037). A story of two cartoon characters, Winthrop and Munchie, who carry on a simple conversation about drinking that young children can understand. The story goes on to explain problems alcoholism can bring and contains illustrations that kids can color.

Pegors, T. (1983). *Learn about alcohol* and *Learn about alcoholism*. Center City, MN: Hazelden. These two pamphlets present the facts on alcoholism in a straightforward way, showing the effects of alcohol on the body and providing illustrations to bring the content alive.

Porterfield, Kay. (1985). *Coping with an alcoholic parent*. New York: Rosen Group. Over seven million children in the United States live in families where one or both parents are alcoholics. This reassuring book helps teens deal with problems and take care of themselves when things aren't right at home. For ages thirteen to eighteen.

Rattray, Jamie, Howells, Bill, & Siegler, Irving. (1982). *Kids and alcohol: Facts and ideas about drinking and not drinking*. Hollywood, FL: Health Communications. Myths about alcoholism are included along with the facts that debunk them. Also includes techniques for exploring feelings and ways to take care of yourself and deal with feelings when a parent drinks.

Ryerson, Eric. (1987). *When your parent drinks too much: A book for teenagers*. New York: Warner. Breaks through the isolation and reaches out to teenage COAs by putting them in touch with those best able to help—other COAs. Draws on ideas from Al-Anon and Alateen.

Seixas, Judith. (1977). *Alcohol: What it is, what it does*. New York: Greenwillow. Includes chapters giving facts about alcohol, the disease concept, and reasons for drinking. Illustrated with cartoon-style pictures, the book concludes with the message that kids have a choice.

Seixas, Judith. (1979). *Living with a parent who drinks too much*. New York: Greenwillow. This book was written especially for children living in a situation where parents are alcoholic. It offers insight into the behaviors of the family members and offers strategies for coping with the environment.

Silverstein, Shel. (1976). *The missing piece*. New York: Harper & Row. This fable gently probes the nature of trying to fit in and not feel so different. Illustrated by line drawings, the missing piece sets out to find what's missing and in search of fulfillment.

Snyder, Anne. (1975). *First step.* Center City, MN: Hazelden. Shows how
Alateen helps children deal with their parent's drinking. In this story, a girl
learns to cope with her mother's alcoholism with the aid of Alateen.

Summers, James. (1966). *The long ride home.* Philadelphia: Westminster. A
brother and sister, high-school age, must cope with their father's alcoholism, which prevents them from carrying on an ordinary social life.

Special Reports

This section includes governmental and advocacy reports that have
relevance for program developers, child advocates, researchers, and
practitioners nationwide.

Blume, S. (1985). *Report of the conference on prevention research.* New York: Children of Alcoholics Foundation, Inc. Summarizes a conference on prevention
research held in New York City in December 1984. High-priority research
needs and proposed strategies to improve prevention research were identified.

Children of Alcoholics Foundation. (1982). *Report of the Children of Alcoholics
Foundation.* New York: Author. Presents an extensive review of the literature; identifies roles for professionals, including educators and mental
health and health care workers; and discusses issues in identification. Recommends high-priority areas of research. Sobering children's art illustrates
the inner pain these children suffer.

Children of Alcoholics Foundation. (1984). *Report of the conference on research
needs and opportunities for children of alcoholics.* New York: Author. Summarizes the conclusions of a conference on research needs and opportunities
for children of alcoholics in New York City in April 1984. High-priority research opportunities were identified, strategies were recommended, and areas of research were reviewed.

Cramer, P. (1977). *An educational strategy to impact the children of alcoholic parents:
A feasibility report.* Arlington, VA: National Center for Alcohol Education.
(ERIC Document Reproduction Service No. ED 199 190) Examines areas in
which supportive services can be provided to children of alcoholic parents
within a school setting. Concludes that the school staff is the best resource
to provide needed care.

National Institute on Alcohol Abuse and Alcoholism. (1981). *Services for children of alcoholics* (Research Monograph 4). Washington, DC: Government
Printing Office. (Document Number: HE 208315:4) Reports on a symposium

about children from alcoholic homes. Deals with identification, intervention, prevention, and treatment issues.

Office for Substance Abuse Prevention. (1988). *Children of alcoholics: Kit for kids, parents, therapists, and helpers.* Rockville, MD: National Clearinghouse for Alcohol and Drug Information. This package includes four kits directed to four audiences: kids, parents, therapists, and helpers. The kit is free and can be copied at will.

Russell, M., Henderson, C., & Blume, S. B. (1985). *Children of alcoholics: A review of the literature.* New York: Children of Alcoholics Foundation. A comprehensive review of the research on COAs, presenting an excellent overview and synthesis of current knowledge on the topic.

Waite, B. J., & Ludwig, M. J. (1985). *A growing concern: How to provide services for children of alcoholic families.* Rockville, MD: National Institute on Alcohol Abuse and Alcoholism. Enlightens caregivers on how to identify, intervene, treat, and prevent further problems with COAs. Also includes sections on training caregivers, referral and support resources, cultural factors, and research directions.

Woodside, M. (1982). *Children of alcoholics.* New York: Children of Alcoholics Foundation. Examines the problems and needs of COAs through literature review and interviews with programs providing services for children from chemically dependent families and site visits to eleven programs. The report was presented to New York Governor Hugh Carey and Joseph Califano, special counselor on alcoholism and drug abuse.

Woodside, M. (1986). *Children of alcoholics on the job.* New York: Children of Alcoholics Foundation. Aimed at corporations and businesses, this report includes a general overview of COAs, preliminary findings by various companies, problems parental alcohol abuse can cause employees, results of the first nationwide survey of corporate medical directors and employee assistance programs on this issue, and practical cost-free recommendations for action.

Organizations

This section details the major organizations concerned with alcoholism as it pertains to children and chemically dependent families. The organizations are divided into two types: resource organizations and professional organizations. Resource organizations provide such services as dissemination of information on the incidence and effects on children of alcoholic parents, methods of supporting children in such

homes, legislative advocacy efforts for these children, replication models for programs, and other types of technical assistance in the area of
alcoholism and the family. Professional organizations are national as-
sociations of professionals dedicated to the improvement of those who
work with children and adolescents. These organizations generally
charge membership dues, publish their own journals, and sponsor an
annual meeting where members gather for seminars, speeches, and
workshops.

Resource Organizations

Addiction Research Foundation, 33 Russell Street, Toronto, Ontario, Canada
    M5S 2S1. Conducts and promotes research in alcoholism and other addic-
    tions; conducts programs for and methods of treatment and rehabilitation
    of alcoholics and other addicts; and disseminates information about alco-
    holism and other addictions through public education and prevention.

Adult Children of Alcoholics Central Service Board, P.O. Box 3216, 2522 West
    Sepulveda Blvd., Suite 200, Torrance, CA 90505. A twelve-step, twelve-
    tradition suggested program of recovery/discovery for adults who were
    raised in an alcoholic family. The board was formed on November 10, 1984,
    by the independent meetings in California, and an interim World Service
    Organization was formed on January 19, 1986. The office now serves as a
    clearinghouse for information to, from, and about the growing fellowship
    of adult COAs around the world.

Al-Anon/Alateen Family Group Headquarters, Inc., P.O. Box 182, Madison
    Square Station, New York, NY 10159-0182. A nationwide fellowship of
    young people, usually teenagers, whose lives have been affected by alcohol-
    ism in a family member or close friend. Help is offered by the sharing of
    personal experiences, strength, and hope.

Alcoholics Anonymous, P.O. Box 459, Grand Central Station, New York, NY
    10163. A fellowship of men and women who share their experience,
    strength, and hope with each other with the goal that they may solve their
    common problem and help others recover from alcoholism. The only re-
    quirement for membership is a desire to stop drinking.

American Council for Drug Education, 5820 Hubbard Drive, Rockville, MD
    20852. The council's goal is to communicate the latest valid information on
    psychoactive drugs, including alcohol, to the public at large.

Center of Alcohol Studies, Rutgers University, P.O. Box 969, Piscataway, NJ
    08854. The multifaceted mission of the center includes research, education,

clinical services, and information services. The center serves as an international source of information on alcohol studies.

Children of Alcoholics Foundation, Inc., 31st Floor, 200 Park Avenue, New York, NY 10166. A nonprofit, public organization created to assist this country's 28 million children of alcoholic parents. The primary goals of the foundation are to raise awareness of the intergenerational links in the disease of alcoholism, help reduce the suffering and pain of those from alcoholic homes, and prevent future alcoholism.

Children's Defense Fund, 122 C Street, N.W., Washington, DC 20001. Publishes information on prevention problems, issues, and news regarding children of all ages. A newsletter and booklets are available for child advocates, community leaders, public health workers, and others interested in improving the lives of children.

Co-Dependents Anonymous, National Service Office, P.O. Box 5508, Glendale, AZ 85312-5508. This is a fellowship of men and women whose common problem is an inability to maintain functional relationships. CoDA bases its meetings on Alcoholics Anonymous's twelve steps and twelve traditions. Its meetings are open to anyone who feels he or she is in a codependent relationship and feels overly responsible for others' feelings and behaviors.

Families Anonymous, P.O. Box 528, Van Nuys, CA 91408. For relatives and friends concerned about the use of drugs or related behavioral problems. Uses the twelve steps of Alcoholics Anonymous to help families recover.

National Clearinghouse for Alcohol and Drug Information, P.O. Box 2345, Rockville, MD 20852. Provides information and services to anyone with questions or concerns about any type of drug problem, including alcohol abuse, illicit drug use, and misuse of prescription drugs. Printed materials, references and referrals, and media are available through the clearinghouse.

National Council on Alcoholism, Inc., 12 West 21st Street, New York, NY 10010. A national nonprofit organization combating alcoholism, other drug addictions, and related problems. Major programs include prevention and education, public information, public policy advocacy, medical/scientific information, conferences, and publications.

National Federation of Parents for Drug-Free Youth (NFP), 8730 Georgia Avenue, Suite 200, Silver Spring, MD 20910. A nonprofit organization committed to raising a generation of drug-free youth. Its principal objective is to assist in the formation and support of local parent and youth groups in communities across the United States to eliminate drug and alcohol use among youth.

National Institute on Alcohol Abuse and Alcoholism, 5600 Fishers Lane, Rockville, MD 20852. Provides a focus in the federal effort to increase knowledge and promote effective strategies to deal with economic, social, and human devastation associated with alcohol abuse and alcoholism. It is committed to promoting and carrying out the long-term basic and applied research required to accomplish treatment, training, and prevention programs.

National Women's Christian Temperance Union, 1730 Chicago Avenue, Evanston, IL 60201. A nonprofit, nonpartisan, interdenominational organization, dedicated to the education of our nation's citizens, especially our youth, on the harmful effects of alcoholic beverages, other narcotic drugs, and tobacco on the human body and the society in which we live.

U.S. Journal, 3201 S.W. 15th Street, Deerfield Beach, FL. Publishes alcohol-related information and three periodicals: *The U.S. Journal of Drug and Alcohol Dependence, Chemical Dependency,* and *Grassroots,* a comprehensive alcohol and drug information service.

Professional Organizations

Association for the Care of Children's Health, 3615 Wisconsin Avenue, N.W., Washington, DC 20016. Formerly the Association for the Care of Children in Hospitals, this organization is committed to humanizing health care for children, adolescents, and their families.

Association for Childhood Education International, 11141 Georgia Avenue, Suite 200, Wheaton, MD 20902. A professional medium for those concerned with the education and well-being of children from infancy through early adolescence: classroom teachers, teachers in training, teacher educators, parents, day care workers, librarians, supervisors, administrators, and other practitioners.

Child Study Association of America, 9 East Eighty-Ninth Street, New York, NY 10028. Concerned with the study and development of young children and the environments that affect them.

Child Welfare League of America, 67 Irving Place, New York, NY 10003. Concerned with any facet of social policy that bears on the welfare of youth and their families. Its membership is composed of professionals who work for child and family welfare through administration, supervision, casework, group work, community organization, teaching, or research.

National Association for Children of Alcoholics, 31582 Coast Highway, Suite B, South Laguna, CA 92677. A national nonprofit organization founded in 1983 to support and serve as a resource for COAs of all ages and for those in a position to help them. NACoA believes that COAs deserve the understanding, information, and help they need to break out of their isolation and silence.

National Association for the Education of Young Children, 1834 Connecticut Avenue, N.W., Washington, DC 20009-5786. NAEYC offers professional development opportunities to early childhood educators designed to improve the quality of services to children from birth through age eight—the critical years of development.

National Association of Social Workers, 2 Park Avenue, New York, NY 10016. NASW is composed of caseworkers in the field of social welfare, many of whom work with chemically dependent families.

National Council on Family Relations, 1910 West County Road B, Suite 147, Saint Paul, MN 55113. NCFR is dedicated to furthering all aspects of family life in terms of program development, education, and research.

National PTA, 700 North Rush Street, Chicago, IL 60611. A professional organization for parents, teachers, and others concerned with bridging the gap between home and school for the welfare of the nation's children.

Society for Research in Child Development, 5801 Ellis Avenue, Chicago, IL 60637. A professional platform for researchers and theoreticians interested in the study and development of children from infancy to adolescence.

Periodicals

This section highlights the major professional journals in the field that publish articles pertaining to alcoholism, chemically dependent families, and children of alcoholic parents.

The ACA Journal, American Council on Alcoholism, Inc., 8501 LaSalle Road, Suite 301, Towson, MD 21204. Published quarterly, this journal presents the latest information in the field of alcoholism.

Addictive Behaviors: An International Journal, Pergamon Journals, Inc., Maxwell House, Fairview Park, Elmsford, NY 10523. Published quarterly, the journal includes original research, theoretical papers, and critical reviews in the area of substance abuse. Attention is given to alcohol, drug abuse, smoking, and eating disorders.

Alcohol Health & Research World, The Editor, P.O. Box 2345, Rockville, MD 20852. This quarterly journal, produced by the National Institute on Alcohol Abuse and Alcoholism, presents current research in an easily readable format.

Alcoholism Treatment Quarterly, The Haworth Press, 12 West 32nd Street, New York, NY 10001. This practical journal is the practitioner's quarterly for individual, group, and family therapy. It provides a balance of practice-oriented material along with selective publication of data-based research.

Child Abuse & Neglect: The International Journal, International Society for Prevention of Child Abuse and Neglect, c/o Pergamon Journals, Fairview Park, Elmsford, NY 10523. Published quarterly, the journal provides a multidisciplinary forum on the prevention and treatment of child abuse and neglect, including sexual abuse.

International Journal of Addictions, The Editor, 417 Garces Drive, San Francisco, CA 94132. An international journal that reports the latest research in the areas of alcoholism and other human addictions.

Journal of Alcohol and Drug Education, Journal Executive, 1120 East Oakland, P.O. Box 10212, Lansing, MI 48901. Published three times a year, the journal reports various educational philosophies and differing points of view regarding alcohol and drugs. Teacher experience, experiments, materials, techniques, and procedures all are possible topics.

Journal of Chemical Dependency Treatment, The Haworth Press, 12 West 32nd Street, New York, NY 10001. Published biannually, this journal provides focused thematic issues dealing with practical clinical topics for drug abuse/substance abuse counselors and treatment professionals, covering both maintenance and drug-free philosophies.

Journal of Drug Issues, P.O. Box 4021, Tallahassee, FL 32315-4021. Published quarterly, this journal provides a forum for discussion of drug policy issues. Includes timely and critical commentaries on social, legal, political, economic, historical, and medical issues related to drug policy making.

Journal of Studies on Alcohol, Center of Alcohol Studies, Rutgers University, P.O. Box 969, Piscataway, NJ 08854. Published bimonthly at the Center of Alcohol Studies, this journal contains original research reports that contribute significantly to fundamental knowledge about alcohol, its use and misuse, and its biomedical, behavioral, and sociocultural effects.

Journal of Substance Abuse Treatment, Editorial Office, Drug Treatment and Education Center, Department of Psychiatry, North Shore University Hospital, 400 Community Drive, Manhasset, NY 11030. Published quarterly, the journal features original contributions and articles on the clinical treatment of substance abuse and alcoholism. Directed toward treatment practitioners in both public and private sectors.

Professional Counselor, 12729 N. E. 20th, Suite 12, Bellevue, WA 98005. Published bimonthly and serving the alcohol and drug addictions field, the journal gives special tips to counselors.

Videotapes

Children of Alcoholics (38 minutes). Order from: KIDRIGHTS, 3700 Progress Boulevard, P.O. Box 851, Mount Dora, FL 32757. Designed for use with therapists, counselors, and other professionals, this video discusses important dynamics for the child of alcoholism. Offers valuable guidance to parents and helping professionals.

Children of Alcoholics (30 minutes). Order from: Onsite Training and Consulting, Inc., 2820 West Main Street, Rapid City, SD 57702. Portrays the dysfunctional behaviors that develop in alcoholic families, with special emphasis on children. Sharon Wegscheider narrates on the roles and potential for change.

Children of Alcoholics: Choice for Growth (55 minutes). Order from: KIDSRIGHTS, 3700 Progress Boulevard, P.O. Box 851, Mount Dora, FL 32757. Features Dr. Robert Ackerman before a live audience discussing the effects of parental alcoholism on COAs who are now adults. Appropriate for anyone raised in an alcoholic home and for those who work with them.

Drinking Parents (10 minutes). Order from: Coronet/MTI Film & Video, 108 Wilmot Road, Deerfield, IL 60015. Twenty million children living in homes with alcoholic parents are often subjected to violence, abuse, and neglect. The special problems of these children are brought to light in this film. Victimized children and their parents give case history accounts of how they coped.

If Someone in Your Family Drinks . . . (30 minutes). Order from: KIDSRIGHTS, 3700 Progress Boulevard, P.O. Box 851, Mount Dora, FL 32757. Helps youngsters who may be growing up in an alcoholic family system to understand the situation and see how it affects their behavior. Recommends specific things they can do to make things better for themselves. For ages ten to fifteen.

Parents with Alcoholism: Kids with Hope (30 minutes). Order from: KIDSRIGHTS, 3700 Progress Boulevard, P.O. Box 851, Mount Dora, FL 32757. Shows how a parent's alcoholism affects the rest of the family. Helps teens who blame themselves for their parent's drinking. Shows how to cope; provides kids with hope. Ages fourteen to eighteen.

Roles (30 minutes). Order from: MAC, 1850 High Street, Denver, CO 80218. Claudia Black presents the four family roles she writes about in her book *It Will Never Happen to Me: The Responsible Child, the Adjuster, the Placater, and the Acting Out Child.*

Soft Is the Heart of a Child (28 minutes). Order from: Operation CORK/PGP, 138B Avenue, Coronado, CA 92118. Deals with the effects of alcoholism on children in a family. Shows different roles children adopt to survive in an alcoholic family. This touching film is excellent for introducing the concept of family dysfunction in alcoholic homes.

A Story About Feelings (10 minutes). Order from: The Johnson Institute, 7151 Metro Boulevard, Minneapolis, MN 55435. Effective, eye-catching film for three- to eight-year-olds. Presented mainly in cartoon form, it helps children understand the role that feelings play in their lives. It also explains that some people drink, smoke, and use drugs to change their feelings.

Strong Kids, Safe Kids (42 minutes). Order from: Mass Media Ministries Films and Videos, 2116 North Charles Street, Baltimore, MD 21218. Henry Winkler and cohosts John Ritter and Mariette Hartley are joined by Scooby Doo, Yogi Bear, and The Flintstones in this special family guide to protecting children against sexual abuse.

The Summer We Moved to Elm Street (Beta and VHS: 28 minutes). Order from: CRM-McGraw-Hill Inc., P.O. Box 64, Del Mar, CA 92014. A nine-year-old girl's feelings are explored in an environment of emotional neglect. The child must take greater responsibility and adjust to a new neighborhood in the midst of problems caused by parental conflicts and a nonsupportive, alcoholic father.

Twelve Steps, The Video. Order from: Perrin & Treggett Booksellers, P.O. Box 190, 5 Glen Road, Rutherford, NJ 07070. A completely new approach for families touched by alcoholism. Based on the twelve steps, this film serves to motivate and provide spiritual strength for living life fully and joyously, one day at a time.

Where's Shelley? (10 minutes). Order from: The Johnson Institute, 7151 Metro Boulevard, Minneapolis, MN 55435. A stimulating story about ordinary children nine to eleven years old faced with a situation where alcohol and drugs are available for their use. Without moralizing, the film helps children understand factors that can affect their decisions about using alcohol and drugs.

REFERENCES ▟

Ackerman, R. (1983). *Children of alcoholics: A guidebook for educators, therapists, and parents* (2nd ed.). Holmes Beach, FL: Learning Publications.

Ackerman, R. (1987). *Same house, different homes: Why adult children of alcoholics are not all the same.* Pompano Beach, FL: Health Communications.

Ainsworth, M. D., Blehar, M. C., Waters, E., & Wall, S. (1978). *Patterns of attachment: A psychological study of the strange situation.* Hillsdale, NJ: Lawrence Erlbaum.

Anderson, S., & Sabatelli, R. (1993). *Family interaction: A multigenerational developmental perspective.* Needham Heights, MA: Allyn & Bacon.

Anthony, E. J. (1978). A new scientific region to explore. In E. J. Anthony, C. Koupernik, & C. Chiland (Eds.), *The child and his family: Vulnerable children* (Vol. 4). New York: John Wiley.

Aronson, H., & Gilbert, A. (1963). Preadolescent sons of male alcoholics. *Archives of General Psychiatry, 8,* 47-53.

Aronson, H., Kyllerman, M., Sable, K. G., Sandin, B., & Olegard, R. (1985). Children of alcoholic mothers: Developmental, perceptual, and behavioral characteristics as compared to matched controls. *Acta Paediatrica Scandanavia, 74,* 27-35.

Bardo, M., & Risner, M. (1985). Biochemical substrates of alcohol abuse. In M. Galizio & S. Maisto (Eds.), *Determinants of substance abuse* (pp. 65-99). New York: Plenum.

Barnard, C. P., & Spoentgen, P. A. (1987). *Alcoholism Treatment Quarterly, 3,* 47-65.

Barrett, R. J. (1985). Drug-taking behavior. In M. Galizio & S. Maisto (Eds.), *Determinants of substance abuse* (pp. 125-175). New York: Plenum.

Baumrind, D. (1967). Child care practices anteceding three patterns of preschool behavior. *Genetic Psychology Monographs, 75,* 43-48.

Begleiter, H., Porjesz, B., & Bihari, B. (1984). Event-related brain potentials in boys at risk for alcoholism, *Science, 225,* 1493-1496.

Bell, B., & Cohen, R. (1981). The Bristol Social Adjustment Guide: Comparison between the offspring of alcoholic and nonalcoholic mothers. *British Journal of Clinical Psychology, 20,* 93-95.

Biek, J. (1981). Screen test for identifying adolescents adversely affected by a parental drinking problem. *Journal of Adolescent Health Care, 2,* 107-113.

Bingham, A., & Bargar, J. (1985). Children of alcoholic families. *Journal of Psychosocial Nursing, 23,* 13-15.

Black, C. (1979, Fall). Children of alcoholics. *Alcohol Health and Research World,* pp. 23-27.

Black, C. (1982). *It will never happen to me!* Denver, CO: MAC Publications.

Black, C. (1986, January-February). Alcoholism and family violence. *Alcoholism and Addiction Magazine,* pp. 46-47.

Black, C. (1987, November 10-11). *Young and adult children of alcoholics.* Seminar presented by the Randolph Clinic, Charlotte, NC.

Black, C., Bucky, S. F., & Wilder-Padilla, S. (1986). The interpersonal and emotional consequences of being an adult child of an alcoholic. *International Journal of Addictions, 21,* 213-232.

Bly, R. (1987). A conversation with Robert Bly on leaving the father's house. In Rachel V. (Ed.), *Family secrets.* New York: Harper & Row.

Bohman, M. (1978). Some genetic aspects of alcoholism and criminality: A population of adoptees. *Archives of General Psychiatry, 35,* 269-276.

Bohman, M., Cloninger, R., Von Knorring, A. L., & Sigvardsson, S. (1984). An adoption study of somatoform disorders. *Archives of General Psychiatry, 41,* 872-878.

Bohman, M., Sigvardsson, D., & Cloninger, R. (1981). Maternal inheritance of alcohol abuse. *Archives of General Psychiatry, 38,* 965-969.

Booz-Allen & Hamilton, Inc. (1974). *Final report on the needs of and resources for children of alcoholic parents.* Rockville, MD: National Institute on Alcohol Abuse and Alcoholism, Alcohol, Drug Abuse, and Mental Health Administration, U. S. Department of Health and Human Services.

Bosma, W. (1972). Alcoholism and the family: A hidden tragedy. *Maryland State Medical Journal, 21,* 34-36.

Bowles, C. (1968). Children of alcoholic parents. *American Journal of Nursing, 68,* 1062-1064.

Braithwaite, V., & Devine, C. (1993). Life satisfaction and adjustment of children of alcoholics: The effects of parental drinking, family disorganization, and survival roles. *British Journal of Clinical Psychology, 32,* 417-429.

Brenner, A. (1984). *Helping children cope with stress.* Lexington, MA: Lexington Books.

Brisbane, F. L. (1985). Using contemporary fiction with black children and adolescents in alcoholism treatment. *Alcoholism Treatment Quarterly, 2,* 179-197.

Butler, K. (1997). The anatomy of resilience. *Family Therapy Networker, 21*(2), 22-31.

Cadoret, A. J., Cain, C. A., & Grove, W. M. (1980). Development of alcoholism in adoptees raised apart from alcoholic biologic relatives. *Archives of General Psychiatry, 37*, 561-563.

Cadoret, R. J., Troughton, E., & O'Gorman, T. W. (1987). Genetic and environmental factors in alcohol abuse and antisocial personality. *Journal of Studies on Alcohol, 48*, 1-8.

Callan, V. J., & Jackson, D. (1986). Children of alcoholic fathers and recovered alcoholic fathers: Personal and family functioning. *Journal of Studies on Alcohol, 47*, 180-182.

Chafetz, M. E., Blane, H. T., & Hill, M. J. (1971). Children of alcoholics: Observations in a child guidance clinic. *Quarterly Journal of Studies on Alcohol, 32*, 687-698.

Chandy, J., Harris, L., Blum, R., & Resnick, M. (1993). Children of alcohol misusers and school performance outcomes. *Children and Youth Services Review, 15*, 507-519.

Chase, N. (1997). *The parentified child: Theory, research, and treatment.* Thousand Oaks, CA: Sage.

Clair, D., & Genest, M. (1987). Variables associated with the adjustment of offspring of alcoholic fathers. *Journal of Studies on Alcohol, 48*, 345-355.

Cloninger, R., Bohman, M., Sigvardsson, S., & Knorring, A. (1981). Inheritance of alcohol abuse. *Archives of General Psychiatry, 38*, 861-868.

Cloninger, R., Bohman, M., Sigvardsson, S., & Knorring, A. (1984). In M. Galanter (Ed.), *Recent developments in alcoholism* (Vol. 3, pp. 37-51). New York: Plenum.

Compas, B. (1987). Coping with stress during childhood and adolescence. *Annual Progress in Child Psychiatry and Child Development*, 211-237.

Connors, G., & Tarbox, A. (1985). Macroenvironmental factors as determinants of substance use and abuse. In M. Galizio & S. Maisto (Eds.), *Determinants of substance abuse: Biological, psychological, and environmental factors* (pp. 283-314). New York: Plenum.

Cork, M. (1969). *The forgotten child.* Ontario, Canada: General Publishing.

Crabbe, J., McSwigan, J., & Belknap, J. (1985). The role of genetics in substance abuse. In M. Galizio & S. Maisto (Eds.), *Determinants of substance abuse* (pp. 13-64). New York: Plenum.

Cutter, C. G., & Cutter, H. S. (1987). Experience and change in Al-Anon family groups: Adult children of alcoholics. *Journal of Studies on Alcohol, 48*, 29-32.

Davis, K. (1996). *Families: A handbook of concepts and techniques for the helping professional.* New York: Brooks Cole.

Deutsch, C. (1982). *Broken bottles, broken dreams: Understanding and helping the children of alcoholics.* New York: Teachers College Press.

DiCicco, L., Davis, R., & Orenstein, A. (1984). Identifying the children of alcoholic parents from survey responses. *Journal of Alcohol and Drug Education, 30*, 1-17.

Donovan, B. E. (1981). A collegiate group for the sons and daughters of alcoholics. *Journal of the American College Health Association, 30*, 83-86.

El-Guebaly, N., & Offord, D. R. (1977). The offspring of alcoholics: A critical review. *American Journal of Psychiatry, 134*, 357-365.

Elkind, D. (1981). *The hurried child.* Reading, MA: Addison-Wesley.

Erikson, E. H. (1963). *Childhood and society* (2nd ed.). New York: Norton.

Famularo, R., Stone, K., Barnum, R., & Wharton, R. (1986). Alcoholism and severe child maltreatment. *American Journal of Orthopsychiatry, 56*, 481-485.

Fassler, D. G. (1987). Children's books about alcoholism. *Childhood Education, 66*, 188-194.

Fine, E. W., Yudin, L. W., Holmes, J., & Heinemann, S. (1976). Behavioral disorders in children with parental alcoholism. *New York Academy of Sciences Annals, 273*, 507-517.

Flake-Hobson, C., Robinson, B. E., & Skeen, P. (1983). *Child development and relationships.* New York: Random House.

Gabrielli, W., Mednick, S., Volavka, J., Pollock, V., Schulsinger, F., & Itil, T. (1982). Electroencephalogram in children of alcoholic fathers. *Psychophysiology, 19*, 404-407.

Gacic, B. (1986). An ecosystemic approach to alcoholism: Theory and practice. *Contemporary Family Therapy, 8*, 264-278.

Goodman, R. W. (1987). Adult children of alcoholics. *Journal of Counseling and Development, 66*, 162-163.

Goodwin, D. W. (1985). Alcoholism and genetics: The sins of the fathers. *Archives of General Psychiatry, 42*, 171-174.

Goodwin, D. W., Schulsinger, F., Hermansen, L., Guze, S. B., & Winokur, G. (1973). Alcohol problems in adoptees raised apart from alcoholic biological parents. *Archives of General Psychiatry, 28*, 238-242.

Gravitz, H. (1985). *Children of alcoholics handbook: Who are they, what they experience, how they recover.* South Laguna, CA: The National Association for Children of Alcoholics.

Haberman, P. W. (1966). Childhood symptoms in children of alcoholics and comparison group parents. *Journal of Marriage and Family, 28*, 152-154.

Hafen, B. Q., & Frandsen, K. J. (1986). *Youth suicide: Depression and loneliness.* Evergreen, CO: Cordillera.

Hammond, M. (1985). *Children of alcoholics in play therapy.* Pompano Beach, FL: Health Publications.

Hegedus, A. M., Alterman, A. I., & Tarter, R. E. (1984). Learning achievement in sons of alcoholics. *Alcoholism: Clinical and Experimental Research, 8*, 330-333.

Hennecke, L. (1984). Stimulus augmenting and field dependence in children of alcoholic fathers. *Journal of Studies on Alcohol, 45,* 486-492.

Holzman, I. R. (1983). Fetal alcohol syndrome (FAS): A review. In M. Frank (Ed.), *Children of exceptional parents* (pp. 13-19). New York: Haworth.

Isaacson, E. (1991). Chemical addiction: Individuals and family systems. In *Chemical dependency: Theoretical appraches and strategies.* New York: Haworth.

Jalongo, M. R. (1983). Bibliotherapy: Literature to promote socioemotional growth. *The Reading Teacher, 36,* 796-803.

Jones, J. W. (1983). *The children of alcoholics screening test and test manual.* Chicago, IL: Camelot Unlimited.

Kammeier, M. L. (1971). Adolescents from families with and without alcohol problems. *Quarterly Journal of Studies on Alcohol, 32,* 364-372.

Kearney, T., & Taylor, C. (1969). Emotionally disturbed adolescents with alcoholic parents. *Acta Paedopsychiatrica, 36,* 215-221.

Keltner, N. L., McIntyre, C. W., & Gee, R. (1986). Birth order effects in second-generation alcoholics. *Journal of Studies on Alcohol, 47,* 495-497.

Kern, J. C., Hassett, C. A., & Collipp, P. J. (1981). Children of alcoholics: Locus of control, mental age, and zinc level. *Journal of Psychiatric Treatment and Evaluation, 3,* 169-173.

Knight, S. (1993). Identifying and labeling school-aged children of alcoholics: Insights voiced by academic attainers who are daughters of alcoholics. *Journal of Health Education, 24,* 196-204.

Knop, J., Teasdale, T. W., Schulsinger, F., & Goodwin, D. W. (1985). A prospective study of young men at high risk for alcoholism: School behavior and achievement. *Journal of Studies on Alcohol, 46,* 273-278.

Krauthamer, C. (1979). Maternal attitudes of alcohol and nonalcoholic upper middle-class women. *International Journal of Addictions, 14,* 639-644.

Kritsberg, W. (1984, November/December). Chronic shock and emotional numbness in adult children of alcoholics. *Focus on Family,* pp. 24-25, 40.

Kritsberg, W. (1985). *The adult children of alcoholics syndrome: From discovery to recovery.* Pompano Beach, FL: Health Communications.

Kroll, P. D., Stock, D. F., & James, M. E. (1985). The behavior of adult alcoholic men abused as children. *Journal of Nervous and Mental Disease, 173,* 689-693.

Lamorey, S., Robinson, B., Rowland, B., & Coleman, M. (in press). *Latchkey kids: Unlocking doors for children and their families* (2nd ed.). Lexington, MA: Lexington Books.

Lerner, R. (1986). Codependency: The swirl of energy surrounded by confusion. In R. J. Ackerman (Ed.), *Growing in the shadow: Children of alcoholics* (pp. 113-121). Pompano Beach, FL: Health Communications.

Levin, J. D. (1995). *Introduction to alcoholism counseling: A bio-psycho-social approach.* Washington, DC: Taylor & Francis.

MacDonald, D. I., & Blume, S. B. (1986). Children of alcoholics. *American Journal of Diseases of Children, 140,* 750-754.

Maisto, S., Galizio, M., & Carey, K. (1985). Individual differences in substance abuse. In M. Galizio & S. Maisto (Eds.), *Determinants of substance abuse: Biological, psychological, and environmental factors.* New York: Plenum.

Maisto, S., Galizio, M., & Connors, G. (1991). *Drug use and misuse.* Orlando, FL: Holt, Rinehart & Winston.

Manning, D. T. (1987). Books as therapy for children of alcoholics. *Child Welfare, 66,* 35-43.

Marcus, A. M. (1986). Academic achievement in elementary school children of alcoholic mothers. *Journal of Clinical Psychology, 42,* 372-376.

Matthews, K. A., & Angulo, J. (1980). Measurement of the Type A behavior pattern in children: Assessment of children's competitiveness, impatience, anger, and aggression. *Child Development, 51,* 466-475.

McElligatt, K. (1986). Identifying and treating children of alcoholic parents. *Social Work in Education, 9,* 55-70.

McGoldrick, M., & Gerson, R. (1985). *Genograms in family assessment.* New York: Norton.

McKenna, T., & Pickens, R. (1981). Alcoholic children of alcoholics. *Journal of Studies on Alcohol, 42,* 1021-1029.

McKenna, T., & Pickens, R. (1983). Personality characteristics of alcoholic children of alcoholics. *Journal of Studies on Alcoholism, 44,* 688-700.

McKenry, P. C., & Tischler, C. L. (1987). Le rapport entre l'usage de drogues et le suicide chez les adolescents. *Médecine et Hygiène, 45,* 2127-2132.

McKenry, P. C., Tischler, C. L., & Kelley, C. (1983). The role of drugs in adolescent suicide attempts. *Suicide and Life-Threatening Behavior, 1*(3), 166-175.

McLachlan, J. F. C., Walderman, R. L., & Thomas, S. (1973). *A study of teenagers with alcoholic parents* (Research Monograph No. 3.) Toronto, Canada: Donwood Institute.

Meddin, B. J., & Rosen, A. L. (1986). Child abuse and neglect: Prevention and reporting. *Young Children, 41,* 26-30.

Merikangas, K. A., Weissman, M. M., Prusoff, B. A., Pauls, D. L., & Leckman, J. F. (1985). Depressives with secondary alcoholism: Psychiatric disorders in offspring. *Journal of Studies on Alcohol, 46,* 199-204.

Miller, D., & Jang, M. (1977). Children of alcoholics: A twenty-year longitudinal study. *Social Work Research and Abstracts, 13,* 23-29.

Moe, J., & Pohlman, D. (1988). *Kids' power: Healing games for children of alcoholics.* Redwood City, CA: Whipple & Alameda.

Moos, R. H., & Billings, A. G. (1982). Children of alcoholics during the recovery process: Alcoholic and matched control families. *Addictive Behaviors, 7,* 155-163.

Morehouse, E. R. (1986). Counseling adolescent children of alcoholics in groups. In R. J. Ackerman (Ed.), *Growing in the shadow.* Pompano Beach, FL: Health Communications.

Morehouse, E. R., & Scola, C. M. (1986). *Children of alcoholics: Meeting the needs of the young COA in the school setting.* South Laguna, CA: National Association for Children of Alcoholics.

National Council on Alcoholism and the American Medical Society on Addiction Medicine. (1990). Editorial: The disease of alcoholism. VIII. Is alcoholism really a disease? *Medical/Scientific Advisory, 5*(4), 7.

National Institute on Alcohol Abuse and Alcoholism. (1981). *Fourth special report to the U.S. Congress on alcohol and health from the Secretary of Health and Human Services* (J. R. DeLuca, Ed.). Washington, DC: Superintendent of Documents, Government Printing Office.

New Games Foundation. (1976). *The new games book.* New York: Headlands Press.

New Games Foundation. (1981). *More new games.* New York: Dolphin, Doubleday.

Newlon, B. J., & Furrow, W. V. (1986). Using the classroom to identify children from alcoholic homes. *The School Counselor, 33,* 286-291.

Not the vintage Margaux. (1988, February 8). *People Magazine,* pp. 95-105.

O'Gorman, P. A., & Oliver-Diaz, P. (1987). *Breaking the cycle of addiction: A parent's guide to raising healthy kids.* Pompano Beach, FL: Health Communications.

Pardeck, J. T., & Pardeck, J. A. (1987). Using bibliotherapy to help children cope with the changing family. *Social Work in Education, 9,* 107-116.

Parker, D. A., & Harford, T. C. (1987). Alcohol-related problems of children of heavy-drinking parents. *Journal of Studies on Alcohol, 48,* 265-268.

Parten, M. B. (1932). Social participation among preschool children. *Journal of Abnormal Psychology, 27,* 243-269.

Pelham, W., & Lang, A. (1993). Parental alcohol consumption and deviant child behavior: Laboratory studies of reciprocal effects. *Clinical Psychology Review, 13,* 763-784.

Pilat, J. M., & Jones, J. W. (1985). Identification of children of alcoholics—Two empirical studies. *Alcohol and Research World, 9,* 27-33.

Poley, W., Lea, G., & Vibe, G. (1979). *Alcoholism: A treatment manual.* New York: Gardner.

Post, P., & Robinson, B. E. (1998). A comparison of school-aged children of alcoholic and non-alcoholic parents on anxiety, self-esteem, and locus of control. *The School Counselor.*

Prewett, M. J., Spence, R., & Chaknis, M. (1981). Attribution of causality by children with alcoholic parents. *International Journal of the Addictions, 16,* 367-370.

Priest, K. (1985). Adolescents' response to parents' alcoholism. *Social Casework: Journal of Contemporary Social Work, 66,* 533-539.

Raikkonen, K., & Keltikangas-Jarvinen, L. (1992). Mothers with hostile, Type A predisposing child-rearing practices. *Journal of Genetic Psychology, 153*(3), 343-354.

Ray, O., & Ksir, C. (1996). *Drugs, society, and human behavior.* St. Louis, MO: C. V. Mosby.

Regan, J. M., Connors, G. J., O'Farrell, T. J., & Wyatt, C. J. (1983). Services for the families of alcoholics: A survey of treatment agencies in Massachusetts. *Journal of Studies on Alcohol, 44,* 1072-1075.

Rimmer, J. (1982). The children of alcoholics: An exploratory study. *Children and Youth Services Review, 4,* 365-373.

Roberts, K., & Brent, E. (1982). Physician utilization and illness patterns in families of alcoholics. *Journal of Studies on Alcohol, 43,* 119-128.

Robins, L. N., West, P. A., Ratcliff, K. S., & Herjanic, B. M. (1977, May). *Father's alcoholism and children's outcomes.* Paper presented at the Annual Medical Scientific Meeting of the National Alcoholism Forum, San Diego, CA.

Robinson, B. E. (1988). *Self-esteem and anxiety level among adult children of alcoholics.* Unpublished manuscript, University of North Carolina at Charlotte.

Robinson, B. (1996). Type A children: Empirical findings and counseling implications. *Elementary School Guidance and Counseling, 31,* 34-42.

Robinson, B. (in press). The workaholic family: A clinical perspective. *American Journal of Family Therapy.*

Rubin, L. (1996). *The transcendent child: Tales of triumph over the past.* New York: Basic Books.

Schaeffer, K. W., Parsons, O. A., & Yohman, J. R. (1984). Neuropsychological differences between male familial and nonfamilial alcoholics and nonalcoholics. *Alcoholism: Clinical and Experimental Research, 8,* 347-351.

Schall, J. (1986). Alcoholism: When a parent drinks, a child struggles. *Instructor, 95,* 54-57.

Schuckit, M. A. (1984a). Behavioral effects of alcohol in sons of alcoholics. In M. Galanter (Ed.) *Recent developments in alcoholism* (Vol. 3, pp. 11-19). New York: Plenum.

Schuckit, M. A. (1984b). Relationship between the course of primary alcoholism in men and family history. *Journal of Studies on Alcohol, 45,* 334-338.

Schuckit, M. A. (1984c). Subjective responses to alcohol in sons of alcoholics and control subjects. *Archives of General Psychiatry, 41,* 879-884.

Schuckit, M. A., Gold, E., & Risch, C. (1987). Serum prolactin levels in sons of alcoholics and control subjects. *American Journal of Psychiatry, 144,* 854-859.

Schuckit, M. A., Goodwin, D. A., & Winokur, G. (1972). A study of alcoholism in half siblings. *American Journal of Psychiatry, 128,* 122-126.

Schuckit, M. A., & Rayses, V. (1979). Ethanol ingestion: Differences in blood acetaldehyde concentrations in relatives of alcoholics and controls. *Science, 203*, 54-55.

Schulsinger, F., Knop, J., Goodwin, D. W., Teasdale, T. W., & Mikkeisen, U. (1986). A prospective study of young men at high risk for alcoholism. *Archives of General Psychiatry, 43*, 755-760.

Seilhamer, R., Jacob, T., & Dunn, N. (1993). The impact of alcohol consumption on parent- child relationships in families of alcoholics. *Journal of Studies on Alcohol, 54*(2), 189-198.

Sgroi, S. (1982). *Handbook of clinical intervention in child sexual abuse.* Lexington, MA: Lexington Books.

Shaywitz, S., Cohen, D., & Shaywitz, B. (1980). Behavior and learning difficulties in children of normal intelligence born to alcoholic mothers. *Journal of Pediatrics, 96*, 978-982.

Sher, K., Walitzer, K., Wood, P., & Brent, E. (1991). Characteristics of children of alcoholics: Putative risk factors, substance use and abuse, and psychopathology. *Journal of Abnormal Psychology, 100*, 427-448.

Skeen, P., & McKenry, P. (1980). The teacher's role in facilitating a child's adjustment to divorce. *Young Children, 35*, 3-12.

Slavenas, R. (1988). The role and responsibility of teachers and child care workers in identifying and reporting child abuse and neglect. *Early Child Development and Care, 31*, 19-25.

Smith, A. (1988). *Grandchildren of alcoholics.* Pompano Beach, FL: Health Communications.

Somers, S. (1988). *Keeping secrets.* New York: Warner Books.

Steinberg, L. (1986). Latchkey children and susceptibility to peer pressure: An ecological analysis. *Developmental Psychology, 22*, 433-439.

Steinhausen, H. C., Gobel, D., & Nestler, V. (1984). Psychopathology in the offspring of alcoholic parents. *Journal of the American Academy of Child Psychiatry, 23*, 465-471.

Steinhausen, H. C., Nestler, V., & Huth, H. (1982). Psychopathology and mental functions in the offspring of alcoholic and epileptic mothers. *Journal of the American Academy of Child Psychiatry, 21*, 268-273.

Steinhausen, H. C., Willms, J., & Spohr, H.-L. (1993). Long-term psychopathological and cognitive outcomes of children with fetal alcohol syndrome. *Journal of the American Academy of Child and Adolescent Psychiatry, 32*, 990-994.

Tabakoff, B., Hoffman, P. L., Lee, J. M., Saito, T., Willard, B., & DeLeon-Jones, J. (1988). Differences in platelet enzyme activity between alcoholics and nonalcoholics. *New England Journal of Medicine, 318*, 134-139.

Talashek, M., Gerace, L., & Starr, K. (1994). The substance abuse pandemic: Determinants to guide interventions. *Public Health Nursing, 11*(2), 131-139.

Tarter, R. E., Hegedus, A. M., Goldstein, G., Shelly, C., & Alterman, A. I. (1984). Adolescent sons of alcoholics: Neuropsychological and personality characteristics. *Alcoholism: Clinical and Experimental Research, 8,* 216-222.

Thomas, A., & Chess, S. (1980). *The dynamics of psychological development.* New York: Brunner/Mazel.

Tischler, C. L., & McKenry, P. C. (1982). Parental negative self and adolescent suicide attempts. *Journal of the American Academy of Child Psychiatry, 21,* 404-408.

Tubman, J. G. (1993). A pilot study of school-age children of men with moderate to severe alcohol dependence: Maternal distress and child outcomes. *Journal of Child Psychology and Psychiatry, 34*(5), 729-741.

Udayakumar, G. S., Mohan, A., Shariff, I. A., Sekar, K., & Eswari, C. (1984). Children of the alcoholic parent. *Child Psychiatry Quarterly, 17,* 9-14.

Use of alcohol linked to rise in fetal illness. (1995, April 7). *New York Times,* p. A27.

Venugopal, M. (1985). Emotional problems of the children of alcoholic fathers. *Child Psychiatry Quarterly, 18,* 114-117.

Visintainer, P. F., & Matthews, K. A. (1987). Stability of overt type A behaviors in children: Results from a two- and five-year longitudinal study. *Child Development, 58,* 1586-1591.

Watkins, C. (1988, March 2). *Reaching adolescent COAs through student assistant programs.* Paper presented at the National Association of Children of Alcoholics Annual Conference, New Orleans, LA.

Weatherford, V. (1988, March 1). *ACAs' transgenerational patterns.* Paper presented at the National Association of Children of Alcoholics Conference, New Orleans, LA.

Wegscheider, S. (1976). *The family trap.* Crystal, MN: Nurturing Networks.

Weinraub, M., & Lewis, M. (1977). The determinants of children's responses to separation. *Monographs of the Society for Research in Child Development, 42*(4, Serial No. 172).

Werner, E. E. (1986). Resilient offspring of alcoholics: A longitudinal study from birth to age eighteen. *Journal of Studies on Alcohol, 47,* 34-40.

Werner, E., & Smith, R. (1992). *Overcoming the odds: High risk children from birth to adulthood.* New York: Cornell University Press.

West, M. W., & Prinz, R. J. (1987). Parental alcoholism and childhood psychopathology. *Psychological Bulletin, 102,* 204-218.

Whitchurch, G., & Constantine, L. (1993). Systems theory. In P. Boss, W. Doherty, R. LaRossa, W. Schuman, & S. Steinmetz (Eds.), *Sourcebook of family theories and methods: A contextual approach* (pp. 325-349). New York: Plenum.

Whitfield, C. L. (1980). Children of alcoholics: Treatment issues. *Maryland State Medical Journal, 29,* 86-91.

Wilson, C., & Orford, J. (1978). Children of alcoholics: Report of a preliminary study and comments on the literature. *Journal of Studies on Alcohol, 39,* 121-142.

Woititz, J. (1983). *Adult children of alcoholics.* Pompano Beach, FL: Health Communications.

Wolin, S. J., Bennett, L. A., Noonan, D. L., & Teitelbaum, M. A. (1980). Disrupted family rituals: A factor in the intergenerational transmission of alcoholism. *Journal of Studies on Alcohol, 41,* 199-214.

Wolin, S., & Wolin, S. (1993). *The resilient self: How survivors of troubled families rise above adversity.* New York: Random House.

Wood, B. (1982). *The COA therapist: When the family hero turns pro.* ERIC.

Wood, B. (1987). *Children of alcoholics: The struggle for self and intimacy in adult life.* New York: New York University Press.

Woodside, M. (1986). Children of alcoholics: Breaking the cycle. *Journal of School Health, 56,* 448-449.

Workman-Davis, K. L., & Hesselbrock, V. M. (1987). Childhood problem behavior and neuropsychological functioning in persons at risk for alcoholism. *Journal of Studies on Alcohol, 48,* 187-192.

Yamasaki, K. (1990). Parental child-rearing attitudes associated with Type A behaviors in children. *Psychological Reports, 67,* 235-239.

INDEX ▪▪

Abuse. *See* Physical abuse; Sexual abuse;
    Substance abuse
Academic achievement:
    factors effecting, 79-81, 82, 96, 97-104,
        133
    in family heroes, 38 (table), 39
    in lost children, 38 (table), 42
    in mascots, 38 (table)
    in resilient children, 68, 102
    in scapegoats, 38 (table), 41
    practitioner suggestions, 109-111
Accomplishments:
    family hero role and, 39-41, 86
    societal emphasis on, 27-28
ACOAs. *See* Adult children of alcoholics
    (ACOAs)
Addiction. *See* Alcoholism; Compulsive
    disorders; Substance abuse; Work
    addiction
Adolescents:
    academic achievement, 98, 103
    Alateen therapy group, 167
    creative activities, 164
    delinquency, 41, 102, 104-105, 106, 107
    denial, 141, 155
    grief reactions, 65
    identity formation, 39, 178 (table),
        182-183
    methods of identifying, 141-142, 143
        (table)
    peer relations, 73, 98
    play deprivation, 162
    psychodrama therapy, 163-164
    self-esteem, 71
    sibling relations, 59

suicide, 108
therapeutic use of genograms for,
    189-191
See also School-age children
Adoption, genetic studies, 186
Adult children of alcoholics (ACOAs):
    compulsive disorders, 40, 83-85, 86,
        87, 117
    denial and, 58
    family heroes, 41, 51
    lost children, 43, 51
    mascots, 44, 51
    personality development, 178 (table),
        183-184
    relationship problems, 58, 73-74, 92,
        183
    scapegoats, 42, 51
    self-esteem, 71
    sense of control, 72
    suicide and, 108-109
    transmission of alcoholism to, 72, 92,
        173-177, 183-189
Adult children of alcoholics syndrome,
    175-177
Advertising, alcohol glamorized by, 24, 25
Age:
    alcohol consumption and, 23
    negative psychological functioning
        and, 65
    See also Adolescents; Adult children of
        alcoholics (ACOAs); Infants;
        Preschool children; School-age
        children
Alateen, 157, 167
Alcohol:

ABOUT THE AUTHORS ▪▪

Bryan E. Robinson, Ph.D., is Professor of Child and Family Development at the University of North Carolina at Charlotte. His clinical practice includes work with children of alcoholics. He has published widely in professional journals and popular magazines and is author and coauthor of numerous books related to the impact of alcoholism and workaholism on children and families. Dr. Robinson has also written scripts for national television programs on child development and has appeared on national radio and television discussing children's needs.

J. Lyn Rhoden, Ph.D., is Visiting Assistant Professor in the Department of Counseling, Special Education, and Child Development at the University of North Carolina at Charlotte. She received a master's degree in special education from the University of North Carolina at Charlotte and a doctoral degree in child development and family studies from the University of North Carolina at Greensboro. Her research interests and publications focus on child and family development in the context of changing contemporary family configurations, gender, race, and class.